PHILOSOPHY AND IDEOLOGY IN HUME'S POLITICAL THOUGHT

PHILOSOPHY AND IDEOLOGY IN HUME'S POLITICAL THOUGHT

by
DAVID MILLER

CLARENDON PRESS · OXFORD
1981

Oxford University Press, Walton Street, Oxford OX2 6DP
London Glasgow New York Toronto
Delhi Bombay Calcutta Madras Karachi
Kuala Lumpur Singapore Hong Kong Tokyo
Nairobi Dar es Salaam Cape Town
Melbourne Auckland
and associate companies in
Beirut Berlin Ibadan Mexico City

Published in the United States by
Oxford University Press, New York

British Library Cataloguing in Publication Data
Miller, David
 Philosophy and ideology in Hume's
 political thought.
 1. Hume, David, 1711-1776
 I. Title
 320'.01   JC176.H/

 ISBN 0-19-824658-7

Typeset by DMB (Typesetting) Oxford
Printed in Great Britain
at the University Press, Oxford
by Eric Buckley
Printer to the University

'Human nature being compos'd of two principal parts, which are requisite in all its actions, the affections and understanding; 'tis certain, that the blind motions of the former, without the direction of the latter, incapacitate men for society: And it may be allow'd us to consider separately the effects, that result from the separate operations of these two component parts of the mind. The same liberty may be permitted to moral, which is allow'd to natural philosophers; and 'tis very usual with the latter to consider any motion as compounded and consisting of two parts separate from each other, tho' at the same time they acknowledge it to be in itself uncompounded and inseparable.'

(Treatise, p. 493.)

Preface

I began writing this book with three aims in mind. The first was to provide a reasonably concise account of Hume's social and political thought which might help students coming to it for the first time. Hume is studied less than he deserves to be in the history of political thought, and one reason, I suspect, is that no book meeting this description has yet been published. The existing studies are long and perhaps somewhat unapproachable. Nor is it easy to direct students to Hume's original texts. Although much can be gleaned from the third book of the *Treatise* and a judicious selection of Hume's essays, a great deal more is buried in his vast and inaccessible *History of England* which no undergraduate and few graduates could be expected to read. So although I am temperamentally opposed to commentaries on the past masters of political theory, there seems no other way of restoring Hume to his proper place in that company.

My second aim was to say something about the relationship between philosophy and politics, with explicit attention to Hume, but implicit reference to a general issue. The question I wanted to address, to put it briefly, was whether a person's philosophical convictions were in any way logically relevant to his political outlook. On this subject two views have each enjoyed some support. One view is that clear connections can be found between general philosophical standpoints and political ideologies; to take a frequently cited example, there is a logical link between empiricist philosophy and liberal politics. The other view is that no such link exists or can exist, and that any appearances to the contrary are simply to be explained by the historical fact that certain philosophies have emerged at the same time as their (seemingly) associated ideologies. A cursory reading of Hume had convinced me that the second view could not be true in his case at least, since he plainly relied on arguments and assumptions taken from his philosophy in developing his social and political thought. It was equally obvious, however, that this link could not be captured by sweeping generalizations, such as that purporting to connect empiricism and liberalism. The connection was weaker than the first view implied, and it depended on philosophical positions that were peculiar to Hume rather than on his affiliation to a broad school such as empiricism. In clarifying the relationship between

Hume's philosophy and his politics, therefore, I hoped also to illustrate the kind of connection that might exist in general between these two fields.

In the third place, I was puzzled about the ideological character of Hume's social and political thought when considered in relation to later political traditions, particularly the conservative and liberal traditions. Historians of conservatism often cite him along with Burke as a leading representative of the distinctively British brand of moderate conservatism. But he is regarded with equal respect by theorists of the liberal economic order (Hayek and his disciples, for example), while being castigated by opponents of liberalism for the 'bourgeois' character of his thought. In an earlier study I had myself used Hume's work to illustrate a hierarchical view of society without attempting to show in any detail how his economic writings (in particular) could be fitted into this picture. The present study offers an integrated account of Hume's thought, and it accounts for the variations in interpretation just noted by arguing that the distinction between liberalism and conservatism had little application in mid-eighteenth-century Britain. Hume's ideology contained elements which we should now identify as 'conservative' and 'liberal' respectively, and so by selective emphasis it is possible to make him seem a thoroughbred conservative or liberal according to choice.

These two problems—the relationship between Hume's philosophy and his politics, and the ideological character of his thought—are pursued through the first and second parts of my book respectively. My aim has been to give the book a plot, as it were, while at the same time presenting Hume's ideas in a reasonably comprehensive manner. The reader will decide, whether these two purposes have been married successfully. Wanting to keep the book as short as possible, I have paid comparatively little attention to Hume's intellectual borrowings, merely drawing attention to the more obvious sources in footnote references. I have also refrained from criticizing Hume's ideas at any length. An account which is intended to bring out the coherence of a system of thought must necessarily take note of areas of confusion or of lacunae in chains of argument, but this is a more modest task than wholesale criticism. I hope that by the end of the book the reader will be convinced, not necessarily that Hume is right in what he says, but at least that his arguments deserve careful rebuttal.

The ideas contained in the book were first tried out on various audiences up and down the country, and I should like to thank everyone who offered comments and criticism on these occasions. Material from chapters 5 and 6 has appeared in *History of Political Thought*, and I am grateful to the publishers for permission to use it here. My greatest debt is to David Raphael, John Mackie, and Geraint Parry, each of whom read the manuscript in full and made numerous suggestions for improvement, most of which I have adopted. Neal Todd agreed to act as a student guinea-pig, but exceeded his brief by offering important criticism of parts of the argument. Susan Hersh gave me valuable assistance in preparing the final manuscript. My final thanks go to Ann Franklin and Judy Godley for converting my illegible writing into typescript with such efficiency and good humour.

Nuffield College,
Oxford

1981

Contents

Abbreviations

Enquiry I: David Hume, *An Enquiry Concerning Human Under-standing* in *Enquiries Concerning Human Understanding and Concerning the Principles of Morals*, ed. L. A. Selby-Bigge, 3rd edn. revised P. H. Nidditch (Oxford, 1975).

Enquiry II: David Hume, *An Enquiry Concerning the Principles of Morals*, ibid.

Essays   David Hume, *Essays Moral, Political and Literary* (Oxford, 1963).

History   David Hume, *The History of England from the Invasion of Julius Caesar to the Abdication of James the Second* (London, 1884).

Letters   *The Letters of David Hume,* ed. J. Y. T. Greig (Oxford, 1932).

Treatise   David Hume, *A Treatise of Human Nature*, ed. L. A. Selby-Bigge, 2nd edn. revised P. H. Nidditch (Oxford, 1978).

Introduction

It is often suggested that the work of the great political thinkers of the past should be interpreted as a response to dramatic events occurring within their personal experience. Hobbes has been tied in this way to the English Civil War, Locke to the Revolution of 1688, Burke to the French Revolution, and Marx to the various upheavals surrounding the birth of an urban proletariat in Western Europe. Although in each case there is good reason to think that the theory in question took substantial shape prior to the events supposed to have provoked it, the general interpretation persists. For anyone inclined to regard political thought in this way, David Hume must stand out as a worrying exception. He is a major political thinker whose work cannot plausibly be viewed as a reaction to any political occurrence in particular. Of course his stature is not unquestionable, and one of the incidental tasks of the present book is to vindicate his claim to be called a major theorist. As to the absence of specific political stimuli, we may observe, first of all, that Hume's life fell neatly in between the more turbulent periods at the beginning and the end of the eighteenth century. When George I mounted the throne in 1714, putting an end to the uncertainty about the Hanoverian succession which lingered on through the reign of Anne, Hume was only three. In relation to the two Revolutions, the American and the French, which so dramatically changed the political climate in the last decades of the century, Hume was on his death-bed when news of the Declaration of Independence reached Britain in 1776, and so escaped the impact of either event. The years between were years of comparative political stability. Britain was governed by rival groups of oligarchs, whose rivalry itself steadily abated in the years after 1714, and whose rule was only disrupted spasmodically—by the Jacobites in 1715 and 1745, and by disorderly mobs in the cities, particularly after 1760. In the second place, Hume's own involvement in political life was minimal. For a short period in the 1760s he served as an Under-Secretary of State, and his letters at this time show some interest in the intrigues and dogfights of day-to-day politics, but the period stands out as exceptional in a life mainly lived at an arm's length from the centres of power. Hume was notoriously not a man of party; he strove consistently to view the political quarrels of the time from the position of the detached spectator. He preferred the seclusion of Edinburgh and the company of philosophers and men of letters to the political hurly-burly of London.

This does not mean that Hume lacked political commitments. It suggests rather that his innovations in political thought were not occasioned by his taking sides in any great contemporary debate. Instead Hume's originality lay in his reconstruction of the philosophical foundations of political thought. He shows us in striking fashion how a superstructure of relatively conventional political attitudes may be erected upon a novel basis. Of course the philosophical rebuilding makes some difference; the superstructure is only *relatively* conventional, which perhaps explains why Hume's writings were never warmly received by any of the great political battalions of his day. But we should look in vain for an arresting new political doctrine in these writings. On the other hand, his philosophical originality is unquestionable. He pushed the empiricism of his predecessors Locke and Berkeley to a sceptical conclusion with unparalleled acuteness and persistence. The fascination of Hume's political thought lies in seeing how a revolutionary philosophy is combined with an establishment ideology to yield what is probably the best example we have of a secular and sceptical conservative political theory. Hume's political thought may lack the rhetorical flair of Burke's, for instance, but it makes up for it by its internal coherence and the clarity of its philosophical underpinnings.

To add some more detail to this general picture, we may briefly review Hume's life and work.[1] He was born in 1711, the second son of Joseph and Katherine Home of Ninewells near Berwick-on-Tweed. His family were well-established country gentry, and the estate at Ninewells brought in a comfortable income, though not sufficient to support the younger son besides the elder in the accustomed style. David Hume therefore needed to take up an occupation to supplement his small allowance, and, after attending the University of Edinburgh, he attempted to train as a lawyer. He found, however, that he had no taste for the subject, and was increasingly drawn towards philosophy and literature. He immersed himself in the work of both ancient and modern writers. After a brief and unsuccessful apprenticeship to a Bristol merchant in 1734 he settled in France to resume his philosophical researches.

---

[1] The standard account of Hume's life is E. C. Mossner, *The Life of David Hume* (Edinburgh, 1954, revised edn. Oxford, 1980). Hume's brief autobiographical essay 'My Own Life' in *Essays* is also well worth reading.

The outcome was *A Treatise of Human Nature*, the book which seems certain to stand as his most lasting monument. It was published in three separate parts during 1739-40. Book I, 'Of the Understanding', addresses such central questions in epistemology as the nature of our belief in an external world and our belief in the relation of cause and effect. Book II, 'Of the Passions', discusses the origin and nature of various feelings and emotions. Book III, 'Of Morals', considers the nature of moral judgement, encompassing not only the dictates of private morality but also our social and political obligations. To Hume's great disappointment the work was neither a financial nor a critical success. He fared better with his *Essays Moral and Political* which appeared at the beginning of 1742. These are by comparison much slighter pieces, some political, some literary, and some philosophical in a non-technical sense. The contrasting reception given to the two works convinced Hume that there was no public audience for 'abstruse' philosophy delivered in the manner of the *Treatise*. Now back in Scotland, he made an unsuccessful bid for the chair of Ethics at Edinburgh which was blocked by the clerical lobby. There followed two brief appointments, one an unhappy period as tutor to the Marquess of Annandale, the other a military office as secretary to General St. Clair. Meanwhile Hume was reworking the material of the *Treatise* in an effort to make it more accessible to his readers. Book I was metamorphosed into *An Enquiry Concerning Human Understanding* which first appeared (under a different title) in 1748, and Book III into *An Enquiry Concerning the Principles of Morals* which followed in 1751. Despite his efforts the latter, he claimed, 'came unnoticed and unobserved into the world'. Once again his political essays proved to be more popular. *Political Discourses*, published in 1752, was like its predecessor a miscellaneous volume, with the largest group of essays being on economic topics. It was, Hume said, 'the only work of mine that was successful on the first publication'.

As early as 1745 Hume had planned to compose a history of England which would serve, among other things, to settle certain outstanding disputes concerning the British Constitution. His appointment as Keeper of the Advocates' Library at Edinburgh in 1751 gave him both the time and the materials to press ahead with the task. *The History of England* was not written chronologically, but began with the two volumes on the Stuarts, published in 1754 and 1756, and then continued with the Tudor volumes and the medieval volumes in that order. The appearance of the first Stuart volume in particular caused a political stir for its sympathetic portrayal of James I and Charles I. Sales were none the less reasonably good, and Hume's *History* became a standard text which retained its authority until well into the nineteenth century. In bulk it far exceeds all his other writings put together.

After completing this Herculean task in a decade, Hume produced no further work of any substance, but spent his remaining years revising and rearranging his earlier output. The *Treatise,* however, was left in the oblivion into which it had fallen, and the controversial *Dialogues Concerning Natural Religion,* written in about 1751, were not published until after his death. The royalties that he received from his essays and *History* were now sufficient to give him a comfortable independence, but this was further supplemented by emoluments from the offices he held after 1760. In 1763 he became Lord Hertford's secretary at the British Embassy in Paris, and in 1767 Under-Secretary of State, Northern Department, in London; both jobs carried pensions. From his stay in Paris dated his friendship with several celebrated French philosophers, including d'Alembert and Diderot, not to mention *salon* hostesses such as the Comtesse de Boufflers. He also met Rousseau, with whom he quarrelled, famously and tragically, in 1766.

In 1769 Hume returned to Scotland where he remained until his death in 1776. He resumed his friendship with other leading Scottish thinkers, most notably Adam Smith, whose *The Wealth of Nations* appeared just soon enough in 1776 to win Hume's warm congratulations. When Hume died Smith wrote a short account of his character which may serve as a personal epitaph.

Thus died our most excellent, and never-to-be-forgotten friend; concerning whose philosophical opinions men will no doubt judge variously, every one approving or condemning them according as they happen to coincide, or disagree with his own; but concerning whose character and conduct there can scarce be a difference of opinion. His temper, indeed, seemed to be more happily balanced, if I may be allowed such an expression, than that perhaps of any other man I have ever known. Even in the lowest state of his fortune, his great and necessary frugality never hindered him from exercising, upon proper occasions, acts both of charity and generosity. It was a frugality founded not upon avarice, but upon the love of independency. The extreme gentleness of his nature never weakened either the firmness of his mind, or the steadiness of his resolutions. His constant pleasantry was the genuine effusion of good nature and good humour, tempered with delicacy and modesty, and without even the slightest tincture of malignity, so frequently the disagreeable source of what is called wit in other men. It was never the meaning of his raillery to mortify; and therefore, far from offending, it seldom failed to please and delight even those who were the objects of it. To his friends, who were frequently the objects of it, there was not perhaps any one of all his great and amiable qualities which contributed more to endear his conversation. And that gaiety of temper, so agreeable in society, but which is so often accompanied with frivolous and superficial qualities, was in him certainly attended with the most severe application, the most extensive learning, the greatest depth of thought, and a capacity in every respect the most comprehensive. Upon the whole, I have always considered him, both in his lifetime, and since his death, as approaching as nearly to the idea of a perfectly wise and virtuous man, as perhaps the nature of human frailty will admit.[2]

In fixing our line of approach to Hume's social and political thought, two questions must be faced at the outset. Both concern the degree of coherence we should look for in Hume's writings. The first, and narrower, question concerns the relationship between the *Treatise* and the two *Enquiries*: do the latter works essentially contain restatements of philosophical positions developed in the former, or had the nature of Hume's philosophical enterprise changed in the intervening period? The broader question has to do with the relationship between Hume's philosophy and his economic, political, and historical writing: did Hume effectively abandon philosophy when he turned his attention to these other subjects, or does his treatment of the latter represent a series of applications of the philosophical principles that he had previously established?

On both counts my disposition is to see Hume's work as a coherent whole. Whether this is an adequate approach can really only be judged in retrospect, when the over-all picture has been presented. But the issues involved can be surveyed immediately. Concerning the relationship between the *Treatise* and the *Enquiries*, three issues must be examined: Hume's expressed attitude towards the *Treatise* in later years; differences in the content of the earlier and later works—that is, topics subtracted or added in the *Enquiries*; and substantial changes in the positions Hume adopted in the two versions of his philosophy.

From all the evidence it appears that Hume came to regard his youthful first production with embarrassment and even positive distaste. This attitude of mind was expressed in the advertisement to the 1777 edition of *Essays and Treatises on Several Subjects*, which contained the two *Enquiries*.[3] Hume complained that his opponents had directed their arguments against the *Treatise*—'that juvenile work, which the Author never acknowledged'—and he expressed

---

[2] Adam Smith, cited in *Letters*, vol. ii, p. 452.
[3] Hume sent this to his publisher in October 1775. See *Letters*, vol. ii, p. 301.

his desire 'that the following Pieces may alone be regarded as containing his philosophical sentiments and principles'.[4] This was not a late change of heart. In 1751 he had advised Gilbert Elliot not to read the *Treatise* and recommended the *Enquiries* instead.[5] However, we should pay close attention to the reasons Hume gives for repudiating the *Treatise*. In general, he came to believe that its contents were badly expressed; its failure 'had proceeded more from the manner than the matter'.[6] This encompassed two more specific criticisms: the arguments tended to be too long and too abstract, and the book's general tone was marred by excess of youthful enthusiasm.[7] In the *Enquiries* these faults were rectified: 'By shortening and simplifying the Questions, I really render them much more complete.' But then Hume adds—and this is the significant point—'The philosophical Principles are the same in both', meaning in both the *Treatise* and the *Enquiries*.[8] The furthest he will go in the way of substantial criticism is to say that 'some negligences' in the reasoning of the *Treatise* are corrected in the latter works.[9]

On Hume's own testimony, therefore, the two versions of his philosophy do not differ in their basic principles, but only in style and quality of argument. I believe that this assessment is substantially correct, though, unlike Hume, I prefer the first version on nearly every occasion when they disagree. We must next look, however, at the respective contents of the two versions. By no means everything contained in the *Treatise* reappears in one or other of the *Enquiries*; some material that does reappear is very much compressed.[10] For instance the discussion of our ideas of space and time in the *Treatise* disappears, and the discussion of our belief in an external world is reduced very considerably. The bulk of Book II, 'Of the Passions', has no counterpart in either of the two *Enquiries*. Several important sections of Book III, 'Of Morals', are hidden away in appendices in the *Enquiry Concerning the Principles of Morals,* and others—for instance the chapters on

---

[4] *Enquiry* I, p. 2.
[5] *Letters,* vol. i, p. 158.
[6] 'My Own Life', *Essays,* p. 610.
[7] See *Letters,* vol. i, pp. 158, 187.
[8] *Letters,* vol. i, p. 158.
[9] *Enquiry* I, p. 2.
[10] Full comparative tables are provided by Selby-Bigge in his edition of *Enquiry* I and *Enquiry* II, pp. xxxiii-xl. The only significant additions in the *Enquiries* are the sections on miracles, providence, and a future state, the first of which at least Hume had removed from the *Treatise* for reasons of prudence.

allegiance to government—vanish entirely. What are we to make
of such changes?

It will be found that the alterations Hume makes in recasting
his philosophy fall into two unequal classes. The much larger
class is composed of changes made for the sake of presentation.
Hume's great object in giving the second version of his philosophy
to the world, was to render it more attractive and accessible to the
cultivated but amateur reader. We ought to recollect how few
men in the eighteenth century could be described as professional
philosophers. It was a great misfortune for Hume that he lacked
proficient critics whose comments might have encouraged him to
continue working the philosophical vein opened by the *Treatise*.[11]
In their absence he decided to act 'as a kind of resident or am-
bassador from the dominions of learning to those of conversation',[12] and in the *Enquiries* he salvaged such material from the
Treatise as could be reworked into a more popular form. It is
surprising how little was entirely discarded; what was not used in
the two later books reappeared in essay form. The best parts of
his epistemology and moral theory were reproduced in *Enquiry* I
and *Enquiry* II respectively. The generally less interesting treatment of the passions in Book II of the *Treatise* was heavily con-
densed and later appeared as 'Of the Passions' with three other
dissertations in 1757; even the analysis of our ideas of space and
time in Book I was intended, it is believed, to reappear as 'Some
Considerations previous to Geometry and Natural Philosophy' in
the same volume, but was withdrawn by Hume before publication.
The sections of the *Treatise* on political allegiance formed the basis
for several of the political essays which gave Hume his popular
success later on. In short, the *Enquiries* do not represent all that
Hume thought worth preserving from the first version of his
philosophy, but rather parts of the argument which were able to
stand in relative independence, and which needed to be presented
at moderate length. Hume's problem was not what to keep, but
how to divide the material of the *Treatise* up into more palatable
chunks.

There are, even so, a small number of genuine omissions.
These may be divided in turn into topics which Hume came to

---

[11] The reception which the *Treatise* received is described in Mossner, *Life,* ch. 10.
Summing up he says: 'By no means totally ignored, the *Treatise* was yet totally
misunderstood and badly misrepresented by all who dealt with it publicly and, what is
worse, it failed to stimulate comment from any of the minds competent to deal with it.'
(*Life*, p. 132.)

[12] 'Of Essay Writing', *Essays,* p. 570.

believe he had failed to handle adequately in the *Treatise* and topics which gave the *Treatise* an unnecessary air of paradox. The best-known example in the former category is his discussion of personal identity, which he admitted was a failure even at the time of writing the appendix to Book III of the *Treatise*. Among topics in the latter category is his theory of artificial virtues, which Hume believed had brought unwarranted opprobrium on to the *Treatise* and which he therefore omitted as a topic from *Enquiry* II (though the substance of the theory is still present—see below ch. 3, p. 60).

In considering omissions of this nature, we are clearly bordering on issues of substance, so let me turn briefly to the question of material differences between the *Treatise* and the *Enquiries*.[13] My view is that such differences in actual doctrine as do exist are of negligible importance. This view can only be verified on a case-by-case basis, and I shall consider particular instances (such as the alleged disappearance of Hume's doctrine of sympathy from *Enquiry* II) as they arise. On the other hand there are significant differences both in *balance* and in *tone* between the two versions which cannot be reduced merely to a matter of presentation. Hume changed his opinion about the relative importance of different parts of his work. The clearest example is his account of the rules governing the association of ideas which figures prominently in Book I of the *Treatise*. In the *Abstract* which he later composed to advertise the *Treatise,* he wrote: 'if any thing can intitle the author to so glorious a name as that of an *inventor,* 'tis the use he makes of the principle of the association of ideas, which enters into most of his philosophy.'[14] This enthusiasm had evaporated by the time that *Enquiry* I was composed, and in the final version of that work only two short pages are devoted to the doctrine. A less striking (though still important) example is provided by his view that moral distinctions are not derived from reason, which plays a large role in Book III of the *Treatise* but a much smaller one in the second *Enquiry*; this, I believe, is not merely a tactical shift on Hume's part, but reflects a change of opinion about the centrality of this doctrine to his moral theory.

---

[13] For some conflicting opinions about the relationship between the two works, see Selby-Bigge's Introduction to *Enquiry* I and *Enquiry* II; N. Kemp Smith, *The Philosophy of David Hume* (London, 1941), ch. 24; J. B. Stewart, *The Moral and Political Philosophy of David Hume* (New York, 1963), Appendix; J. Noxon, *Hume's Philosophical Development* (Oxford, 1973), esp. Part I, sect. 3, Part V, sect. 1-2.

[14] D. Hume, *An Abstract of a Book lately Published; Entituled, A Treatise of Human Nature, etc.,* in *Treatise,* pp. 661-2.

There is also a noticeable difference in tone between the *Treatise* and the *Enquiries*. The *Treatise* is suffused with intellectual passion— what Hume called 'the positive Air, which prevails in that Book, and which may be imputed to the Ardor of Youth'[15]—whereas the *Enquiries* exude ironic detachment. Nowhere is this clearer than in Book I, Part IV of the *Treatise*, where Hume responds to sceptical doctrines concerning our reason and our senses, and comes at time close to complete despair. For instance:

> The *intense* view of these manifold contradictions and imperfections in human reason has so wrought upon me, and heated my brain, that I am ready to reject all belief and reasoning, and can look upon no opinion even as more probable or likely than another. Where am I, or what? From what causes do I derive my existence, and to what condition shall I return? Whose favour shall I court, and whose anger must I dread? What beings surround me? and on whom have I any influence, or who have any influence on me? I am confounded with all these questions, and begin to fancy myself in the most deplorable condition imaginable, inviron'd with the deepest darkness, and utterly depriv'd of the use of every member and faculty.'[16]

No such expressions of philosophical doubt disturb the smooth progress of the first *Enquiry*. We might express the contrast by saying that whereas the *Treatise* is a voyage of discovery undertaken in a spirit of high ambition, in the *Enquiries* the destination is known before the journey commences and the ambition is correspondingly lessened. In the revised version Hume continually seeks to soften the impact of doctrines which, stated bluntly, make the *Treatise* so disturbing a work, and which moreover provide plentiful ammunition for the unscrupulous critic. His aim in the *Treatise* was to establish philosophical truth; in the *Enquiries* it was to present portions of that truth, already established, in a way that was eye-catching without being too shocking. In the transition much that was valuable was lost: precision of expression, rigour, and persistence of argument. The corresponding gain in concision and elegance is by no means adequate compensation.

The *Treatise* is correctly regarded as Hume's greatest work, and it is also the key to everything else that he wrote. It contains a system of philosophy which underlies his more practical studies in economics, politics, and history. The *Enquiries* do not present an alternative system of thought, but merely less well-integrated fragments of the original system. They are valuable as an introduction to Hume's more difficult book, as a source of concise

---

[15] *Letters*, vol. i, p. 187.
[16] *Treatise*, pp. 268-9.

quotation, and occasionally for a more balanced presentation of a position that Hume fails to maintain steadily in the *Treatise*; but for no other reason.

This verdict on the relationship between the *Treatise* and the *Enquiries* immediately raises the wider issue of the connection between Hume's philosophy and his practical studies. Did Hume, as has sometimes been maintained, forsake philosophy for politics, history, and so forth in order to establish a literary reputation that had so far eluded him;[17] or, more respectably, because he had come to doubt whether any further progress was possible in pure philosophy? On my reading Hume lost interest in philosophy only in the way that a builder loses interest in the foundations of a house when he starts to construct the walls. But given that he produced no major new work in philosophy after the *Treatise* (the *Enquiries* being a recasting, as argued above), what evidence is there for this interpretation?

The question may be approached in two ways: by reference to Hume's own intentions, or by reference to the logical structure of his thought (one hopes that both approaches lead to the same destination). If we examine Hume's intentions, the key to the puzzle may be found in his perennial interest in the theory of morals. According to Kemp Smith's well-known thesis, Hume began his philosophical career with an interest in questions of moral philosophy, and arrived at the doctrines of the *Treatise* in reverse order, beginning with the account of moral judgement.[18] From this vantage point, Hume's epistemology appears as a necessary prolegomenon to his moral theory, and his political and historical studies as applications of that moral theory to particular areas of human life. His over-all intention was to found a science of human nature, starting with the most general properties of the human mind and proceeding to the explanation of more specific forms of activity.

This interpretation of Hume's enterprise appears at first sight to run up against a logical difficulty. The philosophical and practical parts of the enterprise seem to be divided by an un-bridgeable gulf. Philosophy is commonly distinguished from the natural and human sciences on the grounds that the sciences ask direct, first-order questions about their respective subject-

---

[17] For examples of this cynical reading of Hume's intellectual career, consult E. C. Mossner, 'Philosophy and Biography: The Case of David Hume' in V. C. Chappell (ed.), *Hume* (London, 1968).

[18] Kemp Smith, *Philosophy of David Hume*, esp. Part I, ch. 1.

matters, whereas philosophy asks second-order questions—questions about the nature of the first-order questions. While a scientist will ask which theory of gravitation is correct, a philosopher will ask what criteria we should use to test the correctness of theories in general. Now it must be said that the distinction just drawn is relatively modern, and not one that would have recommended itself to men in the eighteenth century (including Hume), for whom 'philosophy' and 'science' were often interchangeable terms. Yet the logical point still remains: if first-order and second-order questions are separable, how can Hume's philosophical arguments condition the social and political theories that he intends to rest upon them?

The correct reply, I believe, is that although first-order and second-order questions are distinguishable, they are not mutually irrelevant. There is rather a two-way process of conditioning. The philosopher formulates his principles through trying to rationalize the beliefs that we already have and the methods that we use to verify them. Having arrived at these principles, he may then wish to recommend changing certain of these beliefs and methods. Criteria of scientificity, for example, are formulated through reflection on the practice of scientists; but once formulated, they may be used to criticize some aspects of that practice, and as a result first-order beliefs may be changed. Equally, in the moral sphere, the philosopher will begin by examining the judgements that men customarily make about good and evil, right and wrong. But having done so, and having elaborated general criteria for making these judgements, he may then propose that certain established beliefs are erroneous and ought to be discarded. So in place of a sharp dichotomy between philosophical and substantive questions, we may put forward the idea of an intellectual system in which certain beliefs are more abstract and general, others more concrete and specific.

Hume's thought exemplifies such a system. He would not, of course, have felt the need to examine the relationship between higher-order and lower-order questions as I have here. He was nevertheless aware that his more abstract work in epistemology and moral philosophy formed the basis for his more concrete examination of empirical and moral questions in political science. The fact that he transferred his efforts from pure philosophy to political and historical studies is no embarrassment, since if the foundations are well laid, they need not be continually reinspected. To show that Hume's thought actually had the systematic structure

I have outlined is part of the task of this book. I shall try to demonstrate not merely the dependence of Hume's social and political thought on his epistemology and theory of morals, but the precise nature of the connection between the two.

Such an approach to Hume's political thought, setting it within a coherent intellectual enterprise whose foundations are laid in Book I of the *Treatise*, dictates the answer to a question of method which often troubles historians of political thought. How far should political texts be examined historically, as responses to an intellectual environment in which certain assumptions could be taken for granted, other questions were felt to demand an answer, and so forth; and how far philosophically, as making claims that transcend a particular historical setting and demand to be assessed in accordance with atemporal criteria of logic and evidence? It has never seemed sensible to me to answer this question in general terms. To the extent that a political thinker is a pamphleteer or an ideologue, addressing a particular issue from convenient but unexamined (and possibly inconsistent) assumptions, a historical interpretation will be most illuminating. To the extent that a thinker is genuinely philosophical, developing a *system* of political thought from first principles, a correspondingly philosophical treatment is appropriate. Even in this case some historical groundwork is necessary. To understand a political theorist we must first understand the meanings of the terms he uses, and it is arrogant to think that we can do this without paying any attention to the historical context in which he was writing. Furthermore it is wrong to think that even the most philosophical of political theorists proceeds in a purely deductive fashion. Political conclusions cannot be derived solely from philosophical premisses. Into the system there must be fed a large number of empirical and moral assumptions which, in combination with the premisses, do yield the conclusions. These assumptions—a typical case would be an assumption about the dominance of certain motives in political life—are not self-evident, though they may appear not to stand in need of justification to the thinker being considered. We again need some understanding of the social and political context in which the theory was formed to see why one set of postulates rather than another should have been adopted.

My aim, therefore, is to explore the respective roles played by philosophy and by ideology in Hume's political thought, assuming the latter to form a coherent whole. 'Philosophy' refers to the epistemological and meta-ethical premisses which Hume brought to the study of society and politics; 'ideology' to the set of empirical and moral assumptions which came to him immediately from his social and political environment. That there is no objectively necessary connection between cause and effect, or that moral distinctions cannot be derived by reason alone, is a philosophical premiss. That men are predominantly motivated by ambition and avarice, or that society is naturally divided into a series of ranks, is an ideological assumption. The issue to be explored is how the two types of proposition combine to yield an integrated political theory; and the picture I shall paint is one in which both make an essential contribution.

An interpretation of this kind stands midway between two diametrically opposite views of Hume's thought, which have prevailed in different historical periods, no doubt as a reflection of wider assumptions about the relationship between philosophy and politics. During the nineteenth century it was usual to see a direct link between his philosophical and political standpoints. J. S. Mill put the argument here into a nutshell when he wrote:

[Hume's] absolute scepticism in speculation very naturally brought him round to Toryism in practice; for if no faith can be had in the operations of human intellect, and one side of every question is about as likely as another to be true, a man will commonly be inclined to prefer that order of things which, being no more wrong than every other, he has hitherto found compatible with his private comforts.[19]

In the twentieth century the tendency has, by contrast, been to insist on the irrelevance of Hume's philosophy to his political stance. Bertrand Russell used him to illustrate the absence of any necessary connection between epistemological and political views, claiming to agree very largely with Hume in abstract matters while disagreeing totally with his politics.[20] Geoffrey Marshall developed the argument more fully: distinguishing between Hume's philosophical and practical scepticism, he maintained that

Between '*philosophical*' scepticism and the conservative attitude to change, there is no necessary connection at all. Such scepticism has none of the consequences for social theory which are sometimes imputed to it. What undoubtedly does

---

[19] J. S. Mill, 'Bentham' in *Essays on Politics and Culture*, ed. G. Himmelfarb (New York, 1963), p. 80. For a similar account, see L. Stephen, *English Thought in the Eighteenth Century* (London, 1876), esp. p. 185.

[20] See B. Russell, 'A Reply to my Critics' in P. Schilpp (ed.), *The Philosophy of Bertrand Russell* (Evanston and Chicago, 1944). It should be said that Russell did not adhere consistently to the general view expressed here about the relationship between philosophy and politics. Compare B. Russell, 'Philosophy and Politics' in his *Unpopular Essays* (London, 1950).

have these consequences is the *practical* scepticism and empirical caution of the Hume who mistrusted miracles whether they might be theological or political.[21]

A similar doubt about the relevance of Hume's philosophy to his political thinking is implicit in the recent major study by Duncan Forbes.[22]

In contradistinction to both these interpretations, I shall argue that Hume's philosophy is logically relevant to his political thought without entirely determining its character. More formally, the truth of Hume's philosophical premisses is a necessary but insufficient condition of the truth of his political standpoint. The remaining necessary conditions are provided by his ideological commitments.

In making this claim I am of course dissecting Hume's intellectual system in a way that he might well resist; we saw earlier that the distinction between philosophical and empirical or moral judgements, besides being far from rigid when considered logically, is in any case more characteristic of twentieth-century than of eighteenth-century thought. Nevertheless, the dissection is of value if we wish not merely to do justice to Hume, but to consider his system as a prototypal political theory. It is a matter of the greatest interest (though also of the greatest difficulty) to assess the contributions made respectively by philosophy and ideology to the formation of such a theory. We can try to resolve this problem in an impressionistic way by asking what would result if we were to superimpose a different set of philosophical beliefs on Hume's ideological baggage, and vice versa. The thought-experiment involved necessarily does some violence to the integrity of Hume's theory, but (as the quotation that opens this book is meant to suggest) Hume himself recognized the need for an analogous dismemberment in the pursuit of philosophical insight.

The plan of the book follows this conception of the structure of Hume's political thought. In Part I, I trace the connection between Hume's epistemology, his moral theory, and his social and political thought, the link being provided by the account he gives of belief and judgement. I show, in other words, that a theory of judgement which is first developed in relation to belief in general is then applied more specifically to moral judgement; and more specifically still to judgements about justice and political

---

[21] G. Marshall, 'David Hume and Political Scepticism', *Philosophical Quarterly,* iv (1954), p. 252.

[22] D. Forbes, *Hume's Philosophical Politics* (Cambridge, 1975). Forbes has made the implication clear in 'Linking the Philosophical and Political', *Political Studies,* xxv (1977), 272-3.

allegiance, which for Hume are crucial to the maintenance of social and political life respectively. But Hume's theory also requires first-order moral and empirical assumptions, and these are explored in Part II, where I look in turn at his views about human nature, about economic and social institutions, about political institutions in general, and about the particular institutions of government that had developed in Britain. This part of the book is headed 'Action' to emphasize that it focuses on how men behave, individually and collectively, rather than on how they think or judge. In keeping with my thesis that the assumptions in question are best interpreted as ideology, I have tried at various points to set Hume's thought against the social and political background out of which it grew. We may in this way see how assumptions which to us appear peculiar, or at least to stand badly in need of justification, might to Hume have appeared uncontroversial.

Besides enabling us to assess the respective roles played by philosophy and ideology in the formation of Hume's political thought, this analysis will also help us to place Hume in relation to the different traditions that have emerged in the history of political ideas. His affinities are seen to lie with the conservative tradition, but his conservatism is of an unusual kind, partly because of the revolutionary character of its philosophical premisses, and partly because other assumptions reflect an eighteenth-century (rather than nineteenth- or twentieth- century) background. It is therefore misguided to present Hume as a paradigmatic conservative thinker (even if such a notion makes sense at all). He is, nevertheless, a particularly fine representative of one strand in conservative thinking, whose main characteristics are a cautious and moderate approach to politics (which does not exclude progressive change, provided this is gradual), backed up by a sceptical attitude towards all grandiose schemes for social or political reconstruction erected on rationalist foundations. This has at most time been the dominant element within British conservatism, and Hume might with justice be awarded pride of place in an account of that tradition.

PART I: JUDGEMENT

1

The Natural Workings of the Human Mind

Hume's professed intention, in both the *Treatise* and the first *Enquiry*, was to place the study of the human mind on a scientific footing, analogous to that achieved for the natural world by Newton, Bacon, and the other great scientists of the preceding century. Once the general principles governing the human understanding had been discovered, it would be possible to develop the three applied human sciences—morals, criticism, and politics. These, Hume thought, should be cultivated for their own sake, to satisfy curiosity, but also for practical reasons: the better we understood political life, for instance, the better able we should be to conduct our affairs according to our wishes. Thus it was no accident that increasing accuracy in philosophy went along with increasing stability in government.[1] Everything rested, therefore, on the general science of the mind, and Hume was faithful to his intentions in beginning his intellectual career with a work (*Treatise,* Book I) devoted entirely to it. The fact that later, embarrassed by its reception, he was to insist that the other parts of his philosophy could be understood without reference to his theory of the mind, should not mislead us. Theory B may be comprehensible without reference to theory A, and yet still rest on it, in the sense that assumptions essential to B are derivable only from A. We should take Hume at his word and begin by examining his science of the mind; we shall then be in a position to assess how far his other work—and especially his social and political thought—relies upon it.

The new science was to be governed by two fundamental principles, both Newtonian in inspiration. The first was the reduction of the complex to the simple. Human thought and human behaviour were to be explained in terms of a small number of basic causes, as Newton had explained the movements of the planets through his elementary laws of motion. The second was the 'experimental', or as we should say observational, method. All the propositions of Hume's science were to be verified empirically, by observation; no *a priori* hypotheses were to be allowed.

[1] *Enquiry* I, p. 10.

The basic propositions of this science had simply to be accepted on the basis of evidence, being themselves incapable of further explanation (again following the example of Newton, who had for instance treated gravity as an ultimate, though mysterious, causal force). Hume admitted that there was nothing strictly analogous to the controlled experiments of the natural sciences in the human realm. Instead it was necessary to rely on introspection and careful (though unsystematic) observation of the behaviour of men in society. He never thought that there might be a difference in principle between the natural and the human sciences.

Hume began his science with a conceptual apparatus inherited from his predecessors, especially from Locke. The contents of the mind are divided exhaustively into two categories, impressions and ideas. Impressions occur when we experience the external world through our five senses, or have internal feelings or emotions. Thus to see a table, to feel pain, to experience anger, is in each case to have an impression. Ideas, on the other hand, are said to be the copies of impressions, used in thinking, remembering, imagining, and similar mental activities. Thinking about a table, remembering a friend, imagining that one is in pain, all consist in having ideas. If ideas are copies of impressions, how does one distinguish, say, seeing a table from thinking about one? Hume's answer is that the impression has a greater degree of 'force and liveliness' than the corresponding idea.[2] This qualitative difference informs us directly whether an impression or an idea is occupying our consciousness—though not infallibly, for sometimes (in a fever for instance) our ideas become so vivid that we might mistake them for impressions.

Impressions themselves fall into two categories, those of sensation and those of reflection. The former, comprising sensory experiences and physical sensations such as pain, are said to arise immediately; although they may have causes (e.g. physiological ones) we are not aware of any such preceding events in our inner experience. Impressions of reflection include desires and emotions, and these are generated by prior impressions and/or ideas. Thus seeing an orange (an impression of sensation) may produce in me a desire to eat it (an impression of reflection); or imagining myself on top of a high building (an idea) may produce an emotion of fear (again an impression of reflection).

Among ideas, Hume's main distinction is between the ideas of the memory and those of the imagination, using the latter term

[2] *Treatise*, Book I, Part I, Section I; cf. *Enquiry* I, Section II.

for the moment in its familiar sense, to mean the faculty whereby we combine ideas freely and without regard to empirical fact (when day-dreaming, for instance). He claims that this distinction too can be made in terms of the relative vivacity of the two kinds of ideas, those of the memory being more forceful than those of the imagination.

Having made his classification, Hume advances a maxim that is to be reiterated throughout his analysis of the human mind: 'That all our simple ideas in their first appearance are deriv'd from simple impressions, which are correspondent to them, and which they exactly represent.'[3] He assumes that any complex idea (that of a golden mountain, for instance) can be broken down into elementary parts (that of gold, for instance) which cannot be resolved further, and then asserts that each of these simple ideas must have been derived from a preceding impression. If we have the idea of gold, we must at some time have had an impression of gold, from which the idea is copied. This is not an *a priori* truth but simply a fact about our experience. We do only have ideas derived from impressions, Hume claims; we cannot impart a new idea to someone except by arranging for him to have the corresponding impression. Hume's maxim is of great importance to him, because he uses it as a device to show up the impossibility of certain notions. Philosophers have tried to attach a special meaning to a term like 'power', he believes. They intend it to stand for the idea of an object's secret properties, which explain why the object behaves as it does. But in fact we have no such idea, because there is no impression from which we could have obtained it. If 'power' has a meaning, it cannot be what these philosophers claim.

Despite the importance of this maxim, Hume is remarkably cavalier in allowing an exception to it as soon as it is introduced. He suggests that if we were presented with a spectrum of different shades of blue, one shade being blocked out, we could form an idea of the missing shade even if, by some chance, we had never experienced it directly.[4] Hume seems content to regard this as an isolated case, not significant enough to be worth investigating further, and posing no threat to the use he wishes to make of his principle. Clearly the mechanism involved here is a form of extrapolation, and it might seem to us that once such a possibility is

---

[3] *Treatise*, p. 4.
[4] *Treatise*, pp. 5-6; *Enquiry* I, pp. 20-1.

admitted, Hume's razor will be seriously blunted. Might not 'powers', 'faculties', and the rest be reinstated as extrapolations from the more familiar properties of objects? This is one of the less satisfactory aspects of Hume's theory of ideas.

Up to this point it seems as though Hume is offering us an atomistic theory of the mind. Mental activity appears to be made up of a series of discrete perceptions, each occurring independently of its fellows. It is important, therefore, to see that Hume also has a well-developed theory of mental structure, which explains how the mind links together and arranges its atomic contents. The contrast that is sometimes made between, say, Hume and Kant, on the grounds that Hume regards the mind merely as the passive recipient of sensations (whereas Kant gives it an active role in perception) is thus mistaken. What remains true is that Hume regards the ordering of perceptions as something that happens in us, rather than as something that we do. He stresses the involuntary and unconscious character of the process, and minimizes the extent of deliberate decision. Hume often refers to this structure as 'the natural propensities of the mind'. 'Propensity' indicates that the inclination to connect impressions and ideas in particular ways is not irresistible, but operates for the most part. 'Natural' indicates that the propensities in question are endemic, but also inexplicable, at least so long as we confine ourselves to the study of the mind as such. Hume tosses out a suggestion that these propensities might have a physiological explanation in the structure of the brain[5] but declines to pursue the matter systematically.

The propensities that are announced publicly at the beginning of Hume's two works on the understanding are the three principles of the association of ideas.[6] Although the imagination is at liberty to juxtapose ideas in any way that it pleases, it will naturally connect them on the basis of *resemblance, contiguity* in time or place, and *cause and effect*. Thinking about some object will bring to mind objects that resemble it in appearance, objects that lie in close physical or temporal proximity to it, objects that either produce it or are produced by it. Sometimes this may result in confusion— for instance we may switch from thinking about X to thinking about something like X without realising we have done so— but in general we have to rely on these propensities, especially the third, to engage in directed thought at all. However it must

[5] See for instance *Treatise*, pp. 60-1.
[6] *Treatise*, Book I, Part I, Section IV; *Enquiry* I, Section III.

be stressed that Hume does not in the end succeed in reducing all our constructive mental activity to these three principles, and extra mental propensities are discovered as the need arises. These additional propensities are of great importance for our enquiry, and will be noted in due course.[7]

Having assembled his apparatus—the contents and propensities of the mind—Hume's main task is to explain how we come to make certain kinds of judgement on the basis of our experience. We make judgements, for instance about matters of fact not immediately present to our senses, that cannot be identified with the mere having of impressions or ideas. Hume wants to discover what is involved in making these judgements, and what causes them to be made. The account given will also settle the epistemological status of the judgements concerned—i.e. the question of what, if anything, can be offered in their justification. I assume that the two aspects of Hume's enquiry—the account of how judgements are made, and the assessment of their epistemological status—are interdependent, and so it is misguided to try to separate (as some commentators have done) the strictly 'philosophical' from the 'psychological' parts of Hume's theory of the mind.[8]

Before conducting the reader through discussions that may be found a little intricate in places, I ought to indicate that I regard Hume's theory of judgement as the crucial link between his philosophy and his political thought. The account of the mind's workings that is developed in relation to the understanding is subsequently used to underpin his theory of moral and political

---

[7] Hume also finds a principle whereby impressions are associated. 'All resembling impressions are connected together, and no sooner one arises than the rest immediately follow.' (*Treatise*, p. 283.) The examples given are of emotions, and of course this propensity can only operate where the succeeding impression is an impression of reflection. Kemp Smith has drawn attention to the fact that the five principles of association mentioned in *Treatise*, Book II are reduced to three in Book I. (Kemp Smith, *Philosophy of David Hume*, pp. 239-40). This, however, is hardly surprising given that impressions of reflection are not Hume's concern at the beginning of Book I. The fifth 'principle' is a concurrence of the association of impressions and the association of ideas (via one of the above relations), used to explain the emotions of pride and humility. This, it seems to me, should not be seen as an independent principle but as a resultant of the more basic propensities already mentioned. For a fuller discussion of this and the other principles of association, see J. Bricke, 'Hume's Associationist Psychology', *Journal of the History of the Behavioural Sciences*, x (1974), 397-409.

[8] This is no longer an unusual point of view. Besides Kemp Smith, *Philosophy of David Hume*, see, for instance, W. L. Robison, 'David Hume: Naturalist and Meta-Sceptic' in D. W. Livingston and J. T. King (eds.), *Hume: a Re-evaluation* (New York, 1976); B. Stroud, *Hume* (London, 1977).

judgement.[9] Superficially it might seem that, say, a judgement about cause and effect and a judgement about a government's title to power are so different in nature that no common 'theory of judgement' could be used to explain them both. But Hume does attempt to give just such a theory, with what success we shall have to judge as we proceed.

The most striking feature of Hume's theory of judgement is the reduced role assigned in it to reason. Although he is not always precise in his use of terms, reason in the strict sense is confined to the discovery of certain 'relations of ideas'. For instance, we might discover by reason that the idea designated by '4 x 3' is identical to the idea designated by '6 x 2'. In more modern terminology, reason can only establish the truth of analytic propositions, propositions true by virtue of the meaning of their constituent terms. Hume's test is whether the negation of a proposition is conceivable or not. The proposition 'Every effect has a cause' can be established by reason, because we cannot conceive of an effect without a preceding cause (as he would put it, the ideas are 'inseparable'); the proposition 'Every event has a cause', however, cannot be so established, because we can certainly *conceive* of an uncaused event, even if on empirical grounds we think that there are none such. Reason is said by Hume to establish knowledge, and is thus distinguished from other operations of the understanding which at best can produce 'probability'. This does not stop him presenting, at one point in the *Treatise*,[10] an argument designed to show that even knowledge in the strict sense can be put in doubt; the argument relies upon our known fallibility in following through complex chains of deductive reasoning. However Hume's main intention is to present reason as achieving a degree of certainty which cannot be achieved in judgements concerning matters of fact, and in that light the passage in question stands out as incongruous.

It is unlikely that anyone would consider empirical judgements as being based entirely on reason, in Hume's sense; a much more plausible view is that they are derived from a combination of reason and sense-experience. Reason, in other words, operating on the contents of sense-experience, allows us to form judgements

---

[9] This is intended as a statement about logical priority, not about the temporal order in which Hume worked out the two accounts. Kemp Smith's conjecture, that Hume first formulated a theory of moral judgement, which was then extended by analogy to empirical judgement, is well known. See Kemp Smith, *Philosophy of David Hume*, esp. chs. 1-2.

[10] *Treatise*, Book I, Part IV, Section I.

about matters of fact not present to the senses. This plausible view is subjected to sustained critical attack by Hume. In its place he offers us an account of judgement that depends upon the natural workings of the mind, and in which the imagination takes over the role more normally allotted to reason. The two most important classes of judgement considered are judgements of cause and effect and judgements concerning the external world. As Hume points out, we rely entirely on causal judgements in forming beliefs about the future, and indeed in forming beliefs about the past, apart from events directly remembered, since we can only use present facts as evidence for past events by assuming chains of causation. Judgements about the external world are in a sense still more basic, since they are needed to get beyond our impressions to actual events occurring in the world; but Hume treats causation first, supposing at this stage that judgements about objects and events are possible, and I shall follow his order of exposition.

In making a causal judgement we postulate a connection between two events A and B such that whenever event A occurs, we expect event B to follow immediately. The question at issue is how we can come to form such a judgement. Hume considers and rejects two possibilities. The first is that we discover a logical connection between A and B, so that reason alone can deduce the existence of B given the existence of A (as we can deduce the existence of a husband given the existence of a wife). Hume's reply to this is that cause and effect are always separately conceivable; there is nothing in the idea of the cause that implies the idea of the effect.[11] As a way of dramatizing the point he asks: suppose you were placed in the world without any prior experience to rely upon, how would you set about predicting the outcome of any event?

The same challenge might also be used to rebut the second possibility that Hume wishes to discard: that the judgement is made on the basis of some empirically discoverable property of the cause. The suggestion here is that sensory observation of A might detect some B-producing quality inherent in it. Hume's question here is: what kind of quality might this be, and (supposing it not to be directly observable) what reason have we to assume that it is uniformly connected with those properties that are observable? For instance we believe that bread nourishes human beings.

[11] *Enquiry* I, Section IV, Part I.

But how can we infer from the visible texture and colour of bread that it possesses nutritious powers?[12]

Hence neither reason nor simple experience allows us to make judgements of cause and effect. To find out how such judgements are made, we need to consider the circumstances under which we come to make them. What conditions are necessary for us to judge that A causes B? First, A and B must be spatially and temporally contiguous[13]—there must be no gaps between them, unless these gaps are filled by intermediate causes. Second, A must precede B in time. Third, events similar to A must always have been followed by events similar to B; Hume's phrase for this is that there should be a 'constant conjunction' between cause and effect. Now if all these conditions hold, it is tempting to think that there is a rational inference to the conclusion that A will cause B. But Hume points out that such an inference would require as its premiss 'that instances, of which we have had no experience, must resemble those, of which we have had experience, and that the course of nature continues always uniformly the same'.[14] He has no difficulty in showing that this principle cannot be demonstrated by reason; and regarded as an empirical generalization it has no stronger foundation than the particular causal judgement which it is being used to establish. The conclusion we reach is that, even given the three conditions listed above, there is no rational means of arriving at a judgement of cause and effect.

Since, however, we do as a matter of fact make such judgements, constantly and unavoidably, there must be some other mechanism in the human mind which allows us to do so. Hume finds this in the imagination. Now 'imagination' is used by Hume in two senses, which he is not always careful enough in distinguishing, but whose separation is vital if we are to make sense of his philosophy. In the first and more familiar sense, imagination is the faculty whereby we associate ideas in arbitrary ways, conjuring up creatures and events that have never been met with in experience. Hume emphasizes the freedom of the imagination in this sense, insisting only that its basic materials are limited to copies of impressions previously received. He sometimes refers to it as 'the fancy', thereby underlining its capricious nature.

---

[12] *Enquiry* I, pp. 33, 37.

[13] Hume will later wish to drop the requirement of spatial contiguity for causal relations involving non-material events (which have no spatial location)—but this complication need not concern us here.

[14] *Treatise*, p. 89.

However 'imagination' is also used in a second sense, to mean the faculty whereby we form judgements according to the principles of association of ideas. Here, then, the imagination is not arbitrary but rule-governed—it connects, for instance, the thought of one room in a house with the thought of the neighbouring rooms (principle of contiguity).[15] Although normally wanting to under-line the similarities between the two kinds of imagination (both being contrasted with reason), Hume sometimes separates imagination in the second sense from the mere 'fancy' by referring to it as the 'judgement' or the 'understanding'. This tendency is particularly marked in *Enquiry* I, where Hume seems to want to play down the more disturbing aspects of his theory of the mind. It is *not* the case, however, that 'imagination' in the second sense disappears from the *Enquiry*, as Kemp Smith has claimed.[16] Consider the following passage:

> Whenever any object is presented to the memory or senses, it immediately, by the force of custom, carries the imagination to conceive that object, which is usually conjoined to it; and this conception is attended with a feeling or sentiment, different from the loose reveries of the fancy.[17]

This is precisely the same contrast as is made in the *Treatise*. One might add that there are good reasons for Hume to retain this second sense of 'imagination' (the faculty for combining ideas according to the principles of association), since he will later need to distinguish better and worse uses of this faculty, and wish to reserve the term 'judgement' for the better uses.

The workings of the imagination in the second sense explain

---

[15] Hume also on occasion uses 'imagination' broadly to refer collectively to all mental faculties other than memory. At one point in the *Treatise* he recognizes that this is a possible source of confusion: 'The word, imagination, is commonly us'd in two different senses; and tho' nothing be more contrary to true philosophy, than this inaccuracy, yet in the following reasonings I have often been oblig'd to fall into it. When I oppose the imagination to the memory, I mean the faculty, by which we form our fainter ideas. When I oppose it to reason, I mean the same faculty, excluding only our demonstrative and probable reasonings.' (pp. *Treatise*, 117-8.) In the last sentence 'reason' is expanded to include the rule-governed imagination, which forms all 'probable' judgements (i.e. judgements concerning matters of fact not immediately present to the senses), and contrasted with the 'fanciful' imagination. In seeking to eliminate one source of confusion, Hume has in-advertently introduced another (the broader sense of 'reason' is frequently used by Hume in expounding his moral philosophy). It would be less confusing to say that imagination, in the broad sense, covers reason proper, the rule-governed imagination, and the fancy. For two rather different attempts to systematize Hume's use of 'imagination' see E. J. Furlong, 'Imagination in Hume's *Treatise* and *Enquiry Concerning the Human Understanding*', *Philosophy*, xxxvi (1961), 62-70; J. Wilbanks, *Hume's Theory of Imagination* (The Hague, 1968).

[16] Kemp Smith, *Philosophy of David Hume,* p. 461.   [17] *Enquiry* I, p. 48.

our judgements of cause and effect. These have, in fact, two distinct aspects which need to be explained. First, why do we believe that the effect will occur when we become aware that the cause has occurred? Second, why do we assume a necessary connection between cause and effect; in other words, why do we believe that the effect not only *will* occur but *must* occur? In reply to the first question, Hume argues that repeated observation of events similar to A followed by events similar to B establishes a customary connection in the imagination between the idea of A and the idea of B, so that whenever we think of A we are naturally led (by the force of custom) to think of B as well. Suppose now that we are presented with an actual impression of A. In the terms of Hume's philosophy of mind, this is similar to, but much more vivid than, the mere idea of A. We are at once led to think of B, as before; but the vivacity of the impression is communicated to the associated idea, and we not only contemplate B, but actually believe in its occurrence. For belief, Hume claims, is 'a lively idea related to or associated with a present impression'.[18]

In the course of this explanation we have stumbled across a new propensity of the mind: its capacity to transfer 'vivacity' between associated ideas. There is more to come, however. We have still to explain why we suppose there is a *necessary* connection between cause and effect. Hume has shown that the impressions we receive of A and B themselves do not allow us to make this supposition. Instead the idea of necessary connection has its source in the imagination's own compulsion to pass from the idea of A to the idea of B. When making this transition, we not only pass from one idea to the other, but feel an internal compulsion to do so. This is an impression of reflection. From it we form the idea of a necessary connection between cause and effect.

But if this is so, why do we suppose that the necessary connection holds between the events themselves, rather than merely between our ideas of the events? Why do we say 'B must follow A' rather than 'I can't help thinking of B when I think of A'? Hume answers as follows:

'Tis a common observation, that the mind has a great propensity to spread itself on external objects, and to conjoin with them any internal impressions, which they occasion, and which always make their appearance at the same time that these objects discover themselves to the senses … the same propensity is the reason, why we suppose necessity and power to lie in the objects we consider, not

---

[18] *Treatise*, p. 96.

in our mind, that considers them; notwithstanding it is not possible for us to form the most distant idea of that quality, when it is not taken for the determination of the mind, to pass from the idea of an object to that of its usual attendant.[19]

This implies that our belief in a necessary connection between events is a species of fiction. The imagination projects its internal impression on to the objects whose conjunction gives rise to it, thus endowing that impression with a spurious externality. We begin to see the sceptical conclusion to which Hume is taking us. Not only are beliefs usually thought to be the products of reason in fact the products of the imagination conditioned by custom, but at least one of our essential beliefs—that cause and effect are necessarily connected—is literally false. But to establish the precise nature of Hume's scepticism, we must wait to examine his account of judgements about the external world.

This account is one of the most difficult aspects of Hume's work to comprehend, and the treatment given below will be very inadequate. It is necessary to say something about it, however, partly for the reason just given, and partly because in the course of his account Hume discovers yet more mental propensities which turn out to have some significance for his political thought.[20]

Up to now we have been assuming that our impressions make us directly acquainted with objects and events in the external world. In so doing we have adopted the point of view of 'the vulgar' who, Hume tells us, 'suppose their perceptions to be their only objects, and never think of a double existence internal and external, representing and represented'.[21] As soon as we subject this supposition to critical scrutiny, however, it turns out to be groundless; for it is clear that our impressions of an object can alter while the object remains the same—if, for instance, there is some change in the state of our sensory organs. Once the distinction between perceptions and objects is admitted, it becomes difficult to account for our beliefs about the objects themselves. Since all we actually experience are the perceptions, why should we suppose that there is a material world beyond our perceptions, displaying properties not possessed by those perceptions?

Hume argues that there are two, analytically separable, qualities that we attribute to material objects and that stand in need of

---

[19] *Treatise*, p. 167.

[20] Unlike his account of causation, Hume's treatment of the problem of external objects is confined largely to the *Treatise*. There is merely a passing reference to the problem in *Enquiry* I, Section XII.

[21] *Treatise*, p. 205.

explanation. We suppose that they have a *continued* existence (i.e. exist when not being perceived) and that they have a *distinct* existence (i.e. whether perceived or not, they are specifically different from our perceptions). Clearly neither supposition can be explained by direct reference to the impressions we receive. Instead we must look for some general features of our impressions which, taken together with the natural propensities of the mind, produce these two beliefs.

The two features which Hume believes to be relevant are the *constancy* and *coherence* of our impressions. Many objects provide us with impressions that are more or less uniform; if I glance repeatedly at a mountain, I receive the same visual impression on each occasion. This is what Hume means by 'constancy'. Other objects provide us with changing impressions, but the changes occur in regular ways:

> When I return to my chamber after an hour's absence, I find not my fire in the same situation, in which I left it: But then I am accustom'd in other instances to see a like alteration produc'd in a like time, whether I am present or absent, near or remote.[22]

This illustrates the coherence of impressions.

Hume implies that if our experience did not manifest these two qualities, we should not come to believe in the existence of an external world. But given that it does, how is the belief formed? Hume focuses first on the quality of coherence, and suggests that the imagination, presented with an incomplete series of impressions that nevertheless manifest a pattern, is irresistibly led to complete the series by postulating a continuing object that would have produced the missing impressions had an observer been present. The fire, let us say, was burning fiercely an hour ago; now it shows only a dull glow. These two impressions lack coherence unless we suppose that at the half-hour there was a fire that glowed bright red. Since we have received no such impression, we postulate an external object which has this property, and thus preserve the coherence of our experience.

The difficulty with this account, Hume recognizes, is that we attribute to external objects *complete* continuity of existence, and this exceeds the degree of coherence that we find in our impressions. We may, of course, at some time have stared at the fire for an hour without break; but there is no object that we maintain in view during every hour of the day. How, then, can

----

[22] *Treatise*, p. 195.

we arrive at the idea of fully continuous existence which has no precedent among our impressions? Hume's answer is that

the imagination, when set into any train of thinking, is apt to continue, even when its object fails it, and like a galley put in motion by the oars, carries on its course without any new impulse ... Objects have a certain coherence even as they appear to our senses; but this coherence is much greater and more uniform, if we suppose the objects to have a continu'd existence; and as the mind is once in the train of observing an uniformity among objects, it naturally continues, till it renders the uniformity as compleat as possible.[23]

Here, then, we have found another natural propensity of the imagination, which might be referred to as a perfecting principle. Given incomplete instances of some property, we are told, the imagination can form the idea of a complete instance. This appears to contravene Hume's original doctrine that every idea must be preceded in our experience by a corresponding impression—a doctrine, it now seems, that is violated as often as it is observed.

Perhaps because he is worried by the rather flimsy nature of the argument so far, Hume now turns his attention to the other relevant feature of our experience— the constancy of impressions. He suggests, first, that we obtain our idea of the identity of objects by observing them constantly over a period of time.[24] Suppose now that, instead of gazing constantly at a neighbouring mountain, I look at it intermittently. I thus receive a series of qualitatively similar but numerically different impressions. On the basis of these impressions alone, I have no reason to posit anything continuing in existence throughout the period of time in question. But, Hume suggests—and this is the crux of the argument—the two experiences (constant observation and intermittent observation) *feel* rather similar. I am therefore liable to confuse them, and suppose myself to have been receiving constant impressions when in fact I have merely been receiving intermittent ones. In Hume's words:

An easy transition or passage of the imagination, along the ideas of these different and interrupted perceptions, is almost the same disposition of mind with that in which we consider one constant and uninterrupted perception. 'Tis therefore very natural for us to mistake the one for the other.[25]

---

[23] *Treatise*, p. 198.
[24] Showing this requires some tricky footwork on Hume's part, but there is no space to give the argument here. See *Treatise*, pp. 199-201.
[25] *Treatise*, p. 204.

The argument here is fairly tortuous (as Hume admits in a foot-note: 'This reasoning, it must be confest, is somewhat abstruse, and difficult to be comprehended'), but let us see where it leaves us. The mind has had the experience of an interrupted series of impressions; but it is also inclined to conflate this with the similar experience of constant perception. It is therefore pulled in two ways. The contradiction is removed by inventing a distinction between the object of perception (which is constant) and the perception itself (which is intermittent). By this artifice the mind's uneasiness is resolved. The interruptions in experience are catered for by the positing of perceptions (which have that property); and the (imagined) continuity in experience is taken care of by the positing of objects of perception (which have *that* property).

Hume has now, in a way, explained how we come to believe in the continued existence of objects; he has also shown why we come to think them distinct from our perceptions (i.e. why we are obliged to invent a division between impression and object). But the explanation is hardly satisfactory, nor is Hume at all content with the position he has reached. For one thing, the explanation has had to rely on a most improbable kind of mistake—the confusion of intermittent perception with constant perception. For another, there seems to be no tenable position left for Hume, or anyone else, to hold. Those whom Hume refers to as 'the vulgar' simply identify perceptions and objects. Since each of these has properties which contradict those of the other, such a position can only be maintained so long as the contradiction is overlooked. Any reflection at all will convince us that it is necessary to make a distinction: this leads to what Hume calls 'the philo-sophical system'—the postulation of a dual world of perceptions and objects. But once this distinction is made reflectively, we are no longer able to give any justification for postulating objects having a continued and distinct existence. It seems essential to Hume's mechanism for explaining this belief that it operates without self-reflection; place it under critical scrutiny and it at once collapses. So the logical consequence of the philosophical system is complete scepticism, according to which all that we can assume to exist is a series of discrete and vanishing perceptions. That no one is actually driven to this conclusion testifies only to the hold which the vulgar system has on us, despite its manifest absurdity.

It is hardly surprising that Hume's discussion of judgements concerning the external world should lead him on to some of the most deeply sceptical passages in his philosophical work.[26] But before trying to establish the precise nature of Hume's scepticism, we ought to take stock of his theory of judgement as so far presented. The general outcome of that theory is a reduction in the role assigned to reason in the formation of judgement, and a corresponding increase in the role assigned to the imagination. One consequence is that judgement becomes a matter of feeling rather. than logical compulsion:

> Thus all probable reasoning is nothing but a species of sensation. 'Tis not solely in poetry and music, we must follow our taste and sentiment, but likewise in philosophy. When I am convinc'd of any principle, 'tis only an idea, which strikes more strongly upon me. When I give the preference to one set of arguments above another, I do nothing but decide from my feeling concerning the superiority of their influence.[27]

Next, we have discovered that the main force influencing the imagination is that of custom. The imagination connects ideas, primarily, as a result of the repeated juxtaposition of the corresponding impressions in our experience. There is nothing 'rational' in this, but were it not to occur we should never be able to make judgements that went beyond our immediate impressions:

> Custom, then, is the great guide of human life. It is that principle alone which renders our experience useful to us, and makes us expect, for the future, a similar train of events with those which have appeared in the past. Without the influence of custom, we should be entirely ignorant of every matter of fact beyond what is immediately present to the memory and senses.[28]

Third, the imagination has been found to possess propensities that are not only non-rational but positively irrational; nevertheless these propensities must be invoked to account for judgements that we all make as a matter of course. To single out some of the more striking: the imagination has a propensity to *project* impressions in the mind on to the objects which produce them; it has a tendency to *perfect* its ideas by conceiving of perfect instances of some property X, even though experience has only furnished us with imperfect instances of X; and it is liable to *confuse* resembling modes of experience and so to generate contradictory beliefs. Obviously none of these tendencies is defensible when subjected to rational criticism. So it appears that Hume's science of the

---

[26] These occur in *Treatise,* Book I, Part IV. Hume's avoidance of the problem of the external world in *Enquiry* I is in keeping with the more comfortable general tone of that work.

[27] *Treatise,* p. 103.

[28] *Enquiry* I, pp. 44-5.

mind, although accounting for the judgements we make in terms of the mechanisms that produce them (albeit less tidily than had at first been hoped), has at the same time undermined those judgements by showing them to rest on foundations that are absurdly flimsy. Is Hume, then, a sceptic about human understanding? Is the upshot of his account a generalized doubt about the products of mental activity?

I think that Hume recognizes four distinct positions that one can adopt on this issue.[29] There is first of all the point of view held by 'the vulgar'—'all the unthinking and unphilosophical part of mankind' (Hume adds 'that is, all of us at one time or other'). The vulgar have an unquestioning confidence in our capacity to make judgements, simply because they never reflect on the intellectual processes involved. It does not strike them that every causal judgement requires an unwarranted inference, or that every judgement about material objects involves a contradiction, because they do not subject these judgements to any kind of critical scrutiny. Hume has some sympathy with this position, but it is of course not available to those who have once bitten the philosophical apple. It crumbles upon the slightest amount of reflection.

The second position is ascribed to 'philosophers' in general, and consists in an attempt to rationalize the beliefs that the vulgar take for granted. The philosopher will try to show that, for instance, judgements of cause and effect can be rationally justified. Hume's whole effort has been directed to showing that this position is untenable; it rests on sheer impossibility. It can only be maintained through gross failures of logic and argument.

The third position follows from the second and may be described as extreme scepticism ('Pyrrhonism' is the term that Hume sometimes uses for it). The extreme sceptic sees that the philosopher's arguments are no good, and concludes that we have no rational warrant for believing in anything beyond the immediate contents of our experience. He attempts to doubt all the judgements which the vulgar make unthinkingly. But, Hume argues, this doubt proves to be impossible to sustain, not because it is logically unsound, but because our natural propensities reassert themselves too forcefully:

Nature, by an absolute and uncontroulable necessity has determin'd us to judge as well as to breathe and feel; nor can we any more forbear viewing certain objects in a stronger and fuller light, upon account of their customary connexion with a

---

[29] See *Treatise*, Book I, Part IV, Sections II, III, IV, VII; *Enquiry* I, Section XII.

present impression, than we can hinder ourselves from thinking as long as we are awake, or seeing the surrounding bodies, when we turn our eyes towards them in broad sunshine. Whoever has taken the pains to refute the cavils of this *total* scepticism, has really disputed without an antagonist, and endeavour'd by arguments to establish a faculty, which nature has antecedently implanted in the mind, and render'd unavoidable.[30]

Hume sees extreme scepticism, therefore, as being both irrefutable and unnecessary to refute. No rational arguments can be brought against it, but that does not matter because the would-be sceptic will be unable to maintain his sceptical position in the face of natural instinct. At most such scepticism can produce 'a momentary amazement and confusion', for as long as rational reflection alone can keep nature at bay.

The fourth position is Hume's, and he refers to it as 'moderate' or 'mitigated' scepticism. The difficulty is to explain precisely how it differs from the Pyrrhonism that Hume wishes to reject.[31] From his response to Pyrrhonism, it may appear to consist in the following three theses: (a) reason is incapable of vindicating many of the judgements we normally make; (b) nevertheless we are led by an unavoidable natural necessity to make these judgements; (c) we must therefore recognize the presence of contrary impulses within the mind, and endeavour to achieve some kind of internal balance, giving way neither to naïve confidence in our judgement, nor to extreme scepticism. This is at least a fairly comfortable position to take up, and it may be the one that Hume eventually embraced. In the *Treatise,* however, he seems unable to accept such a solution. In that work he confesses that, so long as he is engaged in philosophical enquiry (and thus subjecting beliefs to rational criticism), it is impossible to avoid falling subject to Pyrrhonian doubt. Relief from this doubt is only to be gained by quitting philosophy and returning to 'life':

The *intense* view of these manifold contradictions and imperfections in human reason has so wrought upon me, and heated my brain, that I am ready to reject all belief and reasoning, and can look upon no opinion even as more probable or likely than another ... Most fortunately it happens, that since reason is incapable of dispelling these clouds, nature herself suffices to that purpose, and cures me of this philosophical melancholy and delirium, either by relaxing this bent of mind, or by some avocation, and lively impression of my senses, which obliterate all these chimeras. I dine, I play a game of back-gammon, I converse, and am

---

[30] *Treatise,* p. 183.

[31] For further discussion see R. H. Popkin, 'David Hume: His Pyrrhonism and His Critique of Pyrrhonism' in V. C. Chappell (ed.), *Hume* (London, 1968); W. L. Robison, 'David Hume: Naturalist and Meta-Sceptic'.

merry with my friends; and when after three or four hour's amusement, I wou'd return to these speculations, they appear so cold, and strain'd, and ridiculous, that I cannot find in my heart to enter into them any farther.[32]

This amounts to denying that any intellectually satisfying solution to the dilemma is possible. Instead of arriving at a balanced position, it seems that we are condemned to a perpetual oscillation between scepticism (while doing philosophy) and naïve belief (while playing backgammon, etc.). Moderate scepticism must then consist in recognizing the oscillation, retrospectively and prospectively (it cannot just consist in *experiencing* the oscillation, since that happens to Pyrrhonian sceptics too). This is equivalent to recognizing that one is, by turns, a philosopher and one of the 'vulgar', but never both at once.

Despite the tortured conclusion to the *Treatise,* however, Hume appears in general to relapse into the more comfortable position identified above,[33] and this is the view that informs his work on morals and politics. The essence of the position is that one should recognize the necessity of making certain kinds of judgement, while denying that these judgements have a foundation in reason. They cannot stand up to rational criticism, but we are naturally obliged to make them, and it is folly to try to resist natural necessity. There is, nonetheless, one difference between judgements about the natural world and judgements about morals and politics that will demand our attention in due course. In the former case scepticism is quickly seen to be absurd, and so is harmless; sceptical arguments, Hume says, 'admit of no answer and produce no conviction'. In morals and politics, however, scepticism may have a disturbing effect by undermining convictions that are necessary to the maintenance of normal social and political life. Here it is more urgent to rebut both extreme scepticism and those philosophical systems which (by attempting to give our judgements a rational foundation) are liable to generate it.

---

[32] *Treatise,* pp. 268-9.

[33] Consider the following passage, for example: 'All sceptics pretend that, if reason be considered in an abstract view, it furnishes invincible arguments against itself, and that we could never retain any conviction or assurance, on any subject, were not the sceptical reasonings so refined and subtile that they are not able to counterpoise the more solid and more natural arguments derived from the senses and experience. But it is evident, whenever our arguments lose this advantage and run wide of common life, that the most refined scepticism comes to be on a footing with them, and is able to oppose and counterbalance them. The one has no more weight than the other. The mind must remain in suspense between them; and it is that very suspense or balance which is the triumph of scepticism.' (Hume, *Dialogues Concerning Natural Religion,* ed. H. D. Aiken (New York, 1948). I assume that Philo speaks for Hume here.)

Before finishing with Hume's account of the natural workings of the mind, there is one further question that must be considered. Does Hume's moderate scepticism effectively leave everything as it was before? Is the consequence of abandoning the attempt to provide a rational foundation for belief, in favour of a reliance on 'nature', to give a blanket endorsement to all the judgements that the vulgar make? Hume would answer in the negative.[34] While the main target of his theory of judgement is philosophical rationalism, he takes occasional sideswipes at 'superstition', 'prejudice', and the like—i.e. at beliefs that are held to have less justification than the rest of our everyday convictions. Since he appears to have removed the ground on which a distinction of this kind might be made, we ought to see how he proposes to draw the contrast.

The key passage is the following:

In order to justify myself, I must distinguish in the imagination betwixt the principles which are permanent, irresistable, and universal; such as the customary transition from causes to effects, and from effects to causes: And the principles, which are changeable, weak, and irregular; such as those I have just now taken notice of. The former are the foundation of all our thoughts and actions, so that upon their removal human nature must immediately perish and go to ruin. The latter are neither unavoidable to mankind, nor necessary, or so much as useful in the conduct of life; but on the contrary are observ'd only to take place in weak minds, and being opposite to the other principles of custom and reasoning, may easily be subverted by a due contrast and opposition. For this reason the former are received by philosophy, and the latter rejected.[35]

Hume is suggesting that we sometimes find tendencies in the imagination that are opposed to one another, leading us to make contradictory judgements in particular cases. When this occurs it is possible, by an act of reflection, to separate tendencies which are inescapable—those which we cannot avoid without abandoning a whole class of ordinary judgements—from those that are dispensable. We can also choose to follow the former propensities and avoid the latter. To give two illustrations, we cannot avoid forming an association between two ideas when their corresponding impressions are uniformly linked in our experience; but we *can* avoid forming a rigid association when the relevant impressions are linked only in the majority of cases, but not uniformly—even though there is a natural tendency to form the

---

[34] Two valuable discussions of this issue are H. H. Price, 'The Permanent Significance of Hume's Philosophy' *Philosophy*, xv (1940), 7-37, and J. A. Passmore, 'Hume and the Ethics of Belief' in G. P. Morice (ed.), *David Hume: Bicentenary Papers* (Edinburgh, 1977).

[35] *Treatise*, p. 225.

association in these circumstances. We observe that most Irishmen are unintelligent (Hume's example, not mine) and conclude that no Irishman can have wit.[36] But, by reflection, we are able to distinguish such partial correlations from complete uniformities and to resist the temptation to convert the one into the other. Again, we tend naturally to suppose that an object superficially similar to A will have causal consequences like those of A. But, by reflection, we can distinguish the features of A which actually produce those effects from other features which may be striking to our senses but have no causal efficacy.[37] Both of these examples illustrate what Hume terms the use of 'general rules', and demonstrate the possibility of correcting our beliefs by using a higher-order general rule to override a lower-order one. Hume in fact lists a number of these higher-order rules in the section of the *Treatise* entitled 'Rules by which to judge of causes and effects'. Obviously there would be no point in his doing this if he did not believe our judgement could be improved by conscious reflection.

When he is discussing this possibility, Hume sometimes speaks in terms of a contrast between imagination and judgement. 'Imagination' refers to the defective belief, 'judgement' to the more adequate belief formed under the influence of higher-level general rules. Although there is some convenience in this distinction, we should be aware that the mechanism involved in generating belief is in both cases that which Hume had previously identified as the imagination. We are in no way escaping from the reign of custom in such cases; rather we use custom to correct custom. For instance we have learnt, by repeated experience, that we are apt to inflate a partial correlation into a complete uniformity, and so fall into error in particular cases. The habit that results—of paying attention to the distinction between partial and uniform correlations—can preserve us from other habits, say of connecting Irishness uniformly with lack of wit. One could equally well speak of better and worse uses of the imagination here.

Not all men are equally skilled at correcting the irregular workings of the imagination, and so Hume draws a contrast between the vulgar, who follow the imagination uncorrected, and the wise, who by reflection succeed in making the necessary corrections.[38] This is an important contrast, but it is *not* the same

---

[36] *Treatise*, pp. 146-7.
[37] *Treatise*, p. 148.
[38] *Treatise*, p. 150.

as the contrast introduced earlier between the vulgar and the philosophers. It is as well to be clear on this point. When distinguishing the vulgar from the philosophers, Hume is contrasting men who take their natural beliefs for granted with men who think (mistakenly) that these natural beliefs can be given a rational justification. When distinguishing the vulgar from the wise, he is contrasting men whose natural beliefs result from every turn and twist of the imagination (as well as its permanent principles) with men whose natural beliefs all flow from the permanent principles. To be included among the wise, it is not necessary to be a philosopher; it is enough to be a careful observer and thinker. Hume's philosophy may of course help to convert one from vulgarity to wisdom, because it explains how the imagination can err, and therefore why and how it needs to be corrected by reflection.

Hume's theory of judgement, as we have examined it so far, has three main features which will prove to be of significance for his social and political thought. First, in accordance with his project of developing a science of the mind, he has given an account of how judgements are made. This account makes primary reference to the imagination and its various natural propensities. Second, it has been shown that the judgements thus made are incapable of being rationally vindicated. Attempts to provide such a vindication end in total scepticism. In the light of this, the appropriate attitude to adopt is one of mitigated scepticism, which involves both conceding that our beliefs cannot be justified rationally and recognizing that we are obliged by nature to believe and judge in the normal way. Third, it does not follow from these theses that our judgement cannot be improved; but such improvement is misconstrued if it is thought to consist in replacing non-rational judgement by rational judgement. Improvement can only take place within the limits set by the natural workings of the mind. The permanent principles of the imagination can be employed to counteract the fluctuating ones. It is not a matter of judging in a way fundamentally different from the vulgar consciousness, but of employing principles recognized by that consciousness in order to correct it. Mitigated scepticism shows how better judgement is possible, but is suitably modest about the character of the improvement.

2

Passion, Reason, and Morality

Despite Hume's assurance that his account of the understanding was meant to provide a grounding for the practical sciences of morals, criticism, and politics, it may seem that on turning from the first book of the *Treatise* to the second and third, we are entering a wholly new realm of enquiry. If, like many readers, we move directly to the opening part of Book III (or to the corresponding portions of *Enquiry* II: Section I and Appendix I), we find Hume asserting a sharp dichotomy between reason, which now comprehends all the operations of the understanding that we have so far examined, and sentiment, which is the essential ingredient both of the passions and of moral judgement. Two of Hume's best-known theses are that moral distinctions cannot be derived solely from reason, and that reason can never provide a motive for action. ' 'Tis not contrary to reason to prefer the destruction of the whole world to the scratching of my finger', Hume had written earlier, and this startling claim appears at first sight to provide the key to his treatment of the passions and morality. In considering these subjects we are still dealing with impressions and ideas, of course, but the perceptions we have now to consider seem wholly distinct from those involved in the workings of the understanding.

First appearances, however, are deceptive. One is likely to arrive at the view just outlined by concentrating too much on the negative side of Hume's theory of morals, just as one can distort Hume's epistemology by looking only at his attack on rationalism and ignoring the positive theory of judgement that he offers in its place. Hume's most clamant denials of reason's role in producing judgement occur when he is attacking ethical rationalism, the view that moral judgements may be derived entirely by the use of reason. Although these arguments have a permanent significance for moral philosophy, they by no means make up the whole of Hume's ethical theory. As Hume develops the constructive side of his position, he gives increasing emphasis to the part played by the understanding in the genesis of moral judgement. He never abandons the view that sentiment is a necessary ingredient of such judgement; but sentiment is only one ingredient, along with other mental operations that are equally necessary. Furthermore, in so far as we are interested in moral disagreements, and the possibilities of resolving them, it is these other operations which should command our attention. Hume assumes that mankind are very much alike in their basic moral sentiments, so such disagreements in moral opinion as do arise are due to the different circumstances in which men find themselves, or to differences in (non-moral) judgement.[1] The latter are resolvable to the extent that the understanding in general is capable of correction, a subject we have already considered.

Over all, Hume's theory of morality depends on his theory of the understanding in two respects. First, processes in the understanding are referred to in order to explain how moral judgements are made. In particular, the imagination has a significant role to play in forming moral judgements, both in general and more especially in the case of judgements about justice and allegiance to government. This is a theme which will be taken up in the following chapters. Second, the general cast of Hume's moral theory may be described as mitigated scepticism, and in this respect it closely parallels his theory of the understanding, the parallelism being not merely a formal similarity, but a result of the connection just noted. This mitigated scepticism can be summed up in three propositions: (1) moral judgements cannot be based entirely on reason, and so are incapable of justification in the strong sense of rational demonstration; (2) we should not, however, embrace the sceptical view that such judgements are entirely arbitrary, for they have a secure foundation in human nature; (3) moral judgements are capable of correction and improvement, but such improvement cannot consist in giving them a fully rational justification; it is limited by the necessary role that sentiment plays in such judgements, and by the general properties of the understanding. As in his account of empirical judgement, we see Hume endeavouring to steer a middle course between rationalism (represented in this case by ethical rationalists such as Clarke and Wollaston) and out-and-out scepticism (here represented by philosophers such as Mandeville who 'have

---

[1] On the uniformity in moral sentiment, see *Treatise*, p. 547, footnote; and Hume, 'The Sceptic', *Essays*, p. 168, footnote. Differences due to the effects of custom and of what Hume calls 'artificial lives' are discussed in Hume, *A Dialogue* in Hume, *Enquiries Concerning Human Understanding and Concerning the Principles of Morals*, ed. L. A. Selby-Bigge, 3rd edn. revised P. H. Nidditch (Oxford, 1975).

represented all moral distinctions as the effect of artifice and education'[2]).

Before moving on to a detailed examination of Hume's account of the passions and moral judgement, a final introductory remark is necessary. It is important to realize that Hume is giving us precisely a theory of moral judgement. That is, he is telling us what is involved in making such a judgement as that Smith is a virtuous man (moral judgements according to Hume are directed primarily at the qualities of individuals, only secondarily at actions, as we shall see). This is to be distinguished from an account of moral sentiment or feeling even though, for Hume, the connection between feeling and judgement is very close. More importantly, it is to be distinguished from an account of moral activity—an account of what is happening when a man acts out of moral conviction. According to Hume the connection between moral judgement and moral activity is contingent and variable. On the one hand, it is possible to acquire a motive for action as a result of making such a judgement; on the other, it is possible to make a moral judgement and yet have no desire to act as a result of it. Unlike some recent philosophers, who see moral judgements as being essentially prescriptive and action-guiding, Hume recognizes that they have a contemplative aspect as well. We may pass judgement, for example, on historical characters even though their circumstances are so different from our own that no practical implications could be drawn from what we say. Hume is interested in what is taking place in such an instance, as well as in the more familiar case when a judgement is made with the intention of affecting our own or others' activities. The question how far men are influenced in practice by moral judgements is separate from the question what is involved in making these judgements, and the first question will not be considered until Part II. All we need say at this point is that Hume must believe moral judgements to have *some* influence on practice, otherwise moral philosophy (which aims in part to improve these judgements) would have no beneficial consequences, and his optimistic remarks at the very beginning of the *Treatise* and the *Enquiry* I[3] would be groundless.

---

[2] *Treatise*, p. 578. Cf. *Treatise*, p. 500 and *Enquiry* II, p. 214; in the latter case ancient sceptics are included as well.
[3] See above, ch. 1, p. 19.

Hume's moral theory is best approached by looking first at his account of the passions.[4] Although he does not actually describe the moral sentiments as passions, there is a close resemblance between the two kinds of feeling. Certain aspects of Hume's theory of morals become clearer when the parallels are observed. This is particularly so in the case of the passions of pride and humility, where the resemblance to moral sentiments is most pronounced.

Both passions and moral sentiments are classified by Hume as impressions of reflection, meaning (we recall) that they are vivid perceptions which arise from some preceding impression or idea. But Hume further classifies the passions as direct or indirect according to the kind of causal mechanism involved in their production. Direct passions are said at first to arise immediately from pleasure and pain; in other words, if contemplating some object or state of affairs produces a sensation of pleasure, this may generate in turn a direct passion, such as a desire to obtain the object or simply a delight at its existence. However Hume also says that certain of the direct passions 'arise from a natural impulse or instinct, which is perfectly unaccountable. Of this kind is the desire of punishment to our enemies, and of happiness to our friends; hunger, lust, and a few other bodily appetites.'[5] It seems wrong to describe these passions as impressions of reflection, since no preceding impression is required to produce them. There is untidiness in Hume's account here, probably attributable to the fact that he is chiefly interested in the indirect passions and includes the direct largely for the sake of completeness. We can see, however, that Hume is no dogmatic hedonist. Since passions such as hunger and revenge can plainly serve as motives for action, not every action is motivated by the thought of pleasure or pain. (Satisfying these passions may of course produce pleasure or pain, but, as Hume acutely observes, that does not make the thought of pleasure or pain their cause.)

Indirect passions are produced by pleasure or pain together with other mental perceptions. Taking the example of pride, to feel proud of a painting it is not enough to gain pleasure from observing it; I must also perceive some connection between the painting and myself—I have produced it or own it, for instance. Besides the preceding impression of pleasure, there must also be

---

[4] In this I follow P. S. Ardal, *Passion and Value in Hume's Treatise* (Edinburgh, 1966).
[5] *Treatise*, p. 439.

a relation of ideas; in this case there is a connection in the imagination between the idea of the picture and the idea of myself.
Hume's label for the whole concatenation is 'the double relation
of ideas and impressions'. The two impressions in the case are
related by similarity: the aesthetic pleasure gained from observing
the picture resembles the pleasurable feeling of pride that ensues.
The two ideas—of the cause of pride and of myself as its object—
may be related by any of the three principles of association which
Hume has recognized in his treatment of the imagination.[6] Pride
is therefore a complex mental state, requiring a simultaneous
transition between the idea of its cause and the idea of myself,
and between the impression produced by the cause and the feeling
of pride itself. Hume offers a somewhat mechanical account of
how these two movements 'mutually assist each other'.

Pride is by no means the only indirect passion that Hume
considers, but I shall continue to examine it because of its close
relation to the moral sentiments. Hume in fact believes that any
personal quality which causes pride is also the subject of moral
approval. This may seem odd in view of the fact that we can feel
proud of intellectual accomplishments and even bodily endow-
ments which are not normally considered to be morally admirable,
but in Hume's book these are all counted as virtues. The common
feature is that the quality gives pleasure when it is contemplated.
For pride to be felt there must of course also be a relation to
oneself, which is not necessary in cases of moral approval.

Given Hume's account of the causal mechanism responsible
for pride, we can see that the direction of this passion will depend
on the properties of the understanding. That is to say, although
the actual sensation of pride, the quality that distinguishes it
from other pleasurable sensations, is original and inexplicable,
the fact that we take pride in certain things rather than others
depends upon the conception that we form of them. To the extent
that this conception is erroneous, we can speak of pride as being
inappropriate. For instance, Hume looks at the influence of
general rules upon feelings of pride. Seeing the various material
advantages possessed by men in different social positions, we are
apt to think that their happiness varies in proportion to these
advantages, overlooking the fact that variables like personal
temperament may in some cases upset the equation altogether.[7]
Thus we might feel pride in belonging to, or being connected

---

[6] See above, ch. 1, p. 22.
[7] *Treatise*, p. 293.

with, the upper class merely as such, as a result of this uncritical generalization. Or again, to take an even more fanciful example, Hume seeks to explain the pride men feel in belonging to a line of distinguished ancestors by male descent. His explanation is that the imagination, when presented with two related objects of unequal magnitude, passes with particular ease from the smaller to the larger (for instance from the moons of Jupiter to the planet itself). In the present case, a child's father is a more striking object than his mother, and so we feel a stronger propensity to pass back along the line of male descent than along the female line. In turn this means that the relation we conceive we bear to our ancestors is more forceful when the connection is entirely by male descent, and the resulting passion of pride is enhanced.[8] Both of these cases illustrate what Hume had earlier called the 'changeable, weak, and irregular' properties of the imagination, but he does not of course mean to suggest that we should dispense with the imagination altogether in forming our passions. Without the imagination no relation of ideas could be established, and so pride and several other passions would become impossible. Even the use of general rules is necessary, for without them we should not be able to judge the relative value of objects and qualities which might be the source of such emotions.[9] Should I feel proud or ashamed of my modest house, for example? Only 'custom and practice' will tell me where it should be placed on the scale of desirability for houses.

In the light of this account of the understanding's role in directing the passions, we are better able to grasp the meaning of Hume's celebrated discussion of reason and the passions in the section of the *Treatise* entitled 'Of the influencing motives of the will'. There he argues that reason alone is incapable of producing desire or action, and therefore to speak of a *conflict* between reason and passion is mistaken.

Since reason alone can never produce any action, or give rise to volition, I infer, that the same faculty is as incapable of preventing volition, or of disputing the preference with any passion or emotion. This consequence is necessary. 'Tis impossible reason cou'd have the latter effect of preventing volition, but by giving an impulse in a contrary direction to our passion; and that impulse, had it operated alone, wou'd have been able to produce volition ... Reason is, and ought only to be the slave of the passions, and can never pretend to any other office than to serve and obey them.[10]

8   *Treatise*, pp. 308-9.
9   *Treatise*, pp. 293-4.
10   *Treatise*, pp. 414-15.

Several points need to be made about this passage. First, when Hume speaks of reason here, he extends the term to cover all the operations of the understanding—that is to say, reason in the strict sense, sensory experience, memory, and the imagination. He claims that none of these faculties singly, nor any combination of them, is sufficient to produce volition or action. Through the understanding we discover either matters of fact or relations of ideas. These are quite distinct from desire and volition, nor can they produce such mental states unaided.

Second, Hume does not intend to claim that passions always produce desire or action. Considered in itself a passion is simply a feeling or emotion; whether it brings a desire in its train is a contingent matter, to be established by experience. On this point Hume contrasts pride and humility with love and hatred.

> For pride and humility are pure emotions in the soul, unattended with any desire, and not immediately exciting us to action. But love and hatred are not compleated within themselves, nor rest in that emotion, which they produce, but carry the mind to something farther. Love is always follow'd by a desire of the happiness of the person belov'd, and an aversion to his misery: As hatred produces a desire of the misery and an aversion to the happiness of the person hated.[11]

But he goes on to indicate that even the connection between love and the desire for a person's happiness, and hatred and a desire for his misery, is contingent and depends upon 'an arbitrary and original instinct implanted in our nature'. 'I see no contradiction in supposing a desire of producing misery annex'd to love, and of happiness to hatred.'[12] So his general point is only that passions can, as a matter of fact, cause desires and aversions, and thereby produce actions, whereas reason by itself cannot.

Third, Hume's point in the celebrated passage is that reason *by itself* cannot produce volition; if no passion is present to the mind, no desire or aversion will be felt. This does not mean that reason (in the extended sense) cannot affect action; it can do so precisely in so far as it can direct the passions, and as we have seen the scope here is considerable. Which passions we feel depends largely on how we conceive of things around us, what relations we think they bear to each other, and so forth (this applies particularly to the indirect passions, but also to a lesser extent to the direct passions, with the exception of those that arise immediately from natural instinct). So it is misleading of Hume to describe reason as the 'slave' of the passions when it is

[11] *Treatise*, p. 367.
[12] *Treatise*, p. 368.

acknowledged to have such a powerful influence upon them. Indeed a few lines earlier he had spoken of reason 'directing' our impulses. Part of the explanation is simply that, fired by youthful enthusiasm, he was out to shock readers of the *Treatise*; another factor is that when considering the relation between reason and passion explicitly, he tends to reduce the role of reason to that of seeking out the most effective means of gratifying passions that already exist. As we have seen, this overlooks the many and complex ways in which the understanding can influence the formation of passions themselves. A similar tendency to offer bold but over-simple statements of his position colours Hume's account of the role of reason in moral judgement.

Fourth, Hume goes on to observe that when we speak loosely of reason combatting passion, we are actually referring to the contest between certain 'calm' passions (which, because they are of low emotional intensity, are mistaken for the operations of the understanding) and others that are 'violent'. This distinction needs careful handling. When Hume introduces it, he makes it clear that 'calm' passions are simply those of low intensity—they 'produce little emotion in the mind'—so any passion may in principle be calm on one occasion, violent on another. But because certain passions are habitually calm in quality, he also uses the term as a labelling device, singling out particularly those passions that direct us towards our long-term future good in contrast to those that prompt us to gratify immediate desires.[13] The love of gain is a typical calm passion in the second sense, lust a typical violent passion. We can now see that there are two more substantial ways in which the calm passions might be described as 'rational': they tend to involve a correct calculation of means to ends, and they tend to direct us towards those objects which, on reflection, we prefer.[14] In other words, they depend not

[13] Kydd suggests that it is a *defining* feature of a calm passion that it is either one whereby we give preference to what is in itself preferable or one that conduces to our greatest possible good. (R. Kydd, *Reason and Conduct in Hume's Treatise* (New York, 1964), ch. 5). Like Ardal (*Passion and Value*, ch. 5) I think this confuses the definition of the calm passions with those features which they do, as a matter of fact, tend to possess. Hirschman has noted the continuities between Hume's doctrine of calm passions and those of Hutcheson and Smith. He argues that the distinction between calm and violent passions is equivalent to that made in other writers between interests and passions. See A. O. Hirschman, *The Passions and the Interests* (Princeton, 1977).

[14] How much room is there in Hume's system for desires to be corrected by 'reflection'? Given his view of the inertness of reason, there is, strictly speaking, no such thing for him as a rational desire. However, it is possible for someone to be mistaken about the relative satisfaction to be gained from realizing each of two desires, and to correct this by reflection on past experience. It is also possible to review the place of one desire within the whole

merely on the workings of the understanding, but on the corrected beliefs that Hume sometimes calls 'judgement'. So although to speak of the combat of reason and passion is 'unphilosophical', it nevertheless points us to an important distinction between two ways in which volition and action can arise and Hume is perfectly ready to make use of it when he comes to analyse human affairs (his *History of England* is replete with references to the victory of passion over reason, or, less often, the converse).

We are now in a position to examine Hume's account of moral judgement, where again it will turn out that he puts his anti-rationalist case in a potentially misleading way. Book III of the *Treatise* opens with sections entitled 'Moral distinctions not derived from reason' and 'Moral distinctions derived from a moral sense', as though 'reason' and 'sense' were two exclusive alternatives. For once, *Enquiry* II gives a more accurate portrayal of Hume's view when it begins with a discussion of the *respective* roles of reason and sentiment in moral judgement. Hume certainly wants to insist that reason (meaning again the understanding in general) is not sufficient to produce judgements of vice and virtue, but he is very far from believing that such judgements arise spontaneously, without the aid of the understanding. Furthermore, to speak of a moral sense is unhelpful, since this suggests that we possess some distinct faculty, analogous to the five senses, by which moral distinctions are perceived. In fact, Hume sees the moral feelings as arising from preceding impressions in much the same way as feelings of pride and the like.

Hume offers four main arguments against the view that moral judgements are based entirely on reason.[15] The first, and perhaps the most important, is that moral judgements may produce volition and action, whereas reason is incapable of doing this. This of course is a direct consequence of his thesis, which we have just considered, that reason is inert, together with the view that moral sentiments, like passions, have practical consequences.

system of our preferences, and to abandon it if it turns out to frustrate a number of others. This is roughly what Hume is doing when, at the end of *Enquiry* II, he gives reasons for thinking that a moral life is personally preferable to its opposite. He admits, quite properly, that such reasons are persuasive rather than logically compelling.

[15] For a fuller analysis, see J. L. Mackie, *Hume's Moral Theory* (London, 1980), ch. 4, and D. D. Raphael, 'Hume's Critique of Ethical Rationalism' in W. B. Todd (ed.), *Hume and the Enlightenment* (Edinburgh, 1974). The latter contains a valuable comparison of *Treatise* and *Enquiry* II. My classification of Hume's arguments is similar to Raphael's, though I do not regard the well-known passage in which Hume challenges the derivation of 'ought' propositions from 'is' propositions as introducing a new argument, but as drawing an implication from those that precede it.

Morals excite passions, and produce or prevent actions. Reason of itself is utterly impotent in this particular. The rules of morality, therefore, are not conclusions of our reason.[16]

What this argument shows is that no judgement of reason is sufficient by itself to produce a moral sentiment. Unfortunately Hume is not always careful enough in separating this claim from the much stronger assertion sometimes attributed to him that reason plays no part at all in the production of such sentiments. This latter assertion would make nonsense of the constructive part of Hume's moral theory.

The second argument is that reason provides judgements that are true or false, whereas the subjects of moral appraisal— passions and actions[17]—cannot have these predicates applied to them. My injuring my neighbour is neither true nor false—so, Hume would claim, it can neither be in accordance with nor contrary to reason. This looks a very odd argument, since one would normally suppose that 'true' and 'false' applied not to the action itself, but to the judgement that the action was right or wrong. Hume provides no evidence that a judgement of this kind cannot be called true or false. Once this is seen, we are left with two residual arguments, one general, the other more specific. The general argument is that the kind of truth and falsehood involved in judgements of reason is different from that which may be involved in moral judgements. 'Morally good' and 'morally bad' are not the same kind of predicate as those used in empirical judgements, for instance. The more specific argument is a rebuttal of Wollaston's claim that all immorality consists in acting in such a way that one is affirming a false proposition and thereby tending to deceive others. If a man steals a horse, he asserts by his action that he owns it, Wollaston had thought. Hume replies that such false judgements may be a consequence of immoral action, but they cannot actually constitute its immorality, since without prior moral conventions no action could imply such a proposition.[18]

---

[16] *Treatise,* p. 457.

[17] Hume departs here from his more usual view that moral appraisals are directed at personal qualities.

[18] For instance Wollaston's example presupposes that the rights of property are understood. In their absence the thief would only be asserting that he *possesses* the horse, which is of course true. Hume has several other arguments against Wollaston, but this alone seems sufficient. Wollaston's views may conveniently be examined in D. D. Raphael (ed.), *British Moralists 1650 - 1800* (Oxford, 1969), vol. i, pp. 272 - 302. For a brief discussion, see Mackie, *Hume's Moral Theory,* ch. 2.

Hume's third and fourth arguments against rationalism take the form of challenges. If moral judgements are founded on reason, they must concern either relations of ideas or matters of fact, these being the only subjects on which reason can pronounce. Hume challenges his opponents to show which relations of ideas or which matters of fact are to provide the grounding for moral appraisals. In the case of relations of ideas, he first argues that the only relations he has so far discovered are those of 'resemblance, contrariety, degrees in quality, and proportions in quantity and number', none of which provide suitable grounds for moral appraisal, and then lays down a condition to be met in case anyone should propose an additional relation. The condition is that the relation should hold *only* between acts of the mind and external objects. This reflects the fact that we do not pass moral judgement on states of the world as such, or on internal thoughts and feelings alone. It is only when an external event results from a mental process that we talk of right and wrong. So, Hume suggests, it will have to be a very odd kind of relation to meet this condition, since the familiar relations all hold between inanimate objects as well.

In the case of matters of fact, the argument consists in a straightforward appeal to introspection. No matter how long we scrutinize a state of affairs, we cannot bring to light any observable quality that constitutes virtue or vice. These properties depend entirely on the feelings of the spectator.

Take any action allow'd to be vicious: Wilful murder, for instance. Examine it in all lights, and see if you can find that matter of fact, or real existence, which you call *vice*. In which-ever way you take it, you find only certain passions, motives, volitions and thoughts. There is no other matter of fact in the case. The vice entirely escapes you, as long as you consider the object. You can never find it, till you turn your reflexion into your own breast, and find a sentiment of disapprobation, which arises in you, towards this action.[19]

Thus Hume has disposed of the two kinds of knowledge which reason (i.e. the understanding) can provide, and prepared the way for his thesis that moral judgement requires a third ingredient, namely a certain kind of sentiment. In turning to that thesis let me stress again that Hume has shown only that moral judgement cannot be *reduced* to analytic or empirical judgement; that reason is not *sufficient* to produce moral appraisals. His hostility to rationalism occasionally makes him overstate his case, and suggest to the unwary reader that the understanding is irrelevant to moral judgement. This is certainly not his real opinion.

Hume maintains that to pass a judgement of moral approval or disapproval, we must have a certain kind of feeling when we contemplate an action or character. What kind of feeling? Like all impressions it is unique and indefinable, but we can characterize it in two ways. First, like the passions of pride and love it is a pleasurable sensation; second, unlike these passions, it is felt when we contemplate actions and characters from an objective point of view, that is to say, without considering how they stand in relation to ourselves. ' 'Tis only when a character is considered in general, without reference to our particular interest, that it causes such a feeling or sentiment, as denominates it morally good or evil.'[20] Had Hume been asked which of these was the defining feature of the moral sentiment, it is difficult to know what he would have replied. He appears to have regarded the sensation and the manner of conceiving its subject as indissolubly connected.[21] If I am right about this, it follows that the sentiment we are now considering has judgement as one of its essential aspects. Moral approval would not *be* moral approval unless its subject were conceived in abstraction from one's personal interest. This requires judgement of a kind that is not necessarily easy to attain. One's capacity to make moral appraisals must depend on one's ability to consider actions and characters impartially. We can see already why Hume's doctrine that moral distinctions are derived from sentiment rather than reason needs careful interpretation.

The next question to ask is how the moral sentiments arise. Like other impressions of reflection they are preceded by primary impressions of pleasure and pain. These impressions occur when we contemplate the personal qualities of other men. Since these qualities may not affect us directly—indeed we are bound to ignore any effects that are specific to us in forming moral judgements —it is difficult to see why we should not remain completely indifferent to them. Hume answers this by invoking the force of *sympathy,* which holds an important place in his account of morals.[22]

---

[20] *Treatise,* p. 472.

[21] In the passage cited above, the emphasis is laid on the quality of the sentiment itself. But cf. *Treatise* p. 499: 'every thing, which gives uneasiness in human actions, upon the general survey, is call'd Vice, and whatever produces satisfaction, in the same manner, is denominated Virtue.' Here the feeling itself is left completely unspecific, and the defining characteristic seems to be the manner of conception—'upon the general survey'.

[22] Selby-Bigge has claimed that in *Enquiry* II sympathy no longer has an explanatory function, but is simply 'another name for social feeling, humanity, benevolence, natural

Sympathy as Hume understands it is best described as a mechanism which allows emotions to be transferred from one mind to another. His use of the term remains close to its sense in physics, where we speak of a vibrating string communicating its resonance sympathetically to a neighbouring string. The second string will duplicate the vibration of the first.[23] In the human case, suppose that I am watching a man in a temper. Seeing his words and movements, I am likely to conclude that he is angry. In Hume's terminology this means that I now have an idea of anger. However more is yet possible. His anger may communicate itself to me; I may actually become angry myself. As Hume would say, I may receive not merely an idea but an impression of anger. This is odd, because the cause of his anger is not the cause of mine; mine is merely sympathetic anger. Sympathy in this sense is a remarkable phenomenon, yet Hume is undoubtedly right in pointing to its existence. Whether it can account for as much of morality as he believes is another matter.

Sympathy underlies moral appraisal in the following way. Suppose I am contemplating a man who has those traits of character which we should normally describe as cruel. I cannot avoid considering the typical effects of those character traits, including the various kinds of suffering which may be caused. Picturing the suffering I am moved sympathetically to feel pain myself. This is the primary impression of pain which is responsible for the secondary impression that constitutes moral disapproval. In the opposite case, sympathetically-experienced pleasure makes us feel approval of those traits which we conceive to cause such pleasure.

This account is peculiar in several respects. First, why should the moral sentiments be directed at character traits rather than at the actions which are the immediate causes of those states of affairs whose contemplation produces pleasure or pain? Suppose I observe or come to learn of a cruel action. The pain aroused by sympathy with the victim would seem to direct my disapproval to the action itself rather than to any permanent disposition of the

philanthropy' (*Enquiries*, p. xxvi). I cannot accept this claim, for on occasion Hume uses 'sympathy' in *Enquiry* II in precisely the same sense as in the *Treatise*—for instance, in explaining why we suffer with someone who cannot pronounce his words. See especially sections 179-82. Furthermore, sympathetic feelings are again represented as the basis for moral sentiments, rather than as being identical with them, since they lack the impartiality of the latter. It is true, however, that Hume's use of terms is looser in *Enquiry* II than in the *Treatise*; towards the end of the later work he speaks of 'the sentiment of humanity' where previously he had spoken of 'sympathy'.

[23] Hume makes explicit use of this analogy at *Treatise*, p. 576.

agent. Hume seems to think it self-evident that the action is only regarded as a sign of some more permanent quality.

> If any *action* be either virtuous or vicious, 'tis only as a sign of some quality or character. It must depend upon durable principles of the mind, which extend over the whole conduct, and enter into the personal character. Actions themselves, not proceeding from any constant principle, have no influence on love or hatred, pride or humility; and consequently are never consider'd in morality.[24]

It is possible that Hume conflates two ways in which an action may fail to issue from permanent character traits. First, an action may be performed unintentionally—for instance as a result of an error of fact concerning its subject (I shoot a man lying in the grass thinking he is a rabbit). In this case no moral blame attaches to the agent, unless his error can be attributed to negligence, and Hume's diagnosis seems correct: the action, though regrettable, is not subject to moral appraisal because it does not issue from the agent's volition. But second, an action may be intentional but a-typical—'out of character'. A normally cowardly man performs a courageous act, say. Here both action and agent may be assessed morally, but the agent will only be credited with the performance of that particular act, and not with possessing the quality of courage in general. This possibility is excluded by Hume's dictum, for no good reason that I can discover.

A second oddity of Hume's account is that it fails to explain *why* we should direct moral attitudes only at human agents and their deeds. Suppose that I witness a man being chased across a field by a bull. Here the mechanism of sympathy seems to operate in exactly the same way as in the case of a human action. Sympathy with the man's fear leads to displeasure when I contemplate the cause of that fear, the bull. Why, then, is the sentiment felt not that of moral disapproval? When considering this point in general terms near the beginning of *Treatise* Book III,[25] Hume simply says that there are different kinds of pleasurable sensation, and that contemplating people gives rise to one kind of sensation, contemplating inanimate objects another.[26] But the question is why there should be such a difference in sensation, given the apparent similarity in the causal mechanisms responsible in the cases of the bull and the human agent. Hume's account of the genesis of moral sentiments in sympathy leaves it as an inexplicable fact about human psychology.

[24] *Treatise*, p. 575.
[25] *Treatise*, pp. 471-2.
[26] Hume omits the natural world here, but I take it this omission is not significant.

A third feature of that account, which bears more directly on our immediate concerns, is that the source of sympathetic feeling is not necessarily taken to be actual pleasure or pain. As the example of cruelty was originally presented, sympathy was induced not by the contemplation of actual acts of cruelty, but by a *picturing* of the effects likely to flow from a particular character trait. This must obviously depend on the workings of the imagination.

'Tis certain, that sympathy is not always limited to the present moment, but that we often feel by communication the pains and pleasures of others, which are not in being, and which we only anticipate by the force of imagination.[27]

That being so, the direction of our sympathetic feelings must depend on all the varied properties of that faculty. Besides the regular transition from cause to effect, there are other cases where the imagination will decide whether and to what extent we respond sympathetically to a trait, and hence what moral attitude we adopt towards it. For instance Hume asks why we approve of people who we know are incapable of conferring actual benefits on others, such as virtuous men locked in prison. His answer is that the imagination still carries our thought forward from character to supposed effects, under the influence of general rules.[28] Hume also asks how the varying proximity of objects affects our sympathetic feelings towards them. Do we sympathize as much with Chinese people as with English people, with the ancients as with the moderns? Hume allows that by nature we do not, but claims that we learn to 'correct' our feelings by abstracting from our particular spatio-temporal location. We imagine ourselves citizens of the world (and of all history) and consider how we would respond to a character trait from that perspective. So moral sentiment does not depend merely on abstracting from our personal interests, from the actual benefits which we receive as individuals from a trait of character, but also from our personal location; we must disregard the 'distance' (in space and time) between ourselves and the person we are evaluating.

We can now see the full extent to which judgement is involved in our moral appraisals. If we approved and disapproved merely on the basis of sense-impressions, we should be incapable of taking up the abstract point of view that morality requires. The imagination frees us from the confines of our personal position.

[27] *Treatise*, p. 385.
[28] See *Treatise*, pp. 584–5.

That faculty, as we know already, can lead to better or worse results. If we follow its irregular principles, our moral appraisals will be based on prejudice. We shall, for instance, approve of character-traits which are not strictly correlated with pleasure-producing effects, even in circumstances where the effect fails. On the other hand, if we follow the permanent principles of the imagination, we shall be able to attain judgement in the proper sense: appraisals that are not only disinterested but soundly based and made from a general point of view.

That is not quite the end of the matter, however, for Hume makes the further suggestion that our feelings may be less corrigible than the judgements which are supposed to direct them. Even though the understanding informs us that two characters are equally productive of good effects, it may be impossible to avoid feeling more strongly about whichever is closer to us in space or time. In that case there will be a divorce between moral feeling and moral judgement: we *feel* more admiration for our compatriot, say, but we *judge* that he and a foreigner are equally meritorious. What does 'judge' mean in this context? I think it must be interpreted dispositionally, as a readiness to say publicly that the two men are equally worthy. Hume's explanation refers to the public character of the language in which we express our appraisals:

We every day meet with persons who are in a situation different from us, and who could never converse with us were we to remain constantly in that position and point of view, which is peculiar to ourselves. The intercourse of sentiments, therefore, in society and conversation, makes us form some general unalterable standard, by which we may approve or disapprove of characters and manners.[29]

Hume had initially stated his position thus: 'To have the sense of virtue, is nothing but to *feel* a satisfaction of a particular kind from the contemplation of a character.' We can now see that this formulation is potentially misleading in two respects. First, it tempts us to overlook the fact that the feeling in question requires

---

[29] *Enquiry* II, p. 229. See also *Treatise*, pp. 582-4, and for discussion J. T. King, 'The Place of the Language of Morals in Hume's Second *Enquiry*' in D. W. Livingston and J. T. King (eds.), *Hume: a Re-evaluation* (New York, 1976). It seems questionable whether language has the right kind of universality for Hume's purpose. One must remember that it is generally specific to one society. The need to communicate with our fellows in a public language may provide a reason to ignore our private interests in forming judgements—i.e. to judge from a *social* point of view—but it gives no reason to judge from a universal point of view, ignoring location in space and time, since this location is shared by our fellow-countrymen. Putting the point analytically: if I use 'good' to mean 'good for me', I shall not be able to engage in moral conversation with others, but if I use it to mean 'good for English people', there is no reason why I should not do so provided others adopt the same convention.

a particular way of conceiving its object, and that to conceive the object appropriately may involve a sophisticated use of the imagination. The feeling is in no sense naïve or immediate. Second, Hume ultimately wishes to separate moral feeling and moral judgement analytically, while still insisting that the latter requires the former. We can only judge that a certain quality is meritorious if it is of a type that generally produces feelings of moral approval, but there is no need for our judgement to be regulated by our feelings in every case.

An incidental consequence of the separation of moral feeling and moral judgement is a further weakening of the practical impact of the latter. Hume thinks in general that the moral sentiments are weak emotions. This reflects the fact that sympathy, although a quality universally shared by human beings, is not a powerful force: the kind of feeling that I have when I contemplate someone else's misfortune is generally much weaker than when I examine some state of affairs that affects me personally. Hence the resulting moral sentiment is correspondingly weak. In so far as moral judgement becomes detached from feeling, it loses connection with the passions and the will entirely. So when Hume comes to examine the practical aspects of morality, he is careful to stress that moral judgements themselves have to be supplemented by other considerations to be an effective influence on conduct: for instance by a person's concern for his social reputation. This is an issue which will be considered more fully in chapter 5.

In this chapter, I have been trying to place in perspective two of Hume's most celebrated theses: that reason is the slave of the passions, and that moral distinctions are not derived from reason. In each case I have argued that his bold statement of the thesis may mislead us as to his real intentions; that the thesis must be taken in conjunction with other aspects of his philosophy. In particular, the understanding has a larger role to play in the genesis of both passions and moral sentiments than one might suppose from those theses alone. Passions like pride depend upon how we conceive of the relations that objects bear to ourselves; moral sentiments depend on how we conceive of the objects which cause pleasure and pain by sympathy. 'Conceiving' is a product of the imagination, which is responsible for all our judgements other than those that are analytic or directly sensory. Variations in conception produce variations in the passions and moral sentiments, and since the other element—feeling—is in practice a constant factor ('there is such a uniformity in the *general* sentiments of mankind'), this accounts for most of the disagreements over moral issues that we encounter.

We may also sum up the interpretation given of Hume's moral philosophy in general as a mitigated form of scepticism. First, against the rationalists, Hume argues that moral judgements cannot be based entirely on reason. They involve an irreducible element of feeling, which, if it were lacking, would prevent any creature from holding moral attitudes. Second, against the extreme sceptics, Hume argues that moral judgements nevertheless have a basis in human nature, and are not merely the expression of arbitrary conventions enforced by social and political pressure. Men have, to a great extent, the same underlying moral feelings, and this is not accidental but a function of their common source in sympathy. Third, moral sentiments and judgements can be corrected to the extent to which the understanding in general can be corrected. We might distinguish three levels of adequacy here. The lowest is occupied by those men whose understanding has been so corrupted by religion or false philosophy that they come to value qualities that are really detrimental. The two most common perversions of the understanding are superstition and enthusiasm. Superstition consists essentially in a suppression of the understanding's critical capacities, so that many beliefs are held merely on the word of authority; enthusiasm, in an intellectual presumption which rejects well-founded beliefs in favour of free-floating speculation.[30] In either of these conditions men are liable to invert normal moral judgements and class as virtues those qualities properly regarded as vicious—'celibacy, fasting, penance, mortification, self-denial, humility, silence, solitude, and the whole train of monkish virtues' are Hume's favourite examples.[31] Such tastes are unaccountable:

When men depart from the maxims of common reason, and affect these *artificial* lives, as you call them, no one can answer for what will please or displease them. They are in a different element from the rest of mankind; and the natural principles of their mind play not with the same regularity, as if left to themselves, free from the illusions of religious superstition or philosophical enthusiasm.[32]

The second level of adequacy is occupied by the 'vulgar' (though Hume does not use the term explicitly in this connection); that

---

[30] See Hume, 'Of Superstition and Enthusiasm', *Essays,* pp. 75-80; Hume, *A Dialogue.* The latter makes it clear that superstition and enthusiasm can take secular as well as religious forms.

[31] *Enquiry* II, p. 270.

[32] Hume, *A Dialogue,* p. 343.

is, those whose understanding is partly governed by the weak, changeable, and irregular principles of the imagination. The effect on moral judgement is that although the appropriate qualities are morally approved in general, inappropriate judgements are made in particular cases. The most obvious source of error is unwarranted generalization. This explains why (to take two of Hume's examples at random) the rich are admired without distinction between those whose riches are a source of pleasure and those whose riches are not; and military virtues are admired excessively in societies which no longer have great need of them.

Such errors are avoided by the wise, who occupy the highest level of adequacy possible in moral judgement. The wise share the same basic sentiments as the vulgar, but use judgement to direct them more accurately. Besides distinguishing partial generalizations from universal generalizations and so forth, they are alive to the distortion which their particular interests and spatio-temporal location may produce, and so endeavour to remedy it by adopting the point of view of an impartial spectator.[33] In short, they satisfy (as far as is humanly possible) all the conditions which Hume has laid down for moral judgement in the strict sense.

This is the quality of Hume's mitigated scepticism as applied to moral judgement in general, and we have now (as students of his social and political thought) to trace its application to judgements about justice and political obligation. In reviewing this chapter, however, I cannot help commenting on one further way in which Hume obscures the character of his own account of morals. In considering the relation of reason to morality, he seems to forget much of what he has said about the understanding in *Treatise*, Book I and *Enquiry* I. In these earlier discussions, as we well know, 'reason' is used to refer exclusively to the analytical operations of the mind, and belief as such is attributed to the workings of the imagination. To dramatize the point, Hume sometimes says that belief is a matter of feeling—'more properly an act of the sensitive, than of the cogitative part of our natures.'[34] In dealing with morality, however, he collects all the workings of the understanding under the heading of 'reason' and *contrasts* this

---

[33] The idea that the responses of the 'impartial spectator' should be taken as the criterion of moral judgement was brought into philosophical currency by Adam Smith, but the basic notion (not the phrase) is certainly to be found in Hume. See the discussion in D. D. Raphael 'The Impartial Spectator', *Proceedings of the British Academy*, lviii (1972), 3-22.

[34] *Treatise*, p. 183.

with 'feeling', which is necessary to moral judgement. In fighting the battle against ethical rationalism, he obscures the nature of his victory over rationalist epistemology. The results can be seen rather clearly in the following passage:

> Thus the distinct boundaries and offices of *reason* and of *taste* are easily ascertained. The former conveys the knowledge of truth and falsehood: the latter gives the sentiment of beauty and deformity, vice and virtue. The one discovers objects as they really stand in nature, without addition or diminution: the other has a productive faculty, and gilding or staining all natural objects with the colours, borrowed from internal sentiment, raises in a manner a new creation. ... The standard of the one, being founded on the nature of things, is eternal and inflexible, even by the will of the Supreme Being: the standard of the other, arising from the internal frame and constitution of animals, is ultimately derived from that Supreme Will, which bestowed on each being its peculiar nature, and arranged the several classes and orders of existence.[35]

Despite what is said in this passage, Hume's real achievement was to have shown that both empirical judgement and moral judgement depend on the 'internal frame and constitution' of the human animal. Although moral judgement may be more variable than empirical judgement, neither can properly be described as 'eternal and inflexible'; each depends on properties of the mind which, although they are universally shared and essential to human survival, are ultimately contingent.[36] (Must the Supreme Being adhere to a notion of causal necessity, for instance?) Furthermore, the same properties are important in both areas of judgement, even if morality relies on an additional kind of sentiment not required for empirical judgement. Hume seems to lose sight of the continuities in his argument; here he is his own worst interpreter.

---

[35] *Enquiry* II, p. 294.

[36] Reason in the *strict* sense may of course be described as 'eternal and inflexible'; and the laws of logic are necessary. But it is clear that Hume in this passage intends that term to cover empirical judgement as well, as the reference to 'objects as they really stand in nature' shows.

3

Justice as an Artificial Virtue

Having completed his account of moral judgement in general, Hume divides the particular virtues into two categories, the natural and the artificial. Justice, which, briefly, consists in a respect for others' property rights, is categorized as artificial. The rationale for this classification (which despite his disclaimers was to cause Hume some embarrassment[1]) needs to be understood to make sense of his theory of justice.

As we have seen, moral judgements are directed at personal qualities which arouse sympathetic pleasure or pain in the spectator. These qualities cannot themselves be dispositions to act morally, or the explanation of morality would fall into a circle; they must be natural motives or traits of character. In the case of the natural virtues, this requirement causes no difficulty. We can conceive how qualities like generosity, parental affection, prudence, and temperance could exist apart from the moral appraisals others make of them. They spring either from natural sympathy or from self-interest. But the case is otherwise with artificial virtues such as justice and promise-keeping. From what original motive are acts of justice performed? To say 'from a sense of moral obligation' would beg the question of how such acts come to be valued morally. Artificial virtues, then, are qualities that correspond to no natural (in the sense of 'original') motive in human beings.

To take a concrete case, Hume considers as an example of behaviour required by justice the return of a piece of borrowed property.[2] What motive could impel me to perform such an act on every occasion (leaving aside, *ex hypothesi*, my sense of justice)? Clearly it could not be self-interest, which in many cases would

---

[1] Hume explained that, in two out of three possible senses, justice was a natural thing; and it was therefore quite proper to refer to the rules of justice as 'Laws of Nature'. Notwithstanding this qualification, the view that justice was an artificial virtue formed the basis of one of the charges laid against Hume by his opponents during the controversy over the Chair of Ethics at Edinburgh. Hume's reply is contained in *A Letter from a Gentleman to his Friend in Edinburgh*, ed. E. C. Mossner and J. V. Price (Edinburgh, 1967), where he admits that he had 'employed words that admit of an invidious construction'. In *Enquiry* II the whole question of the artificiality of justice is dismissed in a footnote, though Hume's substantive doctrine remains unchanged.

[2] See *Treatise*, pp. 479-83.

drive me to keep the property. Equally, sympathy for the owner might fail, because other possible recipients might have more pressing needs. Finally 'regard for the public interest' would not necessarily induce me to return the item to its owner, for he might be 'a miser, or a seditious bigot' whereas I or another would use the property for benevolent purposes. This last consideration applies so long as I consider the proposed action in isolation, ignoring any possible effects on the general practice of returning loans.

It follows that the immediate motive for acts of justice can only be a wish to comply with conventional rules. I return the property to its owner because a rule of justice states that loaned items are to be handed back. This is an artificial motive because the rule in question might not have existed, and indeed Hume can picture circumstances in which it would not exist. The rules which define just behaviour are human conventions, albeit conventions which as we shall see are essential to the well-being of society. By contrast, I shall *always* have a motive (natural sympathy) to relieve another's suffering; there is no need of conventions here.[3]

This contrast between the natural and the artificial virtues has a further implication, namely that acts manifesting the natural virtues are valuable taken singly, whereas acts manifesting the artificial virtues are valuable only as part of a general practice. Every act of generosity (perhaps one should say 'well-directed generosity') has good consequences, whereas an act of justice taken by itself may have bad results, but is redeemed because it forms an essential element in a set of actions which is beneficial over all. Hume expresses this point metaphorically in *Enquiry* II by comparing benevolence to the building of a wall, where every stone increases the height by a certain amount independently of other stones being added, and justice to the building of a vault, where each stone relies on the support of the rest and would fall without them.[4] Clearly we shall need to look at Hume's reasons for thinking that acts of justice form a set which is so close-knit that a single omission may weaken the entire edifice.

[3] It may none the less be true that our practice of natural virtues does in fact involve elements of convention. As J. L. Mackie has recently argued, sympathy alone would induce responses that varied according to such factors as the distance between agent and sufferer. It may therefore be socially useful to develop a convention of impartial generosity, supported by moral judgement, in which case there will be a contrast between the natural motive and the (artificial) moral motive for acts of generosity. See Mackie, *Hume's Moral Theory*, ch. 7.

[4] *Enquiry* II, p. 305.

Having designated justice as an artificial virtue, Hume has set himself three tasks to perform before his analysis of that quality is complete. First, he must show what originally prompted men to adopt rules of justice. Second, he must show what now induces them to abide by the rules. Third, he must show why justice, as the disposition to follow such rules, is considered a moral virtue. Of course, he might answer two or more of these questions in a similar way; in fact he does not, though his answers overlap in certain respects.

To explain the adoption of rules of justice, Hume refers to the general circumstances of human life. There are three main conditions which make it necessary to have rules stabilizing possession by assigning objects to particular people as their property. The first is that men desire more goods than are easily available to them from the hand of nature, and so are placed in competition with one another for scarce resources. The second is that men are not entirely benevolent in their dispositions, and so will not agree to let each person have such goods as will maximize the total stock of happiness. The third is that goods can be wrested fairly easily from one set of hands to another.[5] Given these three conditions,[6] men are liable to come into conflict with one another over the allocation of material goods. If they follow their inclinations in a direct and short-sighted manner, the outcome will be a struggle for goods, which is counter-productive because it gives no one an incentive to develop skills or engage in collaboration with others. Any advantage gained by so doing is liable to be nullified by forcible seizure of goods.

This impasse can be avoided by the adoption of rules which establish rights of property. Each person, surveying the state of affairs before property rights exist, can see that his own interests will best be furthered by having such rules. There is no need that his natural inclinations should change: he must merely become aware that he can follow these inclinations most effectively by following them obliquely—refraining, say, from taking his neighbour's crops on condition that his neighbour will leave him in peace in return. To get rules established, two further conditions are necessary. First, each person must communicate his willingness to engage in mutual restraint to the others who will share in the convention. Second, there must be agreement on the set of

[5] *Treatise*, pp. 484-8.
[6] The justification of these conditions relies upon Hume's view of human nature, consideration of which is postponed until chapter 5.

rules that will be followed: a certain solution to the problem of allocating goods must seem 'natural' to the parties concerned.

I shall postpone examining the second condition for the present. In relation to the first, Hume makes it clear that no explicit act of promising is necessary for the convention to be established—indeed he regards the making and keeping of promises as itself a convention which needs to be explained in a similar way. He is less clear about what kind of communication of intention *is* necessary. Must my intentions be expressed verbally, or is it enough for me to act in a certain way, leaving the other parties to draw the necessary conclusions from my behaviour? He writes:

> When this common sense of interest is mutually express'd, and is known to both, it produces a suitable resolution and behaviour. And this may properly enough be call'd a convention or agreement betwixt us, tho' without the interposition of a promise; since the actions of each of us have a reference to those of the other, and are perform'd upon the supposition, that something is to be perform'd on the other part. Two men, who pull the oars of a boat, do it by an agreement or convention, tho' they have never given promises to each other.[7]

We can certainly think of cases in which no verbal communication is necessary for co-operation of this kind to be initiated, and the fact that Hume describes the conventions governing property as emerging gradually lends support to the view that appropriate action may be sufficient for this purpose.

Once rules of property are established, and are being generally observed, what motive will anyone have to follow them? Several different factors will all point in the same direction. First, enlightened self-interest will dictate that we should keep the rules, provided we accept Hume's assumption that any breaches will weaken the artificial edifice we have constructed,[8] and we regard

---

[7] *Treatise,* p. 490.

[8] Hume never spells out the reasons for this assumption. He is adamant that the rules of justice should be followed inflexibly even where it seems that great benefit (public or private) might be derived from a particular breach. See *Treatise,* pp. 497-8, 531-3; *Enquiry* II, pp. 304-6. There seem to be two possible ways of justifying this standpoint. One is to emphasize the rules' function as instruments of co-ordination, and to argue that no one can be sufficiently certain what the effects of his own action in breaking the rules will be, since those effects depend on what everyone else does at the same time, something he cannot possibly predict. The other is to focus on the problem of motivation, and to argue that one breach may start a chain reaction leading to a breakdown of the whole system of rules (there is a hint of this view at *Treatise,* p. 535). The second argument seems implausible in general, though it might apply in a case where no agency existed to enforce the rules and the system ran entirely on mutual trust.

D. D. Raphael, on the other hand, has suggested that Hume thinks of the rules of property all along as rules of *law* ('Hume and Adam Smith on Justice and Utility', *Proceedings of the Aristotelian Society,* lxiii (1972-3), 87-103). In this case there are good

preserving the edifice as more important than the immediate benefit we may derive from the breach. Second, regard for the public interest will lead to the same conclusion, making similar assumptions with 'public benefit' replacing 'private benefit' in the second clause. Third, mere force of habit is a factor that is far from negligible in Hume's book. Fourth, others will be concerned that we should keep the rules and so will apply various forms of social pressure that influence us through our 'love of reputation'—our desire to stand well with those around us. In Part II we shall want to look at the respective weight that Hume attributes to these four factors, since this is a question of some importance for his social thought. At the moment we need only take note of the fact that, once rules of property are established, additional motives for keeping them come into play which are distinct from the original motive for setting them up, and we should not assume *a priori* that the original motive will remain the strongest.

Finally, there is the question of why justice should come to be regarded as a moral virtue. This is easy to answer in the light of what has been said. If establishing rules of property benefits everyone, and if any breach of the rules is likely to weaken the convention seriously or fatally, then rule-breaking is bound to arouse sympathetic pain in the spectator, such sympathy being directed towards all those liable to be harmed by the weakening of the convention. In line with Hume's general account of moral judgement, this must give rise to sentiments of moral approval towards the rule-keeper and disapproval towards the rule-breaker. Note that the actual object of moral evaluation is the disposition to act justly, and the motive underlying the disposition—which as we have seen may be of different kinds—is not crucial. In case it should seem odd that we should approve morally of someone who acts justly, say, from habit, we ought to take note of Hume's view that personal merit is not confined to those qualities we acquire voluntarily.[9]

---

reasons why those authorized to apply the rules should do so uniformly, but the same reasons do not apply to the ordinary citizen faced with a choice between keeping the law and conferring a benefit illegally.

[9] He argues that we regard as meritorious any quality that is useful or agreeable to the person himself or to others. This includes attributes such as industry, wit, and good humour, as well as other qualities more usually regarded as moral. See *Treatise*, Book III, Part III, Section IV; *Enquiry* II, Appendix IV. I have discussed this view briefly in *Social Justice* (Oxford, 1976), ch. 3, sec. 3.

This completes my general sketch of Hume's conception of justice as an artificial virtue. We must now look in more detail at the content of the rules of justice and ask how, if at all, judgement enters into their formation. What, first, does Hume mean by 'property'? He defines it as 'such a relation betwixt a person and an object as permits him, but forbids any other, the free use and possession of it, without violating the laws of justice and moral equity'.[10] He assumes that the relation of property holds between one individual and a material thing (ruling out joint ownership) and that it consists in a unitary right of possession and use (ruling out the possibility of dividing the rights over a thing between several parties). When dealing with leases, for example,[11] he argues that the hirer has a complete right over the object hired for as· long as the period of hire runs—'however the use may be bounded in time or degree, the right itself is not susceptible of any such gradation, but is absolute and entire, so far as it extends.' From this it appears that Hume conceives of property as an unrestricted right of control over objects, but we should also observe that the original definition contained the rider 'without violating the laws of justice and moral equity'. This is rather vague as it stands, but later we shall see that Hume regards property owners as subject not only to the condition that they should reciprocally respect the property of others, but also to certain natural obligations to dependents and friends, which limit their free use of property. These additional obligations are not, however, matters of justice.

Is there any rational or natural way of allocating titles to property? Hume considers three modes of distribution that seem at first to have such a warrant. The first is a distribution that allocates property according to the deserts of each recipient; Hume thinks that 'a creature, possessed of reason, but unacquainted with human nature' would settle on this:

In a perfect theocracy, where a being, infinitely intelligent, governs by particular volitions, this rule would certainly have place, and might serve to the wisest purposes: But were mankind to execute such a law; so great is the uncertainty of merit, both from its natural obscurity, and from the self-conceit of each individual, that no determinate rule of conduct would ever result from it; and the total dissolution of society must be the immediate consequence.[12]

---

[10] *Treatise,* p. 310.
[11] See *Treatise,* pp. 529-30.
[12] *Enquiry* II, p. 193.

Hume's objection seems to have two parts to it. The first is that distribution according to desert cannot be achieved by a general rule of distribution or by a set of such rules, presumably because it requires a continual adjustment of property to individual character. (I extrapolate this from Hume's remark that such a distribution would be appropriate to a being that governed 'by particular volitions'—i.e. made particular assignments of property to individuals.) The second is that the personal feature used as a basis of distribution—merit—is one over which men will inevitably disagree, and therefore the distribution itself will be contested. Since the whole purpose of rules of property is to stabilize social relationships, such a mode of distribution would be self-defeating.

A second possibility is that property should be distributed according to the use each person could make of it. The person who would derive the greatest benefit from a particular object should be allowed to have it. This suffers from precisely the same difficulties as a distribution according to desert. Instead of a small number of general rules establishing titles to property, we should have to make a decision about the destination of each particular item; and furthermore the basis of distribution—'ability to benefit'—is quite as contestable as personal merit.

The relation of fitness or suitableness ought never to enter into consideration, in distributing the properties of mankind; but we must govern ourselves by rules, which are more general in their application, and more free from doubt and uncertainty.[13]

Third, Hume looks briefly at the possibility of an equal distribution of property which, although not as ideally 'rational' as the mode we have just considered, might be thought to approach it on the grounds that 'wherever we depart from this equality, we rob the poor of more satisfaction than we add to the rich'.[14] The objections here are of a rather different nature, since equality is at least a simple enough mode of distribution. They are (1) that either differences in human 'art, care, and industry' will destroy equality in time or, if this is prevented, there will be no incentive to be industrious or careful; (2) that continual inspection would be required to preserve equality, leading inevitably to authoritarian government; (3) that by destroying social hierarchy the authority of government would also be destroyed, thus making the necessary inspection impossible anyway.[15]

---

[13] *Treatise*, p. 514.
[14] *Enquiry* II, p. 194.
[15] See *Enquiry* II, p. 194.

From these comments we can see what qualities Hume requires of the rules of property if they are to serve the function he has laid down for them. They must consist in a few general maxims which assign objects in relatively stable fashion to persons, and they must refer to features of those persons whose presence is uncontroversial; observable physical relationships between people and material things will obviously fit the bill admirably. Hume meets this requirement by proposing five rules of original acquisition plus the rule that any title to property may be transferred with the consent of the proprietor. The five rules of acquisition are as follows:[16]

(1) Possession: A person shall have a right to whatever objects he currently holds in his possession.

(2) Occupation: A person shall have a right to whatever objects he possessed first; i.e. prior to other persons.

(3) Prescription: A person shall have a right to whatever objects he has held over an extensive period of time.

(4) Accession: A person shall have a right to whatever is 'intimately' connected with objects he already owns (e.g. the fruits of his trees, the offspring of his cattle).

(5) Succession: A person shall have a right to objects owned by his close relatives upon their death.

Plainly these rules may come into conflict with one another. The first rule—possession—would render all the rest superfluous if followed exclusively, and Hume intends it for use only in exceptional circumstances; in particular at the formation of a society. In the case of rules (2) and (3) an arbitrating principle is evidently required to decide when a title acquired through long possession is strong enough to override original possession. Such conflicts will be resolved by more specific conventions adopted by the members of any particular society. Greater specificity is also needed in fixing the meaning of the terms employed in the rules of property. What must I do before I can be said to possess a wild animal, for instance? How much land can I claim to appropriate by driving in a stake? In nearly every case these matters will be settled not merely by convention but by the positive laws of the society in question, for Hume thinks that a social order cannot in normal circumstances remain stable without an authority to enforce its rules.[17] Laws, however, cannot replace the conventional

---

[16] *Treatise*, Book III, Part II, Section III.

[17] The necessary qualification—'in normal circumstances'—is discussed below in chapter 4.

rules of property, since they require the voluntary acquiescence of the population; they merely make the application of the rules more precise.

Hume's five rules of property are not original in themselves; they follow the standard outlines of Roman law,[18] which had been incorporated into the Scottish jurisprudence of his day.[19] His originality lies in the justification which he offers for them. This is not rational justification; we have seen that attempts to find a rational mode of distributing property are self-defeating, in the sense that the criteria of distribution which appear at first sight to be rational turn out to be incompatible with the basic requirements of a stable system of property. On the other hand, the rules of property cannot merely be arbitrary, otherwise they could not serve as a natural point of convergence for people wishing to create a convention to stabilize possessions. Once again Hume's position is one of mitigated scepticism: he seeks a mid-point between extreme versions of rationalism and scepticism. The rules have a basis in the natural workings of the imagination, and so they will necessarily occur to anyone searching for a way of assigning possessions. This justifies them in the twofold sense (a) that a powerful natural inclination impels us to follow the rules when making judgements about the ascription of property rights; (b) that since we need to establish conventions governing property, and since all individuals will, Hume believes, converge spontaneously on the same broad set of rules, this set represents the only possible point of unforced agreement. Hence, even apart from his own natural inclination, anyone wanting to help establish social order ought to embrace these rules as the necessary means to his end.

How does the imagination suggest rules of property to us? It does so by inclining us to link the conventional relation of property to certain natural relations between individuals and objects. Let us suppose we are seeking a way of assigning objects A...M to individuals N...Z. If there is a natural relation between A and N, B and O, and so forth, then in the absence of counter-

---

[18] A point that has been noted by I. F. G. Baxter, 'David Hume and Justice', *Revue Internationale de Philosophie,* xlvii (1959), 112-31 and J. Moore, 'Hume's Theory of Justice and Property', *Political Studies,* xxiv (1976), 103-19.

[19] Compare, for example, Hutcheson, *A System of Moral Philosophy* (Glasgow, 1755), Book II, chs. 6-8 and Smith, *Lectures on Jurisprudence* (Oxford, 1978) with Hume's account. For a general survey, see P. Stein, 'Law and Society in Eighteenth-Century Scottish Thought' in N. T. Phillipson and R. Mitchison (eds.), *Scotland in the Age of Improvement* (Edinburgh, 1970).

vailing reasons the obvious method of allocation will be to assign A to N, B to O, and so on. In Hume's words:

When the mind is determin'd to join certain objects, but undetermin'd in its choice of the particular objects, it naturally turns its eye to such as are related together. They are already united in the mind: They present themselves at the same time to the conception; and instead of requiring any new reason for their conjunction, it wou'd require a very powerful reason to make us over-look this natural affinity ... As property forms a relation betwixt a person and an object, 'tis natural to found it on some preceding relation.[20]

The natural relations in question are of course resemblance, contiguity, and cause and effect. For the explanation of rules of property, the latter two relations are important. Consider first the rule of possession. This is obviously prompted by the natural relation of contiguity between possessor and object possessed; of all individuals he is in the closest physical proximity to the thing in question. However the relation of cause and effect is also important and may be decisive in disputed cases. Typically, the possessor has the power to produce a physical alteration in the thing possessed. To show the influence of this relation Hume contrasts the following two cases. (1) Someone hunts a hare to the point of exhaustion, whereupon a second person intervenes and seizes the animal; here we should say that the hare is the rightful property of the first person. (2) Someone is advancing towards an apple intending to pick it, whereupon a second person runs past him and picks it first; in this case we should say that the apple rightfully belongs to the latter.[21] Now in both cases the intervener is eventual possessor on the basis of contiguity, but in the first case there is also a strong relation of cause and effect between hunter and hare (the hare's abnormal condition being attributable to the hunter's efforts) and this is striking enough for us to deem him possessor of the animal. In the second case the person advancing does not materially affect the apple and no such relation exists. So 'possession' is actually a more complex phenomenon that at first appears, depending both on the relation of contiguity and on the relation of cause and effect.

We may note in passing that 'labour' is not regarded by Hume as creating a distinct title to property, but merely as one of the ways in which we may possess an object (labouring being a species of causal relationship between persons and things). He does not see it as morally superior to the other modes of possession, nor as

[20] *Treatise*, p. 504.
[21] *Treatise*, pp. 506-7.

the source of a stronger title to property, except in so far as the alteration produced by labour forms a relation which the imagination finds especially striking.[22]

The particular claims of the first possessor of an object are not explained in a very satisfactory manner by Hume; he says merely that 'the first possession always engages the attention most'. So the second rule of property (occupation) seems to lack a distinct basis in the imagination, in the sense that Hume fails to explain, using his theory of natural relations, why first possession should generally be thought to override present possession as a title to property. He is more successful with the third rule, prescription or long possession. The greater the time during which someone has possessed an object, the more strongly the habitual connection between our ideas of possessor and possessed is established, and the firmer is the natural relation to which a relation of property can be united. At the same time any countervailing title based on occupation becomes weaker as the fact of occupation recedes into the distance.

Any considerable space of time sets objects at such a distance, that they seem, in a manner, to lose their reality, and have as little influence on the mind, as if they never had been in being. A man's title, that is clear and certain at present, will seem obscure and doubtful fifty years hence, even tho' the facts, on which it is founded, shou'd be prov'd with the greatest evidence and certainty.[23]

This for Hume is a clear proof that property 'is the offspring of the sentiments, on which alone time is found to have any influence'.

The fourth rule of property, accession, depends again on the natural relations of contiguity and cause and effect. Here the relation between person and object is extended to encompass other things intimately related to that object. In paradigm cases, such as the connection between a tree and its fruit, this further relation involves both contiguity and cause and effect. In other cases, however, contiguity alone is sufficient, as shown in the convention whereby the owner of a river bank is held to own the soil alluvially deposited along it. Such cases of juxtaposition cause Hume some difficulty, for he has to explain why, when a large and a small object are juxtaposed (say a large island and a neighbouring islet), the owner of the large object is thought to have a claim upon the smaller rather than vice versa. The difficulty is that 'the imagination passes with greater facility from little to great, than from great to little',[24] hence 'it shou'd naturally be imagin'd, that the

---

[22] For a succinct dismissal of Locke's theory of property, see *Treatise*, p. 505, fn. 1.
[23] *Treatise*, p. 508.   [24] See above, ch. 2, p. 45.

right of accession must encrease in strength, in proportion as the transition of ideas is perform'd with greater facility'.[25] His solution is to consider the relation between the person and one object, and then the relation between the person and both; clearly the step between the two relations is smaller when the object considered first forms the major part of the final composite. 'And this is the reason, why small objects become accessions to great ones, and not great to small.'[26]

The rule of succession, finally, depends on the pre-existing relation between the deceased and his kinsmen. Now this is not entirely a natural relation, although it has a natural element, namely the causal relation of generation between parent and child. Hume does not dig any deeper here, but it seems in this case that we have one conventional rule, the rule of justice, being founded on other conventional rules, the rules of kinship which obtain in any particular society. Justice in this instance is doubly artificial.

Having examined the basis of the five rules of property in the imagination, we should take note of one further consequence following from Hume's explanation. Our judgements about property do in one respect rest upon an illusion. In making them we link a natural relation between a person and an object with a moral relation, namely his being permitted to use and enjoy that object while others have a duty to abstain from it. This moral relation is clearly not a real relation between the person and the object, but rather (on Hume's analysis) a sentiment in the mind of an observer who feels himself obliged not to interfere with that object. Hume hints, however, that the idea of property as normally understood does indeed connote a real relation between person and thing. When we describe someone as owning a house, we mean that there is some external connection between person and property, not merely that we have a certain feeling when contemplating, for instance, entering that house without his consent. The explanation for this lies in the imagination's capacity to project internal impressions on to external things; 'the mind has a great propensity to spread itself on external objects, and to conjoin with them any internal impressions, which they occasion.'[27] In the present case a physical relation (e.g. of possession) suggests the moral relation,

[25] *Treatise*, p. 510.

[26] *Treatise*, p. 511.

[27] See above, ch. 1, pp. 28-9. The similarity between Hume's accounts of necessary connection and of property should be clear. In both cases an internal sentiment of the mind is unavoidably, though mistakenly, conceived to be a feature of the external world.

but in doing so it leads the imagination to project the latter out into the physical world. However, 'the property of an object, when taken for something real, without any reference to morality, or the sentiments of the mind, is a quality perfectly insensible, and even inconceivable.'[28] This deficiency in our conception is not normally noticed, but it comes to the surface in cases where property is transferred from person to person, for a verbal transfer can take place without any alteration at all in the physical relationship between either party and the object. How can the mind grasp the change of ownership in such a case so long as it conceives property to be a real relation? Hume argues that a remedy for this defect may be found in the delivery (real or symbolic) of the object concerned.

> In order to aid the imagination in conceiving the transference of property, we take the sensible object, and actually transfer its possession to the person, on whom we wou'd bestow the property. The suppos'd resemblance of the actions, and the presence of this sensible delivery, deceive the mind, and make it fancy, that it conceives the mysterious transition of the property. And that this explication of the matter is just, appears hence, that men have invented a *symbolical* delivery to satisfy the fancy, where the real one is impracticable. Thus the giving the keys of a granary is understood to be the delivery of the corn contain'd in it: The giving of stone and earth represents the delivery of a mannor.[29]

The fact that our beliefs about property are, in this important sense, fictitious leads Hume to ask, in *Enquiry* II, whether justice might not crumble under examination in precisely the same way as religious superstition. Each set of beliefs relies on distinctions which correspond to no real differences in the relevant objects. According to vulgar superstition 'a fowl on Thursday is lawful food; on Friday abominable'. According to the rules of justice 'I may lawfully nourish myself from this tree; but the fruit of another of the same species, ten paces off, it is criminal for me to touch'.[30] The great difference, however, is that superstitious belief has no social utility, whereas the rules of justice are essential to society's well-being. That having been said, many particular judgements about property exhibit all the weaknesses of superstitious belief; they are 'whimsical', based on 'analogies', dependent on 'the finer turns and connexions of the imagination'. There is an obvious reference here to Hume's earlier distinction between the permanent and universal principles of the imagination and those that are change-

---

[28] *Treatise*, p. 515.
[29] *Treatise*, p. 515.
[30] *Enquiry*, II, pp. 198-9.

able and irregular. In the present context, the permanent principles are manifested in the five rules of acquisition, while the changeable principles are shown in all those conventions which a particular society adopts to make the rules more precise and to adjudicate between them. The point about these conventions is that they have no basis at all, not even the kind of basis in human nature possessed by the general rules of property. What is 'whimsical' or 'superstitious' is the attempt to provide them with an objective grounding, which will mean conjuring up some feature of the objects in question which is supposed to be relevant to their ownership. In fact it is entirely arbitrary whether, say, a cup made by Smith from metal owned by Jones is held to belong to Smith or to Jones.[31]

It has been taken for granted so far that whereas the existence of rules of property can be justified by reference to both private and public interest, the rules themselves depend solely on the workings of the imagination. That is not quite a fair account of Hume's position, however, because he believes that considerations of utility have some part to play in forming the rules. There is a clear difference of emphasis over this between *Treatise,* Book III and *Enquiry* II. In the former work he treats the imagination as primarily responsible for the rules of acquisition, while noting that there are also utilitarian reasons in favour of most of them. The rule of present possession, for example, is supported by the observation that we gain most enjoyment from objects we are used to possessing, and the rule of succession by the observation that we are encouraged to be 'industrious and frugal' by the knowledge that our property will pass to our descendants. In *Enquiry* II the order of argument is reversed. Hume begins by claiming that those rules are adopted which are most beneficial to society, and only later concedes that a number of the rules are derived from connections in the imagination.[32] The general outcome, however, is the same: most of the rules can be justified from either direction, and even where a utilitarian justification is offered for a particular rule, it is much less powerful than the utilitarian case for having some rules in the first place. Hume sums up his position in *Enquiry* II as follows:

[31] A standard case discussed in books of Roman law, and considered by Hume at *Treatise,* p. 513.

[32] See *Enquiry* II, p. 309, fn. 1.

In short, we must ever distinguish between the necessity of a separation and constancy in men's possession, and the rules, which assign particular objects to particular persons. The first necessity is obvious, strong, and invincible: the latter may depend on a public utility more light and frivolous, on the sentiment of private humanity and aversion to private hardship, on positive laws, on precedents, analogies, and very fine connexions and turns of the imagination.[33]

If we were to ask in a spirit of rational reconstruction whether any of Hume's rules of property need support from a utilitarian direction as well as from the imagination, the answer would be that they need such support only at two points. First, the rule that property may be transferred by consent is clearly inspired by considerations of private and social utility; its function is to adjust property to the needs and desires of particular individuals. We have seen already that the imagination has difficulty in grasping such transfers and would not spontaneously suggest them. Second, utility explains the relatively low weight attached to the rule of possession when compared to the other rules. Considering the workings of the imagination, one would expect a present impression of contiguity between person and object to have a marked effect on judgements about property rights. But if the rule were followed consistently it would quickly destroy the institution of property (since every thief would become the rightful owner of what he takes), so there is a social interest in confining its use to residual cases where no other title to property is available. These two cases aside, all other references to a utilitarian rationale for the rules of property are, from the point of view of Hume's theory of judgement, icing on the cake.

A further question is why the theory of justice should not be rendered utilitarian throughout. Why shouldn't the rules with maximally useful consequences be chosen, rather than the rules suggested by the imagination? The answer here has three parts to it. First, Hume is openly doubtful about how much difference it makes, from the point of view of utility, which precise rules are chosen provided they fall within the general range he has mapped out for us. The benefits of the property system do not depend on which goods in particular are assigned to which people. So the pay-off from redesigning the set of rules is likely to be fairly small. Second, Hume is also sceptical about whether we can have sufficient information to predict the results of adopting a new set of rules. Since this obviously bears on the wider question of whether deliberate social improvement is possible, I shall return to the point later. Third, and perhaps most important, the rules are not in any case designed for a set of rational and benevolent beings. They represent a point of convergence for creatures of limited judgement and limited benevolence. Their most important quality is that they should appear 'natural' to every participant in the social convention. So the human imagination sets limits to what is possible in the field of justice. Rules that might appear justifiable to the impartial spectator will not necessarily command the assent of individuals engaged in an existing social practice.

The impartial spectator is moreover not bound to employ utilitarian standards in the first place. Returning to Hume's general account of moral judgement, judgements of approval are based on feelings of pleasure conveyed by sympathy when we contemplate the effects of certain character traits. These effects need not consist in a maximal contribution to social utility. Among the virtues that Hume recognizes are numerous qualities that are 'useful' or 'agreeable' to the person who possesses them. When we admire someone for his prudence or his courage, we do so because of our response to the effects of these qualities on the person himself, not on society at large. Hume is quite specific on this point: 'No views of utility or of future beneficial conse-quences enter into this sentiment of approbation.'[34] All that is necessary, therefore, to secure the impartial spectator's approval is that some pleasure-inducing consequences should flow from a quality. Hume's theory of judgement does not have a utilitarian character over all, even though it includes social utility as one of the features on which moral approval may be based. Returning to justice in particular, the disposition to follow rules of justice has valuable consequences even if the particular rules that are followed are not the maximally useful set according to some calculation. That is sufficient to make the quality of justice a virtue in a theory of moral judgement of this nature.

The question remains whether Hume sees the rules of justice as capable of improvement, and if so, in what improvement should consist. We have seen, both in his theory of the understanding and in his general theory of morals, that after disposing of ration-alism and installing an account of 'natural' judgement in its place, he allows that some improvement in judgement is possible. In each case this forms the basis for a contrast between the vulgar and the wise. Does Hume's theory of justice contain the same

---

[34] *Enquiry* II, p. 260.

possibility? We should begin by noticing one important difference between this case and those examined earlier. Judgements about justice form the basis of a social practice, and so it is of paramount importance that everyone should agree in these judgements. In the case of empirical judgements, by contrast, it matters little if you and I reach different conclusions about some matter of fact; if my conclusions are better founded than yours, that is all to the good as far as I am concerned. But supposing I come to believe that an alternative set of rules of property would have better consequences than those that are now followed, what use is that? Unless I can persuade others to accept my judgement, acting on my belief will be highly damaging rather than beneficial— upsetting the existing conventions without replacing them with anything better.

It follows that the wise man will confine his attention to cases in which there is already practical disagreement over the assignment of property rights. These will be cases where the general rules of property fail to give sufficient guidance because of their unavoidable imprecision. In practice this will almost certainly call for positive legislation, not merely for the adoption of social rules. In such circumstances, the man of judgement will want to insist, first and foremost, that it matters less what law in particular is adopted than that everyone should agree to follow some law whose meaning is clearly understood. Second, he may of course wish to offer suggestions as to how the law should be framed; but these suggestions will be put forward diffidently, in view of the practical uncertainties surrounding any piece of legislation. He will be more than willing to defer to the collective opinion of others, if this is based on greater experience.

To balance a large state or society, whether monarchical or republican, on general laws, is a work of so great difficulty, that no human genius, however comprehensive, is able, by the mere dint of reason and reflection, to effect it. The judgments of many must unite in this work: experience must guide their labour: time must bring it to perfection: and the feeling of inconveniences must correct the mistakes, which they inevitably fall into, in their first trials and experiments.[35]

It seems, therefore, that the third element of Hume's mitigated scepticism—the improvement of judgement— appears in somewhat atrophied form in his theory of justice. This is partly because of the practical difficulty of knowing when a proposed improvement really is an improvement, and partly because judgements

---

[35] Hume, 'Of the Rise and Progress of the Arts and Sciences', *Essays*, p. 125.

here are not intended merely for private use, but form the basis of
a collective practice. It is not surprising that there is no section of
Treatise, Book III headed 'Rules by which to judge of rules of
property' corresponding to the section of Book I headed 'Rules by
which to judge of causes and effects'. There would be no objection,
of course, to speculating about how an ideal set of rules might
look, provided this was recognized as little more than an exercise
in idle curiosity. Hume engages in something analogous when he
constructs an ideal commonwealth which, if winning 'the universal consent of the wise and learned', might some day have an
opportunity of being realized 'either by a dissolution of some old
government, or by the combination of men to form a new one, in
some distant part of the world'.[36] An exercise of this kind must
not be confused with the practical advocacy of change. Confusion
can be avoided provided the spirit of the proposals is made clear.
Hume implies such a distinction in a remark on a related subject:

Though a philosopher reasonably acknowledges, in the course of an argument,
that the rules of justice may be dispensed with in cases of urgent necessity; what
should we think of a preacher or casuist, who should make it his chief study to
find out such cases, and enforce them with all the vehemence of argument and
eloquence?[37]

The implication is: if you want to speculate on improved rules
of justice, do so by all means, but recognize the uncertainty of
such reasoning, and above all do not erode people's attachment to
the rules of justice that they now follow. Improvement here is
limited not merely by the natural boundaries of the imagination,
but also by the necessity of maintaining a set of artificial rules
without which 'society must immediately dissolve, and every one
must fall into that savage and solitary condition, which is infinitely
worse than the worst situation that can possibly be suppos'd in
society'.[38]

[36] Hume, 'Idea of a Perfect Commonwealth', *Essays*, p. 500.
[37] Hume, 'Of Passive Obedience', *Essays*, p. 476.
[38] *Treatise*, p. 497.

4

Allegiance to Government

Just as Hume's discussion of justice is intended primarily to refute those rationalists who believe 'that there are eternal fitnesses and unfitnesses of things, which are the same to every rational being that considers them', so his account of political allegiance is directed against those who attempt to find a purely rational basis for our obligation to government. In this case the main target is quite explicit. It is the theory of a social contract, which settles questions about political obligation by reference to a covenant or contract supposedly entered into by all members of a society at the inception of the state, laying down the terms on which the government possesses its authority. On the assumption that such a contract has been made, and adhered to by the other parties, a man's obligation to obey his government can immediately be demonstrated. Hume wished to demolish this theory without simultaneously falling into the extreme sceptical position that nothing constructive can be said about allegiance to government. The overall shape of the position he wants to maintain should by now be familiar.

A successful social contract theory might indeed provide answers to questions of four different kinds: first, questions about the historical origin of governments, answered by reference to the very act of making the contract; second, questions about the general justification of government, answered by reference to the considerations which induced men to enter the contract in preference to an anarchical 'state of nature'; third, questions about the titles of particular persons to hold authority, answered by reference to the detailed specification of the deed of contract; fourth, questions about the circumstances under which obligation would cease and resistance to government become legitimate, answered by reference to the conditions imposed upon governors in the covenant. Not every contract theory was so ambitious, but one influential specimen—Locke's—did claim to answer each of these four kinds of question.[1] One of Hume's great achievements in

---

[1] Locke's political influence may have been exaggerated, but Hume clearly regarded his work as a prototype of the contractual view he wished to demolish. For the historical question of Locke's influence on eighteenth-century thought, see J. P. Kenyon, *Revolution*

rebutting contract theory was to show that each type of question was distinct and required a separate answer. This is not to say that the answers given could be isolated from one another completely; in particular Hume saw a connection between the question of general justification and the question of resistance, as will be seen later.

Hume offers two rather different sorts of argument against the hypothesis of a social contract as a foundation for political allegiance.[2] The first highlights the gross discrepancy between what people actually believe about governments and what they ought to believe if the hypothesis were true. He points out that, apart from those few people actually in the grip of contract theory, neither rulers nor subjects are inclined to understand their relationship in contractual terms. It is not merely that the fine details of the contract cannot be spelt out; rather, the underlying assumptions are quite different. Rulers claim a right to their subjects' allegiance no matter how their own title was acquired, and subjects regard themselves as born to obedience. The latter either give no thought at all to the question of obligation, or they consider their obligation as flowing directly from the fact of having been born into an established political order. It would be odd, Hume suggests, if a contract to found government had left no trace of itself in current attitudes. If it is claimed instead that the contract is renewed in each generation by tacit consent, this being shown by people's behaviour rather than by their expressed beliefs, Hume replies that the behaviour referred to has no such implications:

Can we seriously say, that a poor peasant or artisan has a free choice to leave his country, when he knows no foreign language or manners, and lives, from day to day, by the small wages which he acquires? We may as well assert that a man, by remaining in a vessel, freely consents to the dominion of the master; though he was carried on board while asleep, and must leap into the ocean and perish, the moment he leaves her.[3]

Apart from this appeal to received opinion, Hume has a more philosophical reason for rejecting the contract theory. Deriving our obligations to government from a contract would make sense

---

Principles (Cambridge, 1977) and H. T. Dickinson, 'The Eighteenth-Century Debate on the "Glorious Revolution" ', *History*, lxi (1976), 28-45. For Hume's relationship to Locke, see M. P. Thompson, 'Hume's Critique of Locke and the "Original Contract" ', *Il Pensiero Politico*, x (1977), 189-201.

[2] These arguments are rather differently weighted in the *Treatise* and the *Essays*. Compare *Treatise*, Book III, Part II, Section VIII with the essay 'Of the Original Contract'.

[3] 'Of the Original Contract', *Essays*, p. 462.

if the obligation to keep promises were self-evident or had a rational justification. In that case the contract theory would be pinning a conventional obligation (conventional because government might not have existed) on to a natural foundation. But as we have seen, the obligation to keep promises is itself artificial, and therefore as much in need of explanation as the political obligation it is being used to underpin:

> Having found that *natural*, as well as *civil* justice, derives its origin from human conventions, we shall quickly perceive, how fruitless it is to resolve the one into the other, and seek, in the laws of nature, a stronger foundation for our political duties than interest, and human conventions; while these laws themselves are built on the very same foundation. On which ever side we turn this subject, we shall find, that these two kinds of duty are exactly on the same footing, and have the same source both of their *first invention* and *moral obligation*. They are contriv'd to remedy like inconveniences, and acquire their moral sanction in the same manner, from their remedying those inconveniences.[4]

In other words the contract theory introduces a needless circuit into the argument about government. The duty of allegiance can be explained directly by reference to the human interests which government serves, and thus has its own independent justification. Supposing a particular regime *were* established by contract (a possibility not ruled out by Hume), we should then have two separate obligations towards it—the obligation arising from the contract and our normal obligation to uphold a functioning government.

We see here how Hume's view of moral judgement supports his position in political theory. He relies upon his anti-rationalist account of the genesis of moral sentiments to develop the distinction between the natural and the artificial virtues. This distinction in turn is used to undermine the idea of a social contract and replace it by Hume's account of allegiance as an artificial virtue. For, as he says, 'Tis reasonable for those philosophers, who assert justice to be a natural virtue, and antecedent to human conventions, to resolve all civil allegiance into the obligation of a promise.'[5] But if justice (stretched here to include the virtue of promise-keeping) can be shown to be artificial, the rationale for a contract theory disappears. The way is open for a new account that is compatible with Hume's moral theory.

Turning now to that account, we may begin with Hume's answer to the question about the general justification of govern-

---

[4] *Treatise*, p. 543.
[5] *Treatise*, p. 542.

ment. He poses this in the form: why would people who have adopted rules of justice in a pre-political condition decide to establish government? Observe that this is not intended to be a thesis about the historical origin of actual governments (this issue is dealt with separately) but an analysis of the basic logic of political authority. Let us return, therefore, to a hypothetical state in which justice and property have been introduced, but there is as yet no separate body authorized to enforce the rules of justice. Why should such a body be required?

Hume thinks there are circumstances in which it will not be needed. In small and relatively poor societies, such as those of the Indian tribes of America, property can remain sufficiently stable without political authority. There is not much incentive to steal your neighbour's possessions when you can procure similar things without difficulty from natural sources. Size is important because an act of rule-breaking is likely to have greater visible repercussions in a small group, and so men will feel a more immediate interest in acting justly.

In 'large and polish'd' societies, however, there is a strong temptation to violate the rules of justice for personal gain. This is not because one can do so without serious repercussions, for Hume (as we have seen) thinks that the rules of justice must be observed 'inflexibly' if the property system is not to collapse. For any person the losses resulting from an act of injustice will therefore outweigh the gains.[6] The problem is that the losses are relatively distant whereas the gains are immediate. The passions are governed by the imagination, and the imagination presents a more forceful idea of objects lying near at hand than of objects lying further off in space or time.

This is the reason why men so often act in contradiction to their known interest; and in particular why they prefer any trivial advantage, that is present, to the maintenance of order in society, which so much depends on the observance of justice. The consequences of every breach of equity seem to lie very remote, and are not able to counterballance any immediate advantage, that may be reap'd from it.[7]

Hume argues that this defect in the human understanding would be irremediable were it not for the fact that we can observe how our attitude changes as a moment of action approaches. Suppose

---

[6] As a result this is not a 'free-rider' problem in the strict sense, though the practical effects are the same: individuals acting independently of each other produce a joint result that nobody wants.

[7] *Treatise*, p. 535.

I am considering an act of injustice which I might commit in twelve months' time. In such a case both the gain and the resulting loss are now more or less equally distant, so I see them in proper perspective and can resolve not to commit the unjust act. As the time of action approaches, however, I find my resolve weakening, and I would be willing to accept an external restraint to hold me to my original decision. Consider by way of analogy the following case: I know that if I drink more than two pints of beer in an evening, I shall have a hangover next morning, but I also know that after two pints the attractions of a third will appear to outweigh the ensuing misery. It is then reasonable for me to ask a reliable friend beforehand to stop me after two pints. In Hume's story we set up governors to compel us to follow those rules of justice which we can see we have an interest in following when we consider each case in its true perspective, from a distance.[8]

It is interesting to notice that it is not selfishness as such which, in Hume's account, makes government necessary. Men might be selfish and yet live in anarchy were it not for the weakness of their imagination. 'Here then is the origin of civil government and allegiance. Men are not able radically to cure, either in themselves or others, that narrowness of soul, which makes them prefer the present to the remote.'[9] Nor does it seem that Hume is referring to one of the permanent principles of the imagination, i.e. one in whose absence a whole class of judgements could not be made.[10] In discussing moral judgement in general, we saw that it was possible (though difficult) for people to abstract from their particular spatio-temporal position in arriving at moral appraisals. However, we also observed that a possible cost was a divorce between moral feeling and moral judgement. In the present case it would be necessary not merely that I should judge my interest in the preservation of rules of justice to be greater than my interest in immediate gain, but that my feelings should follow my judgement. It is this which seems to present the greatest difficulty in the

---

[8] Strategies of this and related kinds for dealing with failures of rationality have recently been discussed with considerable sophistication by J. Elster in *Ulysses and the Sirens: Studies in Rationality and Irrationality* (Cambridge, 1979), ch. 2.

[9] *Treatise*, p. 537.

[10] Hume does not ask whether it might not be rational to discount gains and losses according to their distance from us in time; yet such a 'discount rate' is standardly incorporated into rational choice theories when long-term strategies are being considered. The importance of this in one particular case has been brought out by M. Taylor in *Anarchy and Co-operation* (London, 1976). See especially ch. 5, and the discussion of Hume in ch. 6, sect. 2.

case.[11] If we could both replace the unruly offspring of the imagination by judgement *and* regulate our passions by the judgements we have formed, government would be an unnecessary
invention. Hume's whole case at this point rests on the fact that
these conditions are unlikely to be met as a general rule.

As in the case of the rules of justice, we can see that government
is based on individual self-interest, but once established is morally
approved because of its contribution to the public interest.
Knowing the weakness of our imagination, we appoint specific
persons to enforce the rules of justice by applying sanctions to
those who violate them, thus making the loss arising from a
violation greater and more immediate. Once the institution is
established, we see that actions tending to weaken it—acts of
disobedience or rebellion—are contrary to the common interest,
and so we come to regard loyalty as a virtue and rebelliousness as
a vice. Concerning the governors themselves, Hume argues that
it will in most cases be in their immediate interest to enforce the
rules of justice impartially. They owe their position to the people's
wish that they should carry out this function, and they must fear
deposition if they fail. The exceptions are cases where their own
private interests are directly engaged (for instance disputes over
property between themselves and their subjects) and here Hume
says simply that in a large society such cases will be comparatively
rare.[12] Like Hobbes, he assumes that it is better to suffer occasional
invasion from the powerful few than constant invasion from the
powerless many.

This in Hume's eyes is the basic logic of government. He also
offers two subsidiary arguments in its favour. The first concerns
the government's function in specifying the rules of justice more
precisely than is done by natural judgement, and in settling
disputes over the interpretation of the rules.[13] The second concerns
the government's role in providing public goods—benefits like
bridges and harbours which everyone has an interest in seeing
provided, but no one has an interest in contributing to himself
unless assured that everyone else will do likewise.

[11] It is perhaps surprising that Hume does not return at this point in the argument to
the contrast between the calm and the violent passions. If men only had calm passions
(which are directed by judgement) the difficulty would be overcome. Hume's position
here therefore presupposes the irruption of violent passions.
[12] Later we shall see that governments may vary considerably in the quality of the
justice that they dispense (below, ch. 7), but Hume leaves such variations to one side
while explaining the basic logic of government.
[13] *Treatise*, pp. 537-8; *Enquiry* II, p. 308.

Two neighbours may agree to drain a meadow, which they possess in common; because 'tis easy for them to know each others mind; and each must perceive, that the immediate consequence of his failing in his part, is, the abandoning the whole project. But 'tis very difficult, and indeed impossible, that a thousand persons shou'd agree in any such action; it being difficult for them to concert so complicated a design, and still more difficult for them to execute it; while each seeks a pretext to free himself of the trouble and expence, and wou'd lay the whole burden on others. Political society easily remedies both these inconveniences.[14]

It does so because the magistrates have an interest in ensuring that each person makes his contribution.

Each of these arguments for government has the same basic form, inasmuch as government is viewed as an agency which compels us to do what it is really in our interest to do, but from which we are deflected by inescapable human qualities. The general justification offered unites private and public interest in such a way that we can show both why it is prudent and why it is morally obligatory to obey the state. Hume does not believe, however, that the justification he has given is normally prominent in people's minds either when they establish government or when they continue in their allegiance to it. The most that can be said is that they have an 'implicit notion' of the argument for political authority. To account both for the historical origin of government and for most of the allegiance that is given in practice we need to look elsewhere.

Hume is not particularly concerned about the question of origin except in so far as it provides him with more ammunition to fire at the social contract theory. Most existing governments, he believes, were originally founded on usurpation or conquest.[15] This presupposes, of course, that there was something to conquer or usurp, so we need to look further back to discover the origin of government itself. The most likely hypothesis, in Hume's view, is that government grew up gradually from experience gained in time of war. There is then an obvious and immediate need for an authority to co-ordinate people's actions and, once the advantages of authority are seen, recognition of its scope is likely to be extended (except in the case of a 'small uncultivated society') beyond external defence to include internal policing as well. At this point it is possible, though not essential, for a formal promise of obedience to be made to the leader who has emerged; that

---

14 *Treatise*, p. 538.
15 'Of the Original Contract', *Essays*, p. 457.

much Hume is willing to concede to the social contract theorists.[16] In any case, the obligation to the magistrate chosen soon acquires an independent root, distinct from the obligation arising from the promise. Now it is perfectly true that government cannot be established merely by force, but rests upon the voluntary acquiescence of those subject to it. If that were all the contract theorists meant when they said that government necessarily rested on consent, Hume would have no quarrel with them. He is plainly correct to think, however, that they intended something a good deal stronger than this familiar though important truth. Besides showing that a simpler and more direct justification of government can be given, Hume has now shown that the historical origin of government bears little resemblance to the contractual story.[17]

Next there is the question of who shall have the title to govern. Hume envisages allegiance as being pledged originally to a man, or possibly several men, rather than to any set of constitutional rules. Consequently there may be disputes over authority in the event of death, cleavage in the ruling group, appearance of new claimants to power, and so forth. Such disputes cannot be resolved rationally, in the sense that reason cannot inform us which claimant is best suited to wield authority. If we look at the matter from the point of view of private interest, each of us will favour a different pretender according to how we calculate the benefits likely to accrue to us from his accession to power. From the point of view of public interest, the qualities needed in a ruler are not only disputable but also difficult to detect even when there is agreement about them, given the unpredictable effects that power has on a person's character. Hume draws a strong and explicit analogy here with the case of property.[18] We need fixed rules for allocating property rights, but it would be self-defeating if we tried to design those rules so as to assign property to those most fit to receive it. Instead we need to follow the workings of the imagination, and base titles on those connections between persons

---

[16] I am rationalizing Hume's position a little here. In the *Treatise* he says that such a compact would occur 'naturally'; in the essay 'Of the Original Contract' he describes it as 'an idea far beyond the comprehension of savages'. Otherwise the argument runs along similar lines.

[17] It may be argued that, considered as a critique of Locke, this part of the argument misses its target, since an historical contract was not essential to Locke's theory. But popular versions of contractarianism did presuppose that a contract had actually occurred historically, and Hume's remarks are apposite in relation to the tradition as a whole. See further Thompson, 'Hume's Critique of Locke' and P. F. Brownsey, 'Hume and the Social Contract', *Philosophical Quarterly*, xxviii (1978), 132-48.

[18] See *Treatise*, pp. 555-6.

and things which it naturally establishes. The same is true of titles to government. It matters less who in particular holds power than that everyone should agree to accept the same incumbent; the main benefits of government are certainty and stability in the enforcement of the rules of justice, and to achieve these results no exceptional qualities are required in the ruler. The main quality indeed is that he should follow his interest in a reasonably prudent manner rather than be deflected by violent passions into oppressing some or all of his subjects. In the latter event he is liable to be deposed by the people, justifiably as we shall see later on.

Given that disputes over claims to authority are rationally irresolvable, what rules for assigning authority will occur 'naturally' to people, and so indicate possible points of covergence to those wishing to establish or maintain political authority but uncertain whom to acknowledge as ruler? Hume again proposes five such rules:

(1) Long possession: Authority shall be conferred on the person or family who have held power for an extensive period of time.

(2) Present possession: Authority shall be conferred on the person currently holding power.

(3) Conquest: Authority shall be conferred on the successful conqueror of the previous regime.

(4) Succession: Authority shall be conferred on the son of the previous ruler.

(5) Positive laws: Authority shall be conferred on that person designated by the legislature to wield it.

These rules deserve a few brief comments. First, like the rules of property, they may conflict with each other, in which case the various considerations must be weighed up and a decision reached. If, for example, a well-established dynasty is overthrown by a pretender who acquires effective control of the country, long possession clashes with present possession and each person must judge which criterion takes precedence.

Second, the present possession rule has a much greater role to play in judgements about authority than in judgements about property. This is because the reasons which count against the rule in the case of property have much less force in the new case. It is a good deal harder to transfer the powers of government from one hand to another than to transfer a piece of property. So, on the one hand, recognizing the rule of present possession does not give excessive encouragement to the potential usurper (as it would to the potential thief); on the other hand, *not* recognizing it would commit us to opposing a newly-established regime whenever anyone else had a shred of title left, notwithstanding the possible cost in disorder and bloodshed of an attempt to restore the rightful ruler. Hume does not accept the Hobbesian view that we must always acknowledge the authority of the person who wields effective power in our society; but he does maintain that among 'moderate men' this title and the associated one of conquest will always weigh heavily.[19]

Third, the final rule—positive laws—is plainly different in nature from the first four. Whereas long possession, present possession, conquest, and succession all ground authority on some natural feature of the person whose title is established by the rule,[20] positive laws presuppose the authority of the legislative body which enacts them. Hume avoids circularity here by pointing out that the authority of the legislature itself will ultimately depend on one or more of the first four considerations. A new element is introduced, however, because what commands allegiance in such a case is not the legislature as such but the constitutional framework in which it has a more or less well-defined place; so an attempt by the legislature to change the constitution itself will probably not command the assent of the people. What Hume tries to do here is to amalgamate in a single framework two rather different forms of authority: the authority which is accorded to a person on the basis of some characteristic he is thought to possess, and the authority which is attributed to a whole complex of institutions, and thus derivatively to those persons who hold institutional positions. He does so, it seems evident, because the title to supreme authority in British government could not be understood fully without reference to positive laws, bearing in mind the events of 1688 when a monarch satisfying

---

[19] *Treatise,* pp. 559, fn. 1.

[20] I have deliberately expressed the criterion for assigning authority under rules 1 and 2 as 'holding power', and 'power' is intended to refer to a person's ability to make others comply with his will. In that sense power is a natural relationship between persons. Now it is true that one important source of political power is others' recognition of a person's authority, and it might therefore seem that Hume's criterion cannot be applied without circularity. The circle, however, is only apparent, for there is plainly a difference between observing that others recognize X's authority and recognizing it yourself. The present possession rule, for instance, states thay *you* should accept the authority of whoever currently holds power, although this power may in turn derive from others' having already accepted that person's authority. There would of course be a paradox if everyone in a society tried to apply the rule simultaneously. Hume, however, makes the realistic assumption that judgements about authority have to be made in situations where other people have already made their commitments—at the very least the soldiery will have done so.

the requirements of long possession, present possession, and succession was replaced by a parliamentary nominee.[21] The amalgamation is not, however, particularly satisfactory from a philosophical point of view.

A final footnote to Hume's rules of allegiance is worth appending. If we compare them with the rules of property, we notice that three of the latter have no equivalents among the rules of allegiance. The reason for omitting 'occupation' is fairly clear, but why should 'accession' and 'transference by consent' not be included? Accession would imply that the ruler of a territory might claim the allegiance of those inhabiting a smaller territory intimately connected with the original, which does indeed seem to be a title recognized historically as something over and above mere conquest (consider the Indian annexation of Goa as an example). Transference by consent occurs whenever a governor disposes of some of his territory to another or bequeaths it to a successor. Hume touches upon this method of acquiring authority when he refers to 'the smoothest way by which a nation may receive a foreign master, by marriage or a will'.[22] Both rules are in keeping with Hume's general position on titles to authority, and their omission must be attributed either to oversight or to a belief that they count for relatively little in the scales of judgement.

We must now examine the source of Hume's rules of allegiance. With the exception of the fifth rule, this is to be found in the imagination, which unites the relation of authority to connections which it has previously formed between persons and positions of supreme power. In the case of long possession, for instance, the constant possession of power by a person or line of persons leads the imagination to form a strong association between the thought of that person and the thought of the position of power that he occupies, to which it then 'adds' the moral relation of authority. In Hume's words,

Nothing causes any sentiment to have a greater influence upon us than custom, or turns our imagination more strongly to any object. When we have been long accustom'd to obey any set of men, that general instinct or tendency, which we have to suppose a moral obligation attending loyalty, takes easily this direction, and chuses that set of men for its objects. 'Tis interest which gives the general instinct; but 'tis custom which gives the particular direction.[23]

[21] The only alternative was to regard William of Orange as having a title by virtue of conquest, a view adopted by a small minority of his supporters at the time of the Revolution. See Kenyon, *Revolution Principles,* ch. 3.

[22] *Essays,* p. 458.

[23] *Treatise,* p. 556.

The reference to interest reminds us that people wish to recognize authority because they know it is in their interest to do so; the imagination's role is to single out some particular person as the 'natural' holder of authority. Both elements are necessary to a stable system of government. Without the first there would be no motive to obey the authorities; without the second it would be impossible to agree about which contender for power deserves support (trying to resolve this issue by reference to interest would, we recall, lead to perpetual discord).

Present possession and conquest as titles to authority can both be explained along similar lines, the imagination connecting the actual exercise of power to its continued legitimate exercise. Conquest is the stronger title, since in this case the brute fact of possessing power is 'seconded by the notions of glory and honour, which we ascribe to *conquerors,* instead of the sentiments of hatred and detestation, which attend *usurpers'*.[24]

As for the rule of succession:

> The royal authority seems to be connected with the young prince even in his father's life-time, by the natural transition of the thought; and still more after his death: So that nothing is more natural than to compleat this union by a new relation, and by putting him actually in possession of what seems so naturally to belong to him.[25]

What part do considerations of interest or utility play in the adoption of these rules? As with the rules of property, such considerations are quite definitely secondary to the influence of the imagination. The second and third rules are certainly backed up by the thought that any attempt to change the present ruler is likely to be costly in life and limb. In the case of succession, Hume asks specifically whether 'convenience', may not be the source of the rule, but replies that the rule is only convenient *because* there is an antecedent general tendency to link the father's authority to that of the son. This reply summarizes his general position. The rules of allegiance are not especially useful in themselves (i.e. they do not necessarily select rulers whose conduct creates the greatest possible amount of welfare), but if there is widespread consensus that they should be followed, they become useful by derivation, since they will tend to mark out a candidate for authority who will command general allegiance.

---

[24] *Treatise,* p. 558.
[25] *Treatise,* p. 559.

We have seen earlier that the imagination, although essential in generating various classes of belief, also creates illusions and 'fictions'. To what extent is this true in the present case? Although Hume does not make the point, it seems that ascriptions of authority are in general fictitious on his account, in so far as we are inclined to think that authority is an attribute of the person who wields it and not merely an internal sentiment directed by the imagination towards a particular individual.[26] He does, on the other hand, comment on two particular ways in which the imagination leads us into absurdity here. The first arises from the observation that a people who have justifiably deposed their monarch believe themselves entitled to exclude his son from the succession, despite the fact that the son would naturally have acceded to the throne if the king had merely died. This, Hume claims, is a case where 'the mind naturally runs on with any train of action, which it has begun'; having made a justified break with established practice, it proceeds to make a second, unjustified break. He describes this quality of the imagination as 'very singular'.[27]

The second case might be called 'retrospective legitimation'. If a line of kings succeeds in maintaining power in a particular state, so that the later members have a valid title by long possession, we are inclined to project this newly-acquired legitimacy back on to the original founder of the line, even though at the time we should have called him a usurper.

Time and custom give authority to all forms of government, and all successions of princes; and that power, which at first was founded only on injustice and violence, becomes in time legal and obligatory. Nor does the mind rest there; but returning back upon its footsteps, transfers to their predecessors and ancestors that right, which it naturally ascribes to the posterity, as being related together, and united in the imagination.[28]

In classifying these beliefs as fictitious, I mean that they will not stand up to reflective scrutiny; in examining them we find the imagination torn between contradictory impulses, and we are unable to adopt a clear position on either side. It is clear, however, that Hume wants to place them in the category of 'useful fictions', inasmuch as they tend to strengthen the allegiance of the vulgar to the regime that is now established. This raises the question of how far, if at all, the imagination is capable of correction over the

---

[26] Hume makes the analogous point in the case of property; see above ch. 3, pp. 71-2.
[27] *Treatise*, p. 565. The reference is to the exclusion of James II's son in 1688.
[28] *Treatise*, p. 566.

matter of allegiance to government. Can the wise make judgements about authority that are better founded than those of the vulgar?

The basic difficulty, noted already in the case of judgements about justice, is that there must be a consensus in judgement if the rules of allegiance are to have the desired effect of picking out a single authority. It is no use the wise giving their allegiance to one man and the vulgar to another. So the main advice which Hume offers to the wise is that they should acquiesce in the beliefs formed by the vulgar, no matter how flimsy their basis may seem to be. For example:

As the slightest properties of the imagination have an effect on the judgments of the people, it shews the wisdom of the laws and of the parliament to take advantage of such properties, and to chuse the magistrates either in or out of a line, according as the vulgar will most naturally attribute authority and right to them.[29]

The wise man, therefore, is primarily one who recognizes that consensus about authority is more important than the choice of a particular person to wield it. He is also one who recognizes that there are several criteria for ascribing authority, none of which should necessarily be given precedence over the others. A typical vulgar error, for instance, is to suppose that long possession must always outweigh present possession as a title to power; 'a strict adherence to any general rules, and the rigid loyalty to particular persons and families, on which some people set so high a value, are virtues that hold less of reason, than of bigotry and superstition.'[30]

Finally a wise man will recognize the unavoidable imprecision in the rules of allegiance, and will separate the general rule from undecidable particular issues that arise in relation to it. As in the case of property, a notion such as 'long possession' cannot be made precise except by arbitrary fiat. The rule of succession is an especially fecund source of puzzles and paradoxes. Should an adopted son have the same claim as a natural son? Does a child born after his father's accession to the throne have a stronger or weaker claim than his older brother born before the accession?[31] Analogous questions in the case of property are resolved arbitrarily by positive legislation, but in the present case there can be no such resolution (unless there is a constitutional framework), and the

---

[29] *Treatise*, p. 566.
[30] *Treatise*, p. 562.
[31] 'Of the Original Contract', *Essays*, p. 469; *Treatise*, pp. 562-3.

wisest course of action is simply not to be drawn into the controversy. These difficulties, Hume writes, 'are less capable of solution
from the arguments of lawyers and philosophers, than from the
swords of the soldiery'.[32]

We must turn now to our final question, which concerns resistance to government. Let us suppose that we have a ruler
whose title itself is not in question; are there any circumstances in
which it is justifiable to attempt to resist his power, or in the last
resort to remove him? Hume considers two sets of circumstances,
one applying generally to all forms of government, the other being
specific to constitutional regimes.

The general case in which resistance is justifiable is where a
government frustrates the purpose for which it was established.
Since government was instituted primarily to interpret and enforce
the rules of justice, and so allow its subjects to enjoy their property
in security, it may be resisted if it should begin to oppress the
people. Hume is not very explicit about the meaning of 'oppression' here, but it seems we should take it to mean 'serious
infringement of property rights', in the light of his general position.
In such circumstances the government loses its justification, and
people have neither a prudential nor a moral obligation to obey it.

It is difficult to make this criterion for resistance more specific;
and indeed Hume warns against attempts to spell it out publicly,
for instance by a declaration of the legislature.[33] On the one hand,
Hume plainly does not believe that a regime may be removed
whenever the people can envisage a better alternative—one that
will enforce justice more effectively. On the other hand, I doubt
if he wishes to say that resistance is allowable only when the
present regime is judged to be worse than no government at all,
though that is one interpretation of his statement that 'if interest
first produces obedience to government, the obligation to obedience must cease, whenever the interest ceases'. He seems to have
in mind a minimum standard of performance which we are entitled
to expect from government, though failure to achieve it can only
be described in very general terms: 'public ruin', 'extraordinary
emergencies', 'grievous tyranny and oppression' are some of the
phrases used.

Hume's reason for setting the standard fairly low is that, when
contemplating a change in our system of government, we ought to
consider not only the benefits we expect to derive from the new

---

[32] *Treatise*, p. 562.
[33] *History*, vol. v, pp. 381-2, vol. vi, pp. 133-4.

government, but also the costs of change. These encompass not merely the destruction of life and property which usually attends a revolution; but in addition the longer-term effects on people's attitude towards government. If habits of obedience are weakened, the result will be a rebellious population which can only be governed (if at all) by authoritarian rulers. For that reason, Hume concludes, 'I must confess, that I shall always incline to their side, who draw the bond of allegiance very close, and consider an infringement of it as the last refuge in desperate cases, when the public is in the highest danger from violence and tyranny.'[34]

This reasoning does not, however, apply in the more special case where resistance is justifiable. This occurs under a constitutional government when one branch of the state begins to encroach upon the powers of another. A typical instance is a constitutional monarch usurping some of the powers of the legislature. Here, Hume maintains, 'it is allowable to resist and dethrone him; tho' such resistance and violence may, in the general tenor of the laws, be deem'd unlawful and rebellious.'[35] Resistance may be embarked upon in such a case even though the ruler has not been guilty of 'enormous tyranny and oppression'. This, Hume says, is because constitutional government is an absurdity unless the various parts of the constitutional order are given some remedy against encroachment, and in the last resort this remedy must be the force of arms. It is also worth remarking (though Hume does not do so explicitly) that resistance of this kind is conservative rather than innovatory—it seeks to preserve an established constitutional framework—and so reinforces rather than destroys ingrained loyalties to the regime.

Hume's doctrine of resistance gives us a clear indication of his practical disagreements with partisans of the social contract theory. Rather than rebellion being justified whenever the terms of an imaginary contract were violated by the government, Hume would countenance it only in extreme circumstances or, in the case of constitutional government, for self-protection.[36] His

---

[34] 'Of Passive Obedience', *Essays*, p. 475.

[35] *Treatise*, p. 564.

[36] Of course not all partisans of the contract theory were wild-eyed radicals. Locke was at pains to point out that his doctrine of resistance did not lay 'a *ferment* for frequent *Rebellion*' (J. Locke, *Two Treatises of Government*, ed. P. Laslett (New York, 1965), p. 463), and, to take the limiting case, Hobbes's theory excluded collective resistance altogether. But popular versions of the social contract tended to open the door to resistance more widely than Hume was willing to allow.

position on the issue was fundamentally a conservative one, even though he would not embrace the extreme conservative dogma of passive resistance, according to which active resistance to an established government was never justifiable. This, then, was one practical outcome of his demolition of the contractual theory. There were others. According to Hume's account, no particular form of government could be regarded as uniquely legitimate on the grounds that it either had or would have commended itself to the parties to a contract. Every government must be judged by its effectiveness in creating peace and order in society. This did not mean that Hume had no preferences as to forms of government;[37] that, however, was a separate issue involving empirical judgements, and not one that bore upon the legitimacy of any particular government. As he wrote to Catherine Macaulay, 'I look upon all kinds of subdivision of power, from the monarchy of France to the freest democracy of some Swiss Cantons, to be equally legal, if established by custom and authority.'[38] Again, it followed from Hume's account that no definite limits could be set to the scope of a government's authority. He laid down no fixed boundaries, as the contract theorists had done when they argued that government must never infringe the natural rights of individuals. Hume might prefer that governments did not interfere with religion or meddle with trade, but such preferences did not imply that governments which did these things might properly be resisted. Allegiance was owed to any government that met his minimum standards.

This should remind us that Hume's theory of moral and political judgement was intended to have practical implications; anyone who accepted it would come to hold different political attitudes from those held by, say, a rationalist. Of course to know how to act in a particular case it would also be necessary to make empirical assessments: what precisely had the government done, for example, and for what reasons? But Hume's theory would then supply the terms on which a judgement about the right course of action could be made. So let us now return to the general structure of that theory, and ask how far Hume's political standpoint depends upon his over-all account of belief and judgement.

Like almost every other moral and political philosopher, Hume assumes that men's actions are sometimes affected by their beliefs

[37] These will be discussed below in ch. 7.
[38] R. Klibansky and E. C. Mossner (eds.), *New Letters of David Hume* (Oxford, 1954), p. 81.

about what ought to be done in a given set of circumstances.[39] He does not suppose this is necessarily a dominant influence, but such beliefs must have some power if practical philosophy (which addresses them) is to be a useful activity. Now we have seen that passions must motivate actions, and that moral judgements depend on feelings of sympathy. These sentiments cannot in themselves be produced by belief or judgement alone. However their *direction* can be altered by the judgements we form, and in that oblique manner judgement can affect action. What men do depends partly, though not wholly, on what they believe.[40]

If this is true, a theory of judgement—which examines the justification that may be offered for beliefs, separates the adequate from the inadequate, and indicates the extent to which improvement in judgement is possible—will have practical consequences for anyone who embraces it. Such a theory forms the core of Hume's philosophy. He begins with an account of our most general empirical beliefs, then turns to moral judgement as a whole, before coming finally to social and political judgements. Each part of the theory is a necessary precondition of those that succeed it, in the sense that a general account of judgement is worked out at the first stage and applied at the second. So Hume's epistemology is necessary to his moral theory, his moral theory to his theory of justice, and his theory of justice to his theory of political obligation.

The main feature of Hume's theory of judgement is his attack on rationalism and his substitution of a naturalist position. Most of our beliefs are incapable of being justified by reason, but they result from the natural workings of the imagination and must therefore be taken as given. Some commonly-held beliefs are unfounded, but the extent to which criticism and improvement are possible depends itself on the working of the imagination. This view, which I have referred to as mitigated scepticism, recurs throughout the various parts of Hume's theory of judgement.

[39] I say 'almost' because some political philosophers may be interpreted as assuming that men are self-interested, and that the aim of political philosophy is to instruct self-interested men how they may pursue their interests most effectively. Hobbes and Marx can both be read in this way.

[40] The need to make this assertion in a qualified way is shown by some of Hume's comments about Charles I: 'a lively instance of that species of character so frequently to be met with; where there are found parts and judgment in every discourse and opinion; in many actions, indiscretion and imprudence. Men's views of things are the result of their understanding alone; their conduct is regulated by their understanding, their temper, and their passions.' (*History,* vol. v, p. 100.) The effect of philosophical enlightenment on such people will be slight.

Its over-all effect may be described as conservative, in the sense that most common-sense beliefs are eventually re-endorsed, though from another point of view it appears radical, in so far as it cuts away what is usually taken to be the justification of these beliefs. To take beliefs about political authority as an example, most of what ordinary men believe about their government is confirmed—for instance that they owe their allegiance to a long-established line of rulers—but much of what they might offer to support those beliefs is rejected—for instance that these rulers govern by Divine Right, or as a result of an original contract with the people.

It might be asked at this point how a theory of judgement which remains fairly close to common-sense belief (*fairly* close because some common-sense beliefs are still rejected) can make a practical intervention in social and political life. If the outcome is that people should go on believing most of what they believe already, what difference does the theory make? Part of the answer is that ordinary belief is liable to be corrupted by false philosophy, especially rationalist philosophy. Philosophers may offer the people a new set of beliefs, together with a spurious justification for them, and the people may accept what they say. In the fullness of time, these beliefs will be driven out by the force of experience, but much may have taken place meanwhile. Here there is a contrast between empirical judgement in general and political judgement in particular. False empirical beliefs tend to correct themselves quickly, since the relevant experience is often immediately available. The fallacy of a political doctrine may take longer to show itself. We have seen in the case of moral judgement that there are men leading 'artificial lives' whose judgements have become completely distorted. In the sphere of justice, groups of 'imprudent fanatics' had attempted to establish common ownership of goods, until their beliefs were rudely corrected by experience. Politics, however, offers the greatest opportunities for corrupted beliefs to flourish. Men like the Levellers, described by Hume as 'a kind of *political* fanatics, which arose from the religious species', may propose political innovations which, although ultimately shown to be unworkable, may have the effect of disrupting the social order and even precipitating civil war before the absurdity of their views is seen. Everything depends on whether they find an audience. As Hume remarks in one of his essays, 'Of all mankind, there are none so pernicious as political projectors, if they have power, nor so ridiculous, if they want it'.[41] The main achievement of Hume's theory of judgement is to expose these enthusiasts for what they are—men who claim a justification for their proposals that they could not possibly have. If the theory is accepted, the temptation to embrace such views is removed once and for all.[42]

The thrust of Hume's argument is therefore mainly sceptical and conservative, but it has also a constructive side to it, as we have noted throughout. Some improvement in belief is possible; the wise can be distinguished from the vulgar. In social interaction and in politics, however, the difficulty is that both wise and vulgar must live by common conventions, and so the space within which the wise may act is limited. Yet conventions change slowly, and wise men may properly try to influence the direction of change so long as they can carry the vulgar with them.

In summary,

> It is not with forms of government, as with other artificial contrivances, where an old engine may be rejected, if we can discover another more accurate and commodious, or where trials may safely be made, even though the success be doubtful. An established government has an infinite advantage, by that very circumstance, of its being established; the bulk of mankind being governed by authority, not reason, and never attributing authority to any thing that has not the recommendation of antiquity.
>
> To tamper, therefore, in this affair, or try experiments merely upon the credit of supposed argument and philosophy, can never be the part of a wise magistrate, who will bear a reverence to what carries the marks of age; and though he may attempt some improvements for the public good, yet will he adjust his innovations as much as possible to the ancient fabric, and preserve entire the chief pillars and supports of the constitution.[43]

By no means everything that Hume has to say about society and politics can be derived from his theory of judgement. The formation of a political outlook also requires first-order beliefs— empirical beliefs about human nature, social structure, the effects of institutions and so forth, and moral beliefs about what is valuable in human life. Hume of course assumes that his moral beliefs are uncontroversial, since they belong to a consensus of

---

[41] 'Idea of a Perfect Commonwealth', *Essays,* p. 499.

[42] The corrupting effects of rationalism were not confined to radical proposals. Compare Hume's verdict on the philosophy of Hobbes: 'Hobbes's politics are fitted only to promote tyranny, and his ethics to encourage licentiousness. Though an enemy to religion, he partakes nothing of the spirit of scepticism; but is as positive and dogmatical as if human reason, and his reason in particular, could attain a thorough conviction in these subjects.' (*History,* vol. v, p. 531.)

[43] 'Idea of a Perfect Commonwealth', *Essays,* p. 499.

opinion in moral matters, but we are not bound to accept his assumption. These beliefs are circumscribed by the theory of judgement, in the sense that the theory sets down what counts as justification in each area, but they are not determined by it. Two people might accept Hume's philosophy and yet disagree politically because they differed over important empirical issues, just as two scientists might agree in their conception of scientific method and yet disagree about what was actually the case concerning a particular phenomenon. After we have examined Hume's empirical and moral assumptions in Part II, we shall be able to weigh up the contribution made by each of the two elements—the theory of judgement and the first-order beliefs—to his general political perspective.

PART II: ACTION

5

Human Nature

It is nowadays a commonplace to say that a political outlook must rest on a view of human nature; indeed it is often said that differences in political outlook can ultimately be *reduced* to different views of human nature, an exaggeration which forgets that assumptions made at the holistic level, about the working of social and political institutions, may contribute independently to such standpoints. Not everyone is a methodological individualist. Hume indeed recognized this point when arguing in defence of a science of politics. 'So great is the force of laws, and of particular forms of government, and so little dependence have they on the humours and tempers of men, that consequences almost as general and certain may sometimes be deduced from them, as any which the mathematical sciences afford us.'[1] His social and political thought is none the less strongly conditioned by his assumptions about the human individual, and we shall examine these assumptions in the present chapter. Subsequent chapters are devoted to his social and political assumptions respectively. We shall look both at what Hume takes to be the case empirically, and at his moral preferences. These two aspects of his thought cannot usefully be isolated from each other, for what he holds to be desirable from a moral point of view is greatly affected by what he believes to be possible, empirically speaking. Hume expects no radical alterations in human affairs, and our scope for choice is thus circumscribed by what we can learn through careful observation of human life; thus 'all plans of government, which suppose great reformation in the manners of mankind, are plainly imaginary.'[2] Very often we are forced to choose the lesser of two evils. To take a political example, 'it seems a necessary, though perhaps a melancholy truth, that in every government, the magistrate must either possess a large revenue and a military force, or enjoy some discretionary powers, in order to execute the laws and support his own authority.'[3] That

---

[1] 'That Politics may be reduced to a Science', *Essays*, p. 14.
[2] 'Idea of A Perfect Commonwealth', *Essays*, p. 500. He cites Plato's *Republic* and More's *Utopia* as examples.
[3] *History*, vol. iv, p. 500.

being so, we must choose between granting our rulers money and military support and allowing them to exercise prerogative; we cannot avoid both.

Hume's observations are not, however, narrowly parochial. He ranges widely over societies and historical epochs, drawing lessons from ancient Greece and Rome as well as from comparisons between the modern European nations. In the light of this comparative approach, our first question must be whether he sees human nature as a constant quantity or as socially variable.[4] The question is not hard to answer, though Hume muddies the water somewhat by making striking assertions which are later considerably qualified. For instance:

Mankind are so much the same, in all times and places, that history informs us of nothing new or strange in this particular. Its chief use is only to discover the constant and universal principles of human nature, by showing men in all varieties of circumstances and situations, and furnishing us with material from which we may form our observations and become acquainted with the re ¹ar springs of human action and behaviour. These records of wars, intrig ies, factions, and revolutions, are so many collections of experiments, by which the politician or moral philosopher fixes the principles of his science, in the same manner as the physician or natural philosopher becomes acquainted with the nature of plants, minerals, and other external objects, by the experiments which he forms concerning them.[5]

But later in the same section he appears to retract much of what he has said:

We must not, however, expect that this uniformity of human actions should be carried to such a length as that all men, in the same circumstances, will always act precisely in the same manner, without making any allowance for the diversity of characters, prejudices, and opinions. Such a uniformity in every particular, is found in no part of nature. On the contrary, from observing the variety of conduct in different men, we are enabled to form a greater variety of maxims, which still suppose a degree of uniformity and regularity.[6]

There is really no contradiction here. Hume's general point is that human behaviour is as much susceptible to causal explanation as are natural events, and that the same causes must therefore always produce the same effects. This of course says nothing about the extent to which the same causes do operate in the human world. Hume does, however, believe that there is some uniformity among human beings. We have seen already, in the

[4] For a fuller discussion, see Forbes, *Hume's Philosophical Politics*, ch. 4.

[5] *Enquiry* I, pp. 83-4.

[6] *Enquiry* I, p. 85.

theory of judgement, that men share to a great extent the same underlying moral sentiments. There is also some similarity in motivation: 'avarice, ambition and revenge' are omnipresent, and we should not believe reports of a society composed of perfectly benevolent men. At the same time, men are powerfully affected by the manners and customs of their age, by their education and social position, and by individual differences of temperament. Thus 'each century has its peculiar mode in conducting business; and men, guided more by custom than by reason, follow, without inquiry, the manners which are prevalent in their own time.'[7] Again, 'the skin, pores, muscles, and nerves of a day-labourer are different from those of a man of quality: So are his sentiments, actions and manners. The different stations of life influence the whole fabric, external and internal.'[8]

When considering the sources of variation, Hume lays most stress on what he terms 'moral' factors, meaning those that operate through the human consciousness, and pays little attention to physical factors such as climate which influence the body directly.[9] The category of the moral includes, for example, the economic and political circumstances in which a man lives, and is thus considerably broader than that of ideas as such. Hume does, all the same, give some weight to ideas as causes of behaviour, in particular to religious ideas, which not only influence men's judgement[10] but may affect their behaviour in unexpected ways. 'It is an observation suggested by all history,' he writes, ' ...that the religious spirit, when it mingles with faction, contains in it something supernatural and unaccountable; and that, in its operations upon society, effects correspond less to their known causes than is found in any other circumstance of government.'[11] This is true especially of enthusiastic religion. Explaining the downfall of Charles I, he maintains that 'the spirit of enthusiasm, being universally diffused, disappointed all the views of human prudence, and disturbed the operation of every motive which usually influences society'.[12]

Religion should therefore be seen as a force which overlays and distorts the more usual sources of variation in human nature. These include the type of society and system of government under

---

[7] *History*, vol. ii, p. 83.
[8] *Treatise*, p. 402.
[9] See the essay 'Of National Characters', *Essays*, pp. 202-20.
[10] See above, ch. 2, p. 57.
[11] *History*, vol. iv, p. 441.
[12] *History*, vol. v, p. 64.

which a person lives, and we shall examine this influence in subsequent chapters. Does Hume see any over-all pattern of human development arising from such processes? He certainly does not regard human nature as undergoing a radical transformation through the course of history in the manner of a Hegel or a Marx. Yet he has a view about the arrival of something he calls 'civilization' which softens and refines human nature.[13] This is a composite whole which includes both economic elements, especially the growth of industry and commerce, and political elements, especially the establishment of a government of laws; the two sets of factors being seen as interdependent. We can speak, therefore, of a transition from barbarity to civilization, and of an accompanying change in human nature, though this takes the form of a refining of ingredients already present rather than a radical recasting of the human frame.

Bearing this in mind, we may in the present chapter explore the constant elements in Hume's conception of human nature, and we shall begin by examining the role that he assigns to self-interest. We have seen already that Hume finds the origin both of justice and of government in men's attention to their interests, and it may appear that this hypothesis pervades his thought. Yet closer inspection reveals otherwise. When Hume confronts egoism directly, he explicitly rejects it.

So far from thinking, that men have no affection for any thing beyond themselves, I am of opinion, that tho' it be rare to meet with one, who loves any single person better than himself; yet 'tis as rare to meet with one, in whom all the kind affections, taken together, do not over-balance all the selfish.[14]

Hume is alert to the fact that arguments on this subject may turn out to be merely verbal. Is someone who denies the existence of patriotism, friendship, or parental affection really impervious to these motives, or is he merely redescribing them as esoteric forms of self-love? If the latter, he is abusing language, but there is no material disagreement between him and us. 'That species of self-love which displays itself in kindness to others, you must allow to have great influence over human actions, and even greater, on many occasions, than that which remains in its original shape and form.'[15] Another possible source of confusion is that the performance of unselfish actions is often accompanied by feelings of

---

[13] See especially, 'Of Refinement in the Arts', *Essays*, pp. 275-88.
[14] *Treatise*, p. 487.
[15] 'Of the Dignity or Meanness of Human Nature', *Essays*, p. 86.

pleasure, from which it may falsely be concluded that the pleasure is the motive for such actions.[16] But this is just one example of the fallacy which mistakes the primary objects of our passions for those sensations which accompany their satisfaction, and which can therefore become secondary goals:

Thus, hunger and thirst have eating and drinking for their end; and from the gratification of these primary appetites arises a pleasure, which may become the object of another species of desire or inclination that is secondary and interested. In the same manner there are mental passions by which we are impelled immediately to seek particular objects, such as fame or power, or vengeance without any regard to interest; and when these objects are attained a pleasing enjoyment ensues, as the consequence of our indulged affections.[17]

This last example serves as a reminder that non-selfishness encompasses less savoury motives like anger and revenge as well as benign motives like friendship. Hume is offering us a pluralistic conception of human nature, in which a number of irreducibly distinct forces contend within each breast, self-interest being powerful but by no means predominant; 'a man wholly interested is as rare as one entirely endowed with the opposite quality.'[18]

Might egoism nevertheless serve as a useful guide in explaining political behaviour? Hume appears to think so when he endorses the maxim that 'every man ought to be supposed a *knave*, and to have no other end, in all his actions, than private interest'.[19] He immediately adds, however, that 'it appears somewhat strange, that a maxim should be true in *politics* which is false in *fact*',[20] and explains that the principle only holds because men acting in parties and other corporate bodies have the usual restraints on self-interest removed by the applause of their colleagues. It is therefore a thesis about how men act as members of political institutions, and implies that those institutions should be designed to make private and public interest coincide as far as possible. It is not even the whole truth about political life. Wise men recognize, for instance, 'that reasons of state, which are supposed solely to influence the councils of monarchs, are not always the motives which there predominate; that the milder views of gratitude, honor, friendship, generosity, are frequently able, among princes as well as private persons, to counterbalance

[16] Ibid., p. 87.
[17] *Enquiry* II, p. 301.
[18] *History*, vol. ii, p. 478.
[19] 'Of the Independency of Parliament', *Essays*, p. 40.
[20] Ibid., p. 42.

these selfish considerations'.[21] Again, the allegiance which men in general bear to their governments cannot be explained by self-interest in the narrow sense of advantages expected from any particular set of rulers, though it does depend partly on a sense of the over-all benefits derived from political order. Hume, therefore, maintains that all government is founded upon opinion, and that men can only pursue their private interests within a political framework that is antecedently established.[22]

While rejecting egoism as a hypothesis about human motivation, Hume equally clearly rejects pure altruism, conceived as an impartial regard for the interests of others.[23] 'In general, it may be affirm'd, that there is no such passion in human minds, as the love of mankind, merely as such, independent of personal qualities, of services, or of relation to ourself.'[24] Although every man's happiness and suffering does affect us to a degree, through sympathy, the effect is weak and need not move us to action. Moreover the force of sympathy varies according to the proximity of the person concerned. The plight of a near relation concerns us more than that of a stranger; a fellow-countryman matters more to us than a foreigner. Our benevolence, therefore, is unlikely to be impartial; instead we shall give precedence to those closely connected to us.

This postulate of limited or partial benevolence is one of the most distinctive features of Hume's political thought. He sees each man as standing at the centre of a web of social relationships, made up of family, friends, acquaintances, dependents, etc., and as proportioning his generosity to the strength of each tie. Since this behaviour follows natural sympathies, it wins our moral approval; 'we perceive, that the generosity of men is very limited, and that it seldom extends beyond their friends and family, or, at most, beyond their native country. Being thus acquainted with the nature of man, we expect not any impossibilities from him; but confine our view to that narrow circle, in which any person moves, in order to form a judgment of his moral character.'[25] Providentially it turns out that this is all for the best anyway:

[21] *History*, vol. iv, p. 474.
[22] 'Of the First Principles of Government', *Essays*, pp. 29-34.
[23] I mean by this the attitude that one should always act to confer the maximum benefit on others, no matter who these others are: everyone is to count for one, and no one for more than one. In the dictionary sense, altruism merely means 'regard for others, as a principle of action', which is consistent with giving different weight to different people's interests. In the latter sense Hume portrays men as altruists, as shown below.
[24] *Treatise*, p. 481.
[25] *Treatise*, p. 602.

It is wisely ordained by nature, that private connexions should commonly prevail over universal views and considerations; otherwise our affections and actions would be dissipated and lost, for want of a proper limited object.[26]

Nevertheless partial benevolence has its less fortunate side, for it can bring men into competition with one another as effectively as pure selfishness. My activities as breadwinner, attempting to maximize the stock of goods available for distribution to my family and friends, may directly conflict with your parallel activities. From the point of view of establishing social order through the rules of justice, it matters very little whether we assume egoism or partial benevolence; each offers the same possibility of a divergence between immediate and longer-term interests, with dangerous results:

This avidity alone, of acquiring goods and possessions for ourselves and our nearest friends, is insatiable, perpetual, universal, and directly destructive of society. There scarce is any one, who is not actuated by it; and there is no one, who has not reason to fear from it, when it acts without any restraint, and gives way to its first and most natural movements. So that upon the whole, we are to esteem the difficulties in the establishment of society, to be greater or less, according to those we encounter in regulating and restraining this passion.[27]

To understand why men's concern should extend beyond their own interests to take in the interests of their social circle, we must examine Hume's views about human sociability. It turns out, surprisingly perhaps to those who would like to see him essentially as an individualist, that he regards the need for society as basic to human nature:

In all creatures, that prey not upon others, and are not agitated with violent passions, there appears a remarkable desire of company, which associates them together, without any advantages they can ever propose to reap from their union. This is still more conspicuous in man, as being the creature of the universe, who has the most ardent desire of society, and is fitted for it by the most advantages. We can form no wish, which has not a reference to society. A perfect solitude is, perhaps, the greatest punishment we can suffer.[28]

Elsewhere Hume describes the despair into which the human mind falls when it is deprived of external stimulation. Nothing can provide a stronger stimulus than the companionship of another person who, as Hume puts it, 'communicates to us all the actions of his mind; makes us privy to his inmost sentiments and affections;

[26] *Enquiry* II, p. 229.
[27] *Treatise*, pp. 491-2.
[28] *Treatise*, p. 363.

and lets us see, in the very instant of their production, all the emotions, which are caus'd by any object'.[29]

This powerful impetus to associate with others provides the source of that generosity towards family, friends, and acquaintance which we have already examined. But men's natural sociability also helps to explain a second feature of the human condition which makes rules of justice necessary: the fact that men always desire more goods than they have available at any time. Hume writes that when man enters society 'his wants multiply every moment upon him', even though his ability to satisfy them (through co-operation and the division of labour) increases still more rapidly. That is why he describes the desire for goods as 'insatiable'. This has been taken as grounds for attributing to Hume a view of man as an infinitely desirous consumer of utilities, and for placing him in the tradition of 'possessive individualism'.[30] Yet by paying attention to Hume's beliefs about human sociability, we may see the same data in another light. Man's increasing wants are the wants of a social creature who has them precisely because he is social.

When men associate with others, they do not merely reap the joys of social intercourse; they begin to compare themselves with their neighbours, and motives such as envy and resentment come into play. One of the strongest of human feelings is the esteem we have for the rich and powerful. Hume admits that this rests partly on imaginary belief (since riches are not in every case really productive of happiness), but given that the feeling does as a matter of fact exist, it produces a powerful secondary motive for acquiring riches, namely the esteem we expect to receive from others when we have them. Eventually the secondary motive may come to outweigh the original motive for acquisition, the pleasures directly available to the wealthy. Hume explains the process thus:

There is certainly an original satisfaction in riches deriv'd from that power, which they bestow, of enjoying all the pleasures of life; and as this is their very nature and essence, it must be the first source of all the passions, which arise from them. One of the most considerable of these passions is that of love or esteem in others, which therefore proceeds from a sympathy with the pleasure of the possessor. But the possessor has also a secondary satisfaction in riches arising

[29] *Treatise,* p. 353.
[30] See C. B. Macpherson, *The Political Theory of Possessive Individualism* (Oxford, 1962); also *Democratic Theory: Essays in Retrieval* (Oxford, 1973), and 'The Economic Penetration of Political Theory', *Journal of the History of Ideas,* xxxix (1978), 101-18. I have discussed Macpherson's interpretation of Hume more fully in 'Hume and Possessive Individualism', *History of Political Thought,* i (1980), 261-78.

from the love and esteem he acquires by them, and this satisfaction is nothing but a second reflexion of that original pleasure, which proceeded from himself. This secondary satisfaction or vanity becomes one of the principal recommendations of riches, and is the chief reason, why we either desire them for ourselves, or esteem them in others.[31]

There is an air of paradox about this, since finally we admire the rich for their capacity to obtain satisfactions, chief among which is the admiration we give them! But perhaps Hume is right, and such a paradox does lie at the heart of the socially-induced passion for wealth. It would certainly not be possible for any one individual (having the usual psychological make-up) to break out of the circle by himself.

If the main reason for acquiring wealth comes to be the esteem that it brings, then the expansion of men's wants should be understood as a corollary of their search for recognition and social status, rather than as expressive of their nature as consumers of utilities. By the familiar leap-frogging process, more goods are needed over time to stay in the same place on the social ladder. Hume recognizes this when commenting on the value of James I's revenue: 'the chief difference in expense between that age and the present consists in the imaginary wants of men, which have since extremely multiplied.'[32] 'Imaginary wants', with its derogatory overtones, would be an odd phrase in the mouth of an adherent of possessive individualism.

By the same token, the love of gain should be seen primarily as an effect of men's desire for social standing, not as an attribute of human nature considered in isolation. Hume makes this explicit when he remarks on the peculiarity of Henry VII, as a monarch in whom avarice predominated over ambition.

Even among private persons, avarice is commonly nothing but a species of ambition, and is chiefly incited by the prospect of that regard, distinction, and consideration, which attend on riches.[33]

An implication of this point of view is that where wealth ceases to be an important source of social status, people will stop pursuing it. That is why, for example, absolute monarchies tend to discourage commercial activity:

Commerce, therefore, in my opinion, is apt to decay in absolute governments, not because it is there less *secure*, but because it is less *honourable*. A subordination of rank is absolutely necessary to the support of monarchy. Birth, titles, and

---

[31] *Treatise,* p. 365.
[32] *History,* vol. iv, p. 511.
[33] *History,* vol. iii, p. 68.

place, must be honoured above industry and riches: and while these notions prevail, all the considerable traders will be tempted to throw up their commerce, in order to purchase some of those employments, to which privileges and honours are annexed.[34]

Finally we may observe that, although over time the quantity of goods needed to maintain a given social position may increase, *at* any time the quantity is given, and people's levels of satisfaction will depend on their expectations. This is the conservative aspect of Hume's account of wealth-acquisition.

Every thing in this world is judg'd of by comparison. What is an immense fortune for a private gentleman is beggary for a prince. A peasant wou'd think himself happy in what cannot afford necessaries for a gentleman.[35]

It follows that safeguarding what you have is more important than getting richer: 'And as to practical arts, which increase the commodities and enjoyments of life, it is well known that men's happiness consists not so much in an abundance of these, as in the peace and security with which they possess them.'[36] This has some implications for Hume's attitude towards social hierarchy, for although from one point of view social ranking fuels the love of gain through the search for status, from another point of view it restrains it, for all those whose ambition is modest or non-existent, to whatever is necessary to preserve one's desired position. We shall return to this subject later.

How is Hume's attitude towards the desire for wealth to be summed up? Although it is largely derivative, as we have seen, from other desires, it is none the less a powerful force, capable of being restrained but never extinguished. In its crude form it is destructive of society, and it must therefore be harnessed, partly by redirection (we see that we can serve our interests best by conforming to the rules of justice) and partly by the influence of checking factors whose nature we shall examine shortly. There is no point in condemning acquisitiveness wholesale, since it is inseparable from man's nature as a social being, though it becomes a proper subject for ridicule when it becomes obsessive and defeats its own ends.[37] From a detached point of view, however, one can see that people are happier to the extent that they can free themselves from preoccupation with material success.

---

[34] 'Of Civil Liberty', *Essays*, p. 94.
[35] *Treatise*, p. 323.
[36] 'Of Parties in General', *Essays*, p. 54.
[37] See 'Of Avarice', *Essays*, pp. 563-7.

And in a view to *pleasure*, what comparison between the unbought satisfaction of conversation, society, study, even health and the common beauties of nature, but above all the peaceful reflection on one's own conduct; what comparison, I say, between these and the feverish, empty amusements of luxury and expense?[38]

Let us turn now to a related topic, that of the motive to industry.[39] How far does Hume regard work, and economic activity generally, as undertaken from a desire for financial reward? Those who see man as essentially a consumer of utilities regard work as a necessary, though unpleasant, chore, undertaken only in so far as its extrinsic benefits exceed its costs. Surprisingly for those who would attribute such a view to Hume, we find that he regards occupation as an intrinsic part of human welfare. Happiness, he maintains, has three basic ingredients: action, pleasure, and indolence. Without useful activity life becomes insipid, and neither consumption nor rest is enjoyed.

In times when industry and the arts flourish, men are kept in perpetual occupation, and enjoy, as their reward, the occupation itself, as well as those pleasures which are the fruit of their labour. The mind acquires new vigour; enlarges its powers and faculties; and, by an assiduity in honest industry, both satisfies its natural appetites, and prevents the growth of unnatural ones, which commonly spring up, when nourished by ease and idleness.[40]

Again, 'there is no craving or demand of the human mind more constant and insatiable than that for exercise and employment; and this desire seems the foundation of most of our passions and pursuits.'[41] Thus work and business are undertaken even by those who have no material need to do so; they find that the pursuit of pleasure for pleasure's sake quickly palls. It is necessary that the goal of the activity in question should be regarded as valuable, though that does not imply that the people concerned regard their occupation only as a means to an end, and make a rational calculation of its utility: a point Hume makes when comparing philosophy and hunting as activities pursued for their own sake, but requiring a belief that the product—abstract truth and game for the table, respectively—is of some use.[42] There is, however, a danger of goal displacement, so that a man who enters commerce to find a way of occupying his time may become attached to

---

[38] *Enquiry* II, pp. 283-4.

[39] For a fuller discussion see ch. 2 of Rotwein's introduction to Hume, *Writings on Economics,* ed. E. Rotwein (Edinburgh, 1955).

[40] 'Of Refinement in the Arts', *Essays,* p. 277.

[41] 'Of Interest', *Essays,* p. 309.

[42] *Treatise,* Book II, Part III, Section X.

financial gain as an end in itself.[43] So once more we find that avarice may have extrinsic roots; a love of activity may be converted into a love of its results.

We have now established three general points about men's pursuit of their material interests, a topic which Hume sees as central to the problem of establishing social order. First, this pursuit need not be the result of human selfishness, but of a partiality which seeks to benefit family, friends, and dependents at the expense of society at large. Second, as far as personal motives are concerned, the pursuit of wealth gets much of its force from social aspirations, rather than from an intrinsic desire to consume ever-increasing quantities of goods. Third, human beings are primarily actors rather than consumers, but this does not necessarily conflict with the pursuit of wealth and may in some cases actually foster it. Now all of this throws Hume's remarks about the love of gain into a very different light from that in which they are often seen: it shows that his assumptions about human nature are not those of 'possessive individualism'. At the same time it does not diminish the weight of those remarks; the love of gain remains a powerful and inextinguishable force in human affairs, a useful and yet dangerous passion which needs to be regulated properly if social order is to be preserved. What, in Hume's eyes, can restrain this passion within the bounds set by the rules of justice?

We have seen that enlightened self-interest might have this effect, since each person's interests are actually best served by abiding by the rules of justice; but we have also seen that this motive will almost invariably be defeated by the 'narrowness of soul' which makes people prefer present gains to larger but more remote benefits. For this reason government is instituted to apply sanctions to those who break the rules, but of course government can only operate successfully in a context in which most people obey the law most of the time. Fear of the penalty can therefore only be a supplementary reason for keeping the law, deterring the few and so providing reassurance to the remainder who do so from other motives. Moral restraint—our natural disapproval of rule-breakers being directed reflexively at ourselves—might again be effective, were it not too weak a force in most individuals; that, Hume says, 'is a motive too remote and too sublime to affect the generality of mankind, and operate with any force in actions so contrary to private interest as are frequently those of justice and

---

[43] 'Of Interest', *Essays*, p. 309.

common honesty'.[44] So we must look elsewhere for an adequate check on the immediate pursuit of gain.

Our search will light first on the role of custom in human life. In examining Hume's theory of judgement, we have seen how important a part he attributes to the customary connection of ideas in the imagination; it is hardly surprising that he should attach equal importance to habitual action—that is, action performed in repetition of earlier behaviour rather than as a result of rational consideration. In Book II of the *Treatise* he explains that by repetition we gain greater facility in performing any action, while at the same time our inclination to perform it increases; so that once any action becomes customary, it tends to reproduce itself.[45] This view underlies a persistent theme in his history of England, that we must never be surprised to find people following the customs and conventions of their age, rather than policies which appear rational to us. 'Habits, more than reason, we find in every thing to be the governing principle of mankind.'[46] To take a concrete case, that of the marriage between Henry VIII and Catherine of Aragon, a detached view might suggest that there was no reason why a king should not marry his brother's widow, and that there were therefore no grounds for annulling the marriage. Yet 'Henry had custom and precedent on his side, the principle by which men are almost wholly governed in their actions and opinions' and so managed to win support for his attempt to divorce Catherine.[47]

These observations apply equally to the basic rules of justice which support social order. Once such rules are adopted, their observance becomes customary, and so men will continue to follow them unthinkingly, perhaps losing sight of their origin and underlying rationale. Each new generation is inducted into the conventions from an early age through the family. Parents 'inculcate on their children, from their earliest infancy, the principles of probity, and teach them to regard the observance of those rules, by which society is maintain'd, as worthy and honourable, and their violation as base and infamous. By this means the sentiments of honour may take root in their tender minds.'[48] 'Honour' here means something distinct from the

[44] *Treatise*, p. 481.
[45] *Treatise*, Book II, Part III, Section V.
[46] *History*, vol. v, p. 4.
[47] *History*, vol. iii, p. 184.
[48] *Treatise*, pp. 500-1.

moral attitudes which we adopt through reflection on the consequences of human qualities; it is a sense of what must and must not be done which is implanted in us from the outside, and which is therefore not properly speaking a moral motive at all, though it serves to constrain us to act as morality requires. This deeply-imbedded habit of refraining from acts of injustice is a reason, Hume believes, why his own theory of justice as a conventional artefact may not be readily received.

The views the most familiar to us are apt, for that very reason, to escape us; and what we have very frequently performed from certain motives, we are apt likewise to continue mechanically, without recalling, on every occasion, the reflections, which first determined us. The convenience, or rather necessity, which leads to justice is so universal, and everywhere points so much to the same rules, that the habit takes place in all societies; and it is not without some scrutiny, that we are able to ascertain its true origin.[49]

Besides prompting us to observe the rules of justice in general, custom also creates a habit of obedience to a particular political regime or ruler, so that laws enacted by that authority are regarded as binding without any reflection on the general reasons for obeying government. Hume refers to 'that implicit obedience on which the authority of the civil magistrate is chiefly founded'.[50] After reviewing the resources available to rulers which they may use to reinforce the duty of allegiance, in itself only as powerful as any other moral obligation, he remarks:

Habit soon consolidates what other principles of human nature had imperfectly founded; and men, once accustomed to obedience, never think of departing from that path, in which they and their ancestors have constantly trod, and to which they are confined by so many urgent and visible motives.[51]

We are therefore presented with a general picture of man as a creature whose conformity to the rules of justice and to political authority is in most cases an outcome of habit rather than reason. That does not mean that reasons cannot be given for conformity if reasons are demanded; otherwise Hume's theory of judgement would be otiose. Still, it is important to see why people comply in practice, since this will affect our attitude to radical change either in the rules of justice or in the political regime. Hume's view of the matter implies clearly that such change, by upsetting established habits of behaviour, is likely to be harmful. His general attitude is expressed in the following rather Burkean passage:

[49] *Enquiry* II, p. 203.
[50] *History,* vol. iii, p. 202.
[51] 'Of the Origin of Government', *Essays,* p. 37.

Did one generation of men go off the stage at once, and another succeed, as is the case with silkworms and butterflies, the new race, if they had sense enough to choose their government, which surely is never the case with men, might voluntarily, and by general consent, establish their own form of civil polity, without any regard to the laws or precedents which prevailed among their ancestors. But as human society is in perpetual flux, one man every hour going out of the world, another coming into it, it is necessary, in order to preserve stability in government, that the new brood should conform themselves to the established constitution, and nearly follow the path which their fathers, treading in the footsteps of theirs, had marked out to them. Some innovations must necessarily have place in every human institution; and it is happy where the enlightened genius of the age give these a direction to the side of reason, liberty, and justice: but violent innovations no individual is entitled to make: they are even dangerous to be attempted by the legislature: more ill than good is ever to be expected from them: and if history affords examples to the contrary, they are not to be drawn into precedent, and are only to be regarded as proofs, that the science of politics affords few rules, which will not admit of some exception, and which may not sometimes be controlled by fortune and accident.[52]

The control exercised by custom over human behaviour is supplemented by two other factors, the first of these being our love of fame and reputation. Hume once again sets out the basic mechanism involved in *Treatise*, Book II, where he argues that we enter by sympathy into the pleasurable sensations which constitute the esteem others feel for our good qualities; he adds that the degree of pleasure felt depends on who is manifesting the esteem. Since one important object of esteem is moral virtue, the virtuous man benefits from the good opinion of others, quite apart from the satisfaction he may get from contemplating his own rectitude. In particular 'there is nothing, which touches us more nearly than our reputation, and nothing on which our reputation more depends than our conduct, with relation to the property of others'.[53] Thus the potential rule-breaker may be deterred by the thought that, if his misdemeanour is observed, he will lose more by way of reputation than he will gain materially: a powerful thought since 'our reputation, our character, our name are considerations of vast weight and importance'.[54]

Second, there are the 'artifices of politicians'.[55] Hume does not make it very clear how political leaders are supposed to reinforce our attachment to the rules of justice, but we may assume that they make persuasive pronouncements appealing either to our interests or to our sense of honour; exaggerating, perhaps, the

[52] 'Of the Original Contract', *Essays*, pp. 463-4.
[53] *Treatise*, p. 501.
[54] *Treatise*, p. 316.
[55] See *Treatise*, pp. 500, 533-4, 578; *Enquiry* II, p. 214.

misfortunes that will follow acts of injustice. Hume tends to couple references to political artifice with a reminder that it could not be the *source* of moral distinctions, since if we were not already responsive to moral language, the speeches (or parts of them, anyway) would fall on deaf ears.[56] That reminder might also be attached to what has been said about custom and the love of reputation. Custom presupposes a prior disposition to follow certain rules; it could not create that disposition. Equally, the love of reputation acts as a motive only because other people are already prepared to admire virtuous conduct. So all three checks on narrowly selfish behaviour presuppose that certain rules of conduct have been established (through enlightened self-interest) and that conforming to them is morally approved (through sympathy). But once the secondary motives come into operation, they may turn out to be more powerful than the primary motives; this will be true of the greater part of mankind, whose notions of self-interest are narrow and whose moral sympathies are weak. For these people, custom, the love of reputation, and political propaganda are the most effective restraining forces.

Many thinkers who share Hume's anxieties about the destructive effects of human selfishness would wish to include religion in this list of restraints. Does Hume himself see it as performing any function as an instrument of social control? We saw earlier that in general he depicted religion as a force that disturbed the operation of normal human motives. The furthest he will go in allowing it a positive social function is to concede that, in barbaric ages, where the rules of justice are often disregarded, it may sometimes be useful in restraining violent passions. In civilized times its effects are damaging or at best neutral.[57] Religion is liable to be harmful when it becomes either superstitious or enthusiastic. The intellectual character of these tendencies has been noted above:[58] their primary concrete manifestations were, respectively, the

---

[56] This sums up Hume's debt to, and difference from, Mandeville. Mandeville had argued that moral rules were invented by moralists and politicians in order to harmonize public and private interest; see Raphael, *British Moralists,* vol. i, pp. 229-34, and T. A. Horne, *The Social Thought of Bernard Mandeville* (London, 1978), esp. ch. 3. Hume rejects Mandeville's account of morality, while accepting what he says about the social role of politicians. The rejection follows the criticism made earlier by Hutcheson; see Raphael, *British Moralists,* vol. i, pp. 267-8.

[57] Hume takes a more positive view in an unpublished preface to the second Stuart volume of his *History,* which is reproduced in Mossner, *Life,* pp. 306-7. But this is by way of an apology for his treatment of religion in the body of the *History,* and should not I believe be taken at face value.

[58] See above ch. 2, p. 57.

Roman Catholic Church, and the Protestant sects of the sixteenth and seventeenth centuries. In either case religion may serve as a cloak under which private advantage and ambition can be pursued free of the normal social restraints; it loosens the hold of custom, the love of reputation, and morality by providing specious justifications for the most reprehensible conduct.[59] Thus Hume writes of twelfth-century churchmen: 'The spirit of superstition was so prevalent, that it infallibly caught every careless reasoner, much more every one whose interest, and honor, and ambition were engaged to support it ... The spirit of revenge, violence, and ambition which accompanied their conduct, instead of forming a presumption of hypocrisy, are the surest pledges of their sincere attachment to a cause which so much flattered these domineering passions.'[60] Exactly the same processes could be seen at work in seventeenth-century Puritans:

Among the generality of men educated in regular, civilized societies, the sentiments of shame, duty, honor, have considerable authority, and serve to counterbalance and direct the motives derived from private advantage: but, by the predominancy of enthusiasm among the parliamentary forces, these salutary principles lost their credit, and were regarded as mere human inventions, yea, moral institutions, fitter for heathens than for Christians. The saint, resigned over to superior guidance, was at full liberty to gratify all his appetites, disguised under the appearance of pious zeal. And besides the strange corruptions engendered by this spirit, it eluded and loosened all the ties of morality, and gave entire scope, and even sanction, to the selfishness and ambition which naturally adhere to the human mind.[61]

The best policy towards religion is therefore to neutralize its effects by preventing it becoming either superstitious or enthusiastic. Religious belief itself is ineradicable, but it can be channelled in harmless directions. For that reason Hume is in favour of an established church: by paying the clergy's salaries from the public purse, you remove the need for them to pander to the worst instincts of their audiences in order to increase their popularity (and so their income); you make it 'superfluous for them to be

---

[59] Hume does not imply that men who act in this way are wholly hypocritical. They usually embody a mixture of hypocrisy and genuine zeal. See *History*, vol. v, n. I (pp. 542-3).

[60] *History*, vol. i, pp. 322-3.

[61] *History*, vol. v, p. 331. I do not think it is reading too much into this passage to see shame, honour, and duty as distinct sentiments, shame corresponding to the love of reputation, honour to those precepts that are implanted in us by early education, and duty to the moral sentiments themselves. Enthusiasm erodes honour and duty by giving us new justifications for our conduct, discovered by spiritual inspiration; it erodes shame by making our reputation depend on the degree of our religious fervour, and nothing else.

further active than merely to prevent their flock from straying in quest of new pastures'.[62] He sees the advantages of retaining the external trappings of a particular faith which 'acquire a veneration in the eyes of the people, appear sacred in their apprehensions, excite their devotion, and contract a kind of mysterious virtue, which attaches the affections of men to the national and established worship'.[63] In general, he believes, it is easy to be too dismissive of sacred ritual, which may help to dissipate the intensity of religious feeling:

> Whatever ridicule, to a philosophical mind, may be thrown on pious ceremonies, it must be confessed that, during a very religious age, no institutions can be more advantageous to the rude multitude, and tend more to mollify that fierce and gloomy spirit of devotion to which they are subject.[64]

Religion, therefore, is not a prop of social order; it is rather a dangerous acid which may dissolve the other props unless contained in the proper vessels. Hume speaks here as a typical man of the eighteenth century, living in a country where religious controversies had to a great extent died down (though less so in Scotland where 'cant, hypocrisy and fanaticism...is still ready to break out on all occasions',[65] as Hume had discovered to his cost when the clerical lobby had blocked his appointment to the Chair of Ethics at Edinburgh, and later when the Assembly of the Church of Scotland began moves to excommunicate him[66]). If his political stance can be described as conservative (and we shall see later in what sense this is true) it is a wholly secular conservatism; far removed in this respect from that of nineteenth-century conservatives for whom the defence of religion was integral to their ideology.

We have now surveyed the various facets of Hume's conception of human nature. He sees men less as selfish than as partial in their benevolence, serving the interests of those connected to them at the expense of mankind in general; as intensely social creatures, delighting in company and conversation, but at the same time jealous of their reputation and anxious to stand well with their associates; as driven by this quest for status and also by an innate love of activity to pursue material gain; and as held within the

---

[62] *History*, vol. iii, pp. 128-9.
[63] *History*, vol. iv, p. 116.
[64] *History*, vol. v, p. 298.
[65] *History*, vol. iv, p. 22.
[66] For those two episodes, see Mossner, *Life*, chs. 12 and 25. The excommunication move was stopped at the committee stage before reaching the full Assembly.

bounds of justice by custom and social pressure. It is a mildly pessimistic picture, both in the obvious sense that men are not seen as potentially angelic, and in the sense that the restraints on anti-social behaviour depend upon an elaborate web of convention which, although strong, is not indestructible. Although he describes the state of nature as a 'philosophical fiction', he is prepared to use it as a reminder of what might occur if conventional restraints were removed: 'every one must fall into that savage and solitary condition, which is infinitely worse than the worst situation that can possibly be suppos'd in society.'[67] Occasionally a society may come close to relapsing into that condition. Following the breakdown of authority in France in 1358, for example, 'the wild state of nature seemed to be renewed: every man was thrown loose and independent of his fellows: and the populousness of the country, derived from the preceding police of civil society, served only to increase the horror and confusion of the scene.'[68] But Hume's pessimism is not that, say, of Hobbes; there is no sense of *homo homini lupus*. Nor is the upshot that the power of the sword must terrify men into respecting one another's rights. Instead Hume lays his stress, as we have seen, on the need to preserve existing conventions, and to innovate when necessary in such a way that these conventions are least disturbed. The main threat comes from political or religious fanatics who provide a licence for egoism in the guise of principle. 'No character in human society is more dangerous than that of the fanatic; because, if attended with weak judgment, he is exposed to the suggestions of others; if supported by more discernment, he is entirely governed by his own illusions, which sanctify his most selfish views and passions.'[69] Hume's theory of judgement is of course intended to disarm the fanatic by showing that there can be no justification for the claims he makes.

Such a view of human nature is an intelligible reflection of the social milieu in which Hume found himself: the fashionable world of the nobility and the gentry, revolving around the club, the coffee-house, the salon, and the country estate. Against this background Hume's views about natural sociability, about men's concern with their reputation and standing, and indeed about work as something undertaken more from a love of activity than from necessity, fall into place. This point can be made too about the

---

[67] *Treatise*, p. 497.
[68] *History*, vol. ii, pp. 248-9.
[69] *History*, vol. v, p. 492.

virtues which Hume sees as natural and therefore as appropriate
sources of esteem. Besides justice and benevolence, he mentions
pride (in proper degree), wit, good manners, gentility, and decency
('a proper regard to age, sex, character and station in the world').[70]
These are qualities appropriate to the aristocrat who has leisure
enough to enjoy a good helping of company and conversation. At
the same time Hume does not omit enterprise, industry, assiduity,
and frugality,[71] all of them qualities serving to advance a person's
economic interests, so we can see that this is not the morality of a
class that is merely leisured. The man most admired is the one who
strikes a proper balance between business and leisure, neither
letting his fortune decay through inattention nor becoming so
preoccupied with money-making that he loses sight of its proper
purpose: avarice is censured because 'it both deprives a man of all
use of his riches, and checks hospitality and every social enjoyment'.[72] We shall later look more closely at the character of the
eighteenth-century aristocracy, which will throw these observations into an appropriate light. On the other hand, Hume has
no time at all for that austere manner of life which was characteristic of the Puritan sects, and which has often been seen as the
source of the bourgeois mentality.[73]

Celibacy, fasting, penance, mortification, self-denial, humility, silence, solitude,
and the whole train of monkish virtues; for what reason are they everywhere
rejected by men of sense, but because they serve to no manner of purpose; neither
advance a man's fortune in the world, nor render him a more valuable member
of society; neither qualify him for the entertainment of company, nor increase
his power of self-enjoyment?[74]

Preferences of this kind do not derive from philosophical
reflection; they mirror a social outlook which Hume has absorbed
from his environment, and therefore properly belong to the
ideological component of his thought. They cannot be justified,
but neither do they seem to the person who has them to stand in
need of justification.

[70] See *Enquiry* II, Sections VII-VIII.
[71] See *Treatise,* p. 587; *Enquiry* II, p. 242.
[72] *Enquiry* II, p. 238.
[73] For instance by M. Weber in *The Protestant Ethic and the Spirit of Capitalism* (London, 1930).
[74] *Enquiry* II, p. 270.

6

Economy and Society

Like many of his contemporaries, especially the group often referred to collectively as the Scottish enlightenment,[1] Hume was deeply interested in social variety and change. It is true that this interest never disturbed his confidence in the superiority of the social order that he inhabited—'civilized' is the adjective he most often uses to describe it—as happened to many of his successors in the nineteenth century. But Hume's interest carried him beyond regarding past societies as poor imitations of the present. He was aware that the whole mode of life of these societies was different, behaviour passing for normal which would now be regarded as repugnant or absurd. There was no point in moralizing in a naïve way about such behaviour, since men must be expected to follow the customs of their time; and yet the final result of studying alien societies ought to be an increased affection for the manners and practices of our own.

He was interested particularly in two effects of this variety, the first being its consequences for human nature. His interest here was both empirical and moral. I have commented on the fact that Hume saw socially derived characteristics as overlaying the basic and uniform traits of human nature, so a full explanation of any individual's behaviour would have to make reference to the peculiarities of his social milieu. At the same time, Hume wanted to defend the refinement characteristic of men in modern societies against those who wished to return to the heroic virtues associated with a simpler mode of life.[2] A theme often repeated in his work is

---

[1] For general surveys of this group, see G. Bryson, *Man and Society: The Scottish Enquiry of the Eighteenth Century* (Princeton, 1945); A. C. Chitnis, *The Scottish Enlightenment: a Social History* (London, 1976).

. [2] See 'Of Refinement in the Arts', *Essays* pp. 275-88. For the objects of Hume's attack, see J. Moore, 'Hume's Political Science and the Classical Republican Tradition', *Canadian Journal of Political Science*, x (1977), 809-39, sect. VIII; Horne, *The Social Thought of Bernard Mandeville,* ch. 5. The general debate in the eighteenth century over commerce, luxury, and republican virtue has been analysed in several works by J. G. A. Pocock, especially *The Machiavellian Moment* (Princeton, 1975), ch. 13; 'Early Modern Capitalism—the Augustan Perception' in E. Kamenka and R. S. Neale (eds.), *Feudalism, Capitalism and Beyond* (London, 1975); 'The Mobility of Property and the Rise of Eighteenth Century Sociology' in A. Parel and T. Flanagan (eds.), *Theories of Property: Aristotle to the Present* (Waterloo, Ontario, 1979).

the connection between sophistication of taste, education, and virtue. Thus 'it must be acknowledged, in spite of those who declaim so violently against refinement in the arts, or what they are pleased to call luxury, that, as much as an industrious tradesman is both a better man and a better citizen than one of those idle retainers who formerly depended on the great families, so much is the life of a modern nobleman more laudable than that of an ancient baron.'[3]

A second interest was the connection between social conditions and forms of government. Hume was clear that a political constitution had to be appropriate to its social environment. So, for instance, whatever one might feel about the merits of the ancient republics, one could not disregard the fact that they emerged in small, simple, and relatively egalitarian societies, and it was therefore impossible to translate that form of government unaltered to a large modern society.[4] In writing his history of England, Hume made a break roughly at the end of the reign of Henry VII. Before that, he said, conditions were so different that a study of government was valuable chiefly as a means of providing a contrast with the modern establishment; only afterwards was it possible to draw 'instructive lessons' for our own political conduct.[5] Even in Henry's reign, for example, 'it must indeed be confessed, that such a state of the country required great discretionary power in the sovereign; nor will the same maxims of government suit such a rude people, that may be proper in a more advanced stage of society'.[6] However, the causal relationship between society and state did not run exclusively in one direction; political institutions might also foster or retard social change. This is an issue we shall need to explore more fully in a moment.

Hume never attempted to produce a systematic social typology, but one can find in his writings sketchy delineations of four kinds of society.[7] First, there were very simple systems with no settled form of authority. In this category we should place the Indian tribes of America referred to in the *Treatise,* and also the German

---

[3] *History,* vol. iii, pp. 71-2.

[4] See 'Of Commerce, *Essays,* pp. 264-5; 'The Populousness of Ancient Nations', *Essays,* pp. 400-2; *Letters,* vol. ii, p. 306.

[5] *History,* vol. iii, p. 77. See also vol. ii, pp. 507-14.

[6] *History,* vol. iii, p. 453.

[7] Notice also that Hume's social types do not correspond to the four historical stages commonly distinguished by Scottish writers (including Smith) later in the eighteenth century. Hume's categories are not based on the mode of subsistence. For the development of the 'four stages' theory see R. Meek, *Social Science and the Ignoble Savage,* (Cambridge, 1976); the absence of the theory from Hume's work is noted on pp. 30-1.

peoples whom Hume considers at somewhat greater length early in his *History*. Rudimentary social order was provided by temporary allegiance to a chieftain, who gained his ascendancy by his military talents. The main preoccupation of these societies was indeed making war upon their neighbours; agriculture was neglected, there was no opportunity for industry or commerce, and any improvement was discouraged by the lack of a stable property system. (Hume notes especially the Germans' practice of redistributing land annually among the inhabitants of each village.[8]) In short, these societies were 'barbarous' and 'little removed from the original state of nature'.[9]

Next, there were the societies of ancient Greece and Rome, known to Hume through his wide reading of classical authors. These, he thinks, were predominantly agricultural, composed mainly of independent property-owning farmers, who also served as soldiers in the rather frequent periods of war. There was a large degree of equality among the citizens (accompanied, however, by domestic slavery). Industry did not flourish, though there was some trade in agricultural products. The form of political regime varied, but in many cases these societies managed to inspire their members with a degree of public spirit not to be found elsewhere. Although their manners were in some respects crude, they encouraged the first flourishing of the arts and sciences.[10]

Third, there were feudal societies. Hume's view was that their economy must remain based on simple agriculture, since serfs had neither the means nor the incentive to improve their methods of cultivation, and lords were discouraged by the prevailing mores, which regarded every profession except that of arms with contempt. Between these two estates there was a vast economic gulf, and also a great social distance, since no 'middling rank of men' stood between the great landowner and his serfs. In place of a uniform system of law, social order was maintained by the local lord acting on behalf of his dependents—thus the society tended to break up into petty principalities at war with one another, to the further detriment of agricultural improvement and commerce. The main aim of the barons was to increase the

---

[8] *History*, vol. i, p. 13.

[9] *History*, vol. i, p. 166. See in general vol. i, pp. 12-13, 152-77.

[10] See 'Of the Populousness of Ancient Nations', *Essays*, pp. 381-418; 'Of Commerce', *Essays*, pp. 264-5; 'Of the Rise and Progress of the Arts and Sciences', *Essays*, pp. 112-38.

number of their retainers, and they had no interest in cultivating refined tastes.[11]

In contrast to this unflattering picture of feudalism, Hume offers a favourable picture of modern commercial societies, his fourth social type. They are based upon a harmonious inter-marriage of agriculture and industry, the luxuries made available by the latter acting as a spur to improvement in the former. There is less inequality of wealth than in feudal societies (though more than in ancient societies), since property is more widely diffused, and the lot of the common people is improved. Artisans and farmers replace the serfs of the former period. Between these labourers and the great landowners stand the lesser gentry, merchants, manufacturers, and professional men; because there are many gradations of status, it is easier for individuals to move up or down the scale. Everyone is equal before the law, and law is applied uniformly by the state. Tastes are more refined than in the other forms of society; the arts and sciences flourish as never before.[12]

Hume's enthusiasm for civilized, commercial societies cannot be concealed; but it is worth examining the terms on which he defends his preference. Although he sees these societies as both wealthy and containing their own sources of further improvement, he does not favour them primarily on these grounds. This reflects his view, already noted, that happiness consists less in having an abundance of commodities than in enjoying what you have in peace and security.[13] Instead, industrial progress is commended for extrinsic reasons: it encourages men to be active, it brings them into closer contact with one another, and in so doing it renders them more humane.

The more these refined arts advance, the more sociable men become: nor is it possible, that, when enriched with science, and possessed of a fund of con-versation, they should be contented to remain in solitude, or live with their fellow-citizens in that distant manner, which is peculiar to ignorant and barbarous nations. They flock into cities; love to receive and communicate knowledge; to show their wit or their breeding; their taste in conversation or living, in clothes or furniture. Curiosity allures the wise; vanity the foolish; and pleasure both. Particular clubs and societies are everywhere formed: both sexes meet in an easy and sociable manner; and the tempers of men, as well as their behaviour, refine

---

[11] See *History*, vol. i, p. 360, pp. 441-74; vol. ii, pp. 507-14; 'Of Refinement in the Arts', *Essays*, pp. 283-4; 'Of Interest', *Essays*, pp. 305-6.

[12] See 'Of Commerce', *Essays*, pp. 261-74; 'Of Refinement in the Arts', *Essays*, pp. 276-85; *History*, vol. iv, pp. 373-4.

[13] See above, ch. 5, p. 110.

apace. So that, beside the improvements which they receive from knowledge and the liberal arts, it is impossible but they must feel an increase of humanity, from the very habit of conversing together, and contributing to each other's pleasure and entertainment.[14]

Hume also defends commercial societies against the charge that they weaken the state while cosseting its individual members. He argues that the skills and commodities produced by improvements in agriculture and industry can be seen as a fund on which a political leader may draw in time of war. Because productivity has been increased, he is able to lay taxes on all sections of the community without reducing the labourer to destitution, and the money obtained can be used to employ men in military service. The troops so raised may be less ferocious than those drawn from barbarous societies, but they are more skilful and better disciplined. All in all, a rich commercial society is likely to be a greater military power than its less advanced rivals.[15]

What conditions are necessary for a commercial society to develop? To answer this, we need to examine Hume's account of the transition from feudal to modern England, looking for the causes which propelled English society in the direction of civilization. This task turns out to be harder to accomplish than one might suppose. Hume's statements about causal priority cannot easily be reconciled with one another. Some commentators have detected a contrast between the *Essays,* where Hume lays stress on the political preconditions for economic growth, and the *History,* where economic factors appear to be primary.[16]

The source of the difficulty, I believe, is Hume's acute awareness of the interaction between four sets of factors: economic,

[14] 'Of Refinement in the Arts, *Essays,* p. 278.

[15] There is a nice story to illustrate this point. Travelling together to Bath, Hume, Adam Ferguson, and John Home debated what would happen if each were the ruler of an adjoining state. Hume, recalled his cousin, knew, 'the great opinion we had of military virtue as essential to every state; that from these sentiments rooted in us, he was certain he would be attacked and interrupted in his projects of cultivating, improving and civilizing mankind by the arts of peace; that he comforted himself with reflecting, that from our want of economy and order in our affairs, we should be continually in want of money; whilst he would have his finances in excellent condition, his magazines well filled and naval stores in abundance; but, that his final stroke of policy, upon which he depended, was to give one of us a large subsidy to fall upon the other, which would infallibly secure to him peace and quiet, and after a long war, would probably terminate in his being master of all three kingdoms.' (John Home cited in Moore, 'Hume's Political Science and the Classical Republican Tradition', p. 830.) Hume is here attacking another bastion of classical republicanism; see the references in fn. 2 above.

[16] See C. N. Stockton, 'Economics and the Mechanism of Historical Progress in Hume's *History*' in D. W. Livingston and J. T. King (eds.), *Hume: a Re-evaluation* (New York, 1976).

cultural, social, and political. More specifically, the changes to be explained are these: that from crude agriculture to advanced agriculture and industry; that from a taste for military display, 'rustic hospitality', etc. to a taste for luxury, polite society, and the liberal arts; that from a polarized society of nobles and serfs to a graduated society with a prosperous 'middling rank' of gentry, merchants, and manufacturers; and that from a political order where security (such as it was) was provided primarily by the arbitrary power of the great barons to a government where law is enforced equally and uniformly. Now Hume sees a number of connections between these changes. First, the economic and the cultural changes are for obvious reasons mutually reinforcing: it is the appearance of luxury goods which first begins to change the tastes of the nobility, but once the change has occurred, the market for manufactured goods expands, their production increases, and this in turn leads to improvements in agriculture. Second, the economic change provokes a social change, in so far as the numbers of merchants and manufacturers grow to meet the new demands of the nobility, while the fortunes of the latter are dissipated by their purchases of luxury goods; but there is again a reciprocal effect, for Hume argues that merchants and manufacturers (unlike landowners) are able to accumulate capital for new investment. Third, social change provokes political change: the 'middling rank' see that it is in their interests to check first the power of the barons and later the power of the king, and so are instrumental in bringing about a government of laws. But fourth, political change is itself a precondition for economic development, since without the security that law provides, there is no incentive to improve agriculture or develop new industrial techniques.

We seem now to have come full circle; but this is only because we are looking for a monocausal (or perhaps a 'main cause') theory of historical change, whereas Hume is offering us an account in which several distinct factors assist one another in bringing about an over-all transformation. From this perspective there is no contradiction between the *Essays* and the *History*; at one moment Hume will emphasize economic factors, at another political factors, and so on, depending on which aspect of the process he is describing. Even in the *History,* the political transformation is not presented as occurring after and as a result of the economic and social transformation, but alongside it. It was important, for instance, that the fact of conquest gave the Norman kings greater power in England than was usual in a feudal society, forcing the barons to contain that power, which they did through the Great Charter; but to win popular support they were obliged to insert clauses safeguarding the interests of the other orders of the state; articles, Hume says, which 'involve all the chief outlines of a legal government, and provide for the equal distribution of justice, and free enjoyment of property'.[17] Although the Charter was imperfectly observed, it began a process of political change which led eventually to a civilized government.[18] These events took place at the political level: they had economic repercussions, but no economic causes. To take a second example, Hume attaches considerable importance to the rediscovery of Roman law which occurred in the twelfth century.[19] The old English system of law, he argues, with all its absurdities, was incapable of giving enough personal security to allow the practical arts to develop; and the study of Roman law was a stimulus to learning generally. So again we find that a political event helped to create the conditions under which economic and cultural changes could take place.

This complex picture of historical causality implies that there is no simple set of necessary and sufficient conditions for the emergence of civilization. Its growth in Western Europe had been contingent, inasmuch as it had resulted from the concurrence of four distinct processes of change which we have identified. Equally, its survival was not certain. Hume had the example of the Roman Empire before him, whose collapse had also destroyed a whole form of civilization:

> Those who cast their eye on the general revolutions of society, will find that, as almost all improvements of the human mind had reached nearly to their state of perfection about the age of Augustus, there was a sensible decline from that point or period; and men thenceforth relapsed gradually into ignorance and barbarism.[20]

The cause of decline in that case was the extent of the Roman Empire and the despotic political system which it necessitated. Modern states have other sources of decay: we shall touch on one of these later.

[17] *History,* vol. i, p. 431.

[18] See the general assessment in *History,* vol. i, pp. 473-4.

[19] See *History,* vol. ii, pp. 509-11.

[20] *History,* vol. ii, p. 508. Hume's work helped to inspire Gibbon's great chronicle of that decline. The two men held one another in mutual esteem: Gibbon wrote that Hume's favourable opinion of the first volume of *Decline and Fall,* delivered shortly before his death, 'overpaid the labour of ten years'.

Hume has a certain amount to say about the economic policy which ought to be pursued in a commercial society.[21] His underlying assumption is that there exists a harmony of interests between man and man, between trade and trade, between agriculture and industry, and between nation and nation; so allowing each person to pursue his own interests in the economic market will produce the results that benefit others most. He is therefore in favour of freedom in industry and trade as a matter of general policy.

Most of the arts and professions in a state are of such a nature, that, while they promote the interests of the society, they are also useful or agreeable to some individuals; and, in that case, the constant rule of the magistrate, except, perhaps, on the first introduction of any art, is to leave the profession to itself, and trust its encouragement to those who reap the benefit of it. The artisans, finding their profits to rise by the favor of their customers, increase as much as possible their skill and industry; and as matters are not disturbed by any injudicious tampering, the commodity is always sure to be at all times nearly proportioned to the demand.[22]

A number of concrete implications flowed from this general assumption. Price and wage controls were to be avoided.[23] Trying to hold prices down when commodities were in short supply merely made things worse; 'in reality the increase of prices is a necessary consequence of scarcity; and laws, instead of preventing it, only aggravate the evil, by cramping and restraining commerce.'[24] Equally, laws against usury were 'unreasonable', 'iniquitous', and 'hurtful to trade'.[25] But Hume's strongest condemnations were reserved for the monopolies which had been allowed to flourish in Tudor and Stuart times. He calls them 'grievances, the most intolerable for the present, and the most pernicious in their consequences, that ever were known in any age or under any government'.[26] Of the bill which was eventually passed to abolish them he says:

It was there supposed, that every subject of England had entire power to dispose of his own actions, provided he did no injury to any of his fellow-subjects; and

---

[21] A fuller treatment is provided by Rotwein in ch. 3 of his introduction to Hume, *Writings on Economics*.

[22] *History*, vol. iii, p. 128.   [23] *History*, vol. iii, p. 73.

[24] *History*, vol. ii, p. 172.

[25] *History*, vol. iii, p. 72. Hume notes that in the reign of Elizabeth 'by a lucky accident in language, which has a great effect on men's ideas, the invidious word *usury* which formerly meant the taking of any interest for money, came now to express only the taking of exorbitant and illegal interest.' (*History*, vol. iv, p. 369.)

[26] *History*, vol. iv, p. 336.

that no prerogative of the king, no power of any magistrate, nothing but the authority alone of laws, could restrain that unlimited freedom. The full prosecution of this noble principle into all its natural consequences, has at last, through many contests, produced that singular and happy government which we enjoy at present.[27]

What was true for domestic industry held for international trade as well. Along with monopolies Hume condemned the exclusive companies which had been given the sole rights to conduct trade with various parts of the globe.[28] His general view was that freedom of trade benefited all the countires that engaged in it. By allowing the unimpeded import and export of commodities, each nation could profit from the improvements made by others; either it would learn to make the products it now imported for itself, or it would participate in a beneficial international division of labour whereby each nation specialized in those commodities which it was naturally suited (by soil, climate, etc.) to produce.[29] Trying to protect domestic industry by banning or restricting the import of foreign products was therefore short-sighted. On the other hand, Hume was prepared to countenance the use of taxation to boost the home economy. 'All taxes, however, upon foreign commodities, are not to be regarded as prejudicial or useless... A tax on German linen encourages home manufactures, and thereby multiplies our people and industry.'[30] This should perhaps be seen as a pump-priming operation, in line with Hume's caveat in the passage cited above that professions are to be left to themselves 'except, perhaps, on the first introduction of any art'.[31] We are reminded that Hume has the national interest firmly in mind when pronouncing on economic policy. His general preference for *laissez-faire* reflects a belief that this normally serves the nation best.

Monetary policy attracted a good deal of Hume's attention. Against the mercantilists, who held that a nation's prosperity was measured by the stocks of bullion it possessed, he argued that money always adjusted itself to the quantity of labour and commodities in a country. It would, in other words, flow from one country to another until the amount of money in each was proportional to the volume of labour and commodities it contained.

[27] *History*, vol. iv, p. 486.
[28] *History*, vol. iv, pp. 394-5.
[29] 'Of the Jealousy of Trade', *Essays*, pp. 334-8.
[30] 'Of the Balance of Trade', *Essays*, p. 332.
[31] See further Stockton, 'Economics and the Mechanism of Historical Progress in Hume's *History*'.

Supposing the quantity of money in a given country were miraculously to double, therefore, that country would not become twice as prosperous. The immediate effect would be a doubling of all commodity prices (since prices depended simply on the proportion between commodities and money) which would stifle exports and cause a flood of imports. Money would flow out until prices had regained their international level. The practical upshot of this was that politicians could not hope to increase national prosperity by hoarding money or interfering with international flows of bullion. Hume's message was: look after domestic industry, and money will take care of itself.[32]

There was, however, one qualification to be added to this point of view. In the interval between an increase of money taking place and natural equilibrium being resumed, home manufacturing might be stimulated so that more labour was performed and more commodities produced; in which case not all of the additional money would flow out and national prosperity really would have increased. If it were possible for the magistrate to arrange a slow but steady increase in the supply of money, the effect might be prolonged (though Hume does not explain how the magistrate should set about arranging this). The arrival of West Indian gold and silver after 1600 provided an illustration; 'while money thus flowed into England, we may observe, that, at the same time, and probably from that very cause, arts and industry of all kinds received a mighty increase; and elegance in every enjoyment of life became better known and more cultivated among all ranks of people.'[33]

One method which the government might use to increase the money supply was to issue paper money; but Hume was doubtful of the wisdom of this course of action, suggesting that it would merely impede the inflow of gold and silver. He acknowledged the convenience of paper money from the user's point of view, but preferred that the bank which issued it should simply lock up the specie it received in exchange, rather than return it to circulation.[34]

On monetary matters, therefore, Hume's advice was to proceed very cautiously and in most cases allow commercial forces

---

[32] 'Of Money', *Essays*, pp. 289-302; 'Of the Balance of Trade', *Essays*, pp. 316-33.

[33] *History*, vol. iv, pp. 413-4. See in general 'Of Money', *Essays*, pp. 292-6; Letter to Oswald, *Letters*, vol. i, pp. 142-3; and for discussion Stockton, 'Economics and the Mechanism of Historical Progress in Hume's *History*', pp. 309-13, and Hume, *Writings on Economics*, pp. liv-lxvii.

[34] 'Of Money', *Essays*, pp. 291-2; 'Of the Balance of Trade', *Essays*, pp. 324-8.

to operate unhindered. This reflected his general conviction that the effects of economic intervention were very difficult to predict. 'The more simple ideas of order and equity are sufficient to guide a legislator in every thing that regards the internal administration of justice: but the principles of commerce are much more complicated, and require long experience and deep reflection to be well understood in any state.'[35]

Hume also addressed himself to the subject of taxation.[36] Here he wished to rebut two contemporary doctrines: one the view that taxes might in principle be increased indefinitely, since the effect of imposing taxation was to make the victim work harder to pay the impost; the other the view of the physiocrats that taxes should always be laid on land, since they must ultimately fall on the landowner in any case. In response to these doctrines, Hume argued that the best taxes were taxes on commodities, especially on luxury goods, and he proceeded to analyse the effects of imposing them. Labourers might do one of three things: work harder to raise their income, cut back on consumption, or demand higher wages. *A priori* one could not say which of these was most likely, though experience showed that increasing output or cutting consumption were quite probable responses. This disposed of the physiocrats, since in neither case was the tax passed on to manufacturer or landowner through a wage rise.[37] On the other hand, it showed that tax increases should always be very moderate, since there were obviously limits to the extent to which productivity could be raised or consumption retrenched. 'Taxes, like necessity, when carried too far, destroy industry, by engendering despair; and even before they reach this pitch, they raise the wages of the labourer and manufacturer, and heighten the price of all commodities.'[38] So although Hume had no rooted objection to taxation, and indeed expected politicians to use it as far as was prudent for the purposes of strengthening the state, one had to avoid slaughtering the milch cow.

There was an alternative means of raising public funds which became the object of one of Hume's great obsessions later in his life.[39] This was the issuing of government stocks bearing a fixed

---

[35] *History*, vol. iii, p. 69.   [36] See 'Of Taxes', *Essays*, pp. 349-54.
[37] Hume argued that labourers would, of course, try to pass on a tax increase in this way; but their success would depend on their bargaining strength *vis-à-vis* their employers, and there was no reason to think that they would necessarily prevail (*Essays*, p. 353.).
[38] 'Of Taxes', *Essays*, p. 351.
[39] Besides the essay 'Of Public Credit', *Essays*, pp. 355-71, which was enlarged in later editions, see 'Of Civil Liberty', *Essays*, pp. 96-7; *History*, vol. ii, p. 444; *Letters*, vol. ii, pp. 237, 242, 245, 248.

interest. Hume's fear was that this would prove too attractive a way of raising revenue, since compared to the alternative of taxation it was initially quite painless. But to pay the interest due to the stockholders one had either to increase taxation or (again this was the less painful course) issue more stock. In this way the national debt would begin to spiral upwards at an alarming pace, and Hume indeed thought that such a spiral was developing before his eyes. He argued that in any case public stocks had a number of disadvantages: they could be bought and sold, and thus in effect served as paper money; they could be purchased by foreigners, thus rendering the nation economically vulnerable; and they created a class of idle stockholders. If the national debt continued to increase, two cataclysmic outcomes were possible. One was that taxation would increase to the point where all sections of the community were ground down to pay the stockholders; we shall examine the social consequences of this in a moment. The other was a sudden bursting of the bubble. A government, finding that all its resources were needed to pay the interest on its stock, and facing some emergency such as a foreign war, would order a delay in interest payments; at which point the stocks would collapse. This, Hume says, 'may be called the *natural death* of public credit'.

Those of Hume's assumptions and attitudes that we have so far examined—his preference for commercial societies, his predisposition towards *laissez-faire* policies, his fears about increases in taxation, his condemnation of public borrowing—might seem to categorize him as an apostle of rising capitalism, a nineteenth-century liberal before his time. To several commentators this has seemed the appropriate interpretation of his work.[40] But now we must counterpose other attitudes whose ideological affiliations seem at first sight rather different; they seem so until we realize that nineteenth- and twentieth-century ideological patterns may not fit the eighteenth century very well. Let us take the attitudes themselves first, and look at their social context later.

The picture we have been forming of Hume's social thought needs to be corrected in the following general way. Hume saw the industrial and commercial activity of which he so much approved taking place within a ranked social order whose existence was

[40] See, for example, Stewart, *The Moral and Political Philosophy of David Hume*, esp. chs. 5, 7, 12; F. A. Hayek, 'The Legal and Political Philosophy of David Hume' in V. C. Chappell (ed.), *Hume: A Collection of Critical Essays* (London, 1968); E. Roll, *A History of Economic Thought* (London, 1961), pp. 117-21; P. W. Larkin, *Property in the Eighteenth Century* (Cork, 1930), pp. 98-102.

both natural and essential to political stability. The merchant and the manufacturer took their positions within a social hierarchy that had been inherited (with modifications) from the feudal period; there was no question, in Hume's eyes, of social equality coming to replace inequality of rank. We have looked already at the nature of the modifications involved. In commercial societies, rank had no legal basis since everyone was equal before the law; the hierarchy was finely graduated, with an extensive 'middling rank' standing between the landowners and the labourers; and rather more social mobility was possible than in the preceding system. None of this, however, amounted to an abolition of hierarchy as such, and there is ample evidence, as we shall see, that Hume would have regarded such an abolition with abhorrence.

Essential to Hume's outlook was his assumption that the landed and commercial sections of society had identical interests. Improvements in industry spurred on improvements in agriculture, so there was no economic basis for hostility between the two sections. Moreover land and commerce were tied to one another by personal connections, and it was therefore unlikely that the landed sector, which held the political reins, would act against the commercial sector, even when the latter's interest diverged from that of the public as a whole.[41] Thus 'there has been an attempt in England to divide the *landed* and *trading* part of the nation; but without success. The interests of these two bodies are not really distinct, and never will be so, till our public debts increase to such a degree as to become altogether oppressive and intolerable.'[42] An exorbitant national debt does in fact produce the only circumstance in which Hume sees a real conflict of interests between the commercial sector and the rest of society. He never regards merchants and manufacturers as being constrained, economically or socially, by a social order dominated by the landed interest. Hostility towards the landlord, a recurrent feature of nineteenth-century liberalism, is completely absent from his thought.

Hume regards rank itself as arising naturally in any society. Casting around in *Treatise*, Book II for examples to illustrate the regularity of human life, he cites the fact that 'different stations arise necessarily, because uniformly, from the necessary and uniform principles of human nature'.[43] The mechanism at work

---

[41] See 'Of Public Credit', *Essays*, pp. 370-1; and *Letters*, vol. ii, p. 248, where Hume comments on the fact that representatives of the landowners may be expected to protect the interests of the stockholders even to the detriment of national security.

[42] 'Of Parties in General', *Essays*, p. 58.   [43] *Treatise*, p. 402.

here is not explained, but one might look for it either in the inbuilt human propensity to compare oneself with others—so that
each person naturally generates his own hierarchy of esteem—or
in the more instrumental consideration that rank is necessary to
social stability. This second thought appears to lie behind Hume's
comment on John Ball's rebellion in his *History*:

> But of all the evils incident to human society, the insurrections of the populace,
> when not raised and supported by persons of higher quality, are the least to be
> dreaded: the mischiefs consequent to an abolition of all rank and distinction
> become so great, that they are immediately felt, and soon bring affairs back to
> their former order and arrangement.[44]

Since ranking is inevitable, rules of behaviour have evolved to
govern the interactions of men in different ranks, and Hume
counsels us to abide by them:

> There are certain deferences and mutual submissions, which custom requires of
> the different ranks of men towards each other… 'Tis necessary, therefore, to
> know our rank and station in the world, whether it be fix'd by our birth, fortune,
> employments, talents or reputation.[45]

This piece of advice also reveals that an individual's position in
the order of rank may be decided by various factors: personal
merit plays a part, but does not necessarily predominate over
birth and fortune. Comparing the royalist and parliamentary
armies in the Civil War, Hume remarks that in the King's army
'every man there, as in a regular established government, was
confined to the station in which his birth had placed him'. The
parliamentarians, lacking sufficient men of the social rank from
which officers would normally be drawn, had to promote 'citizens
and country gentlemen', but this turned out not to be to their
disadvantage; they produced the best generals.[46] So here at least
Hume concedes that hierarchies governed predominantly by birth
may stifle individual talents; but he offers nothing by way of
criticism on the grounds of justice. He is no apostle of meritocracy.

For further light on Hume's attitude to the bases on which a
hierarchy may be erected, we may consider the contrast he draws
between societies such as France where a person's rank is fixed
primarily by birth, and contemporary Britain where (he believes)
wealth is the major determinant. It was not always so. Of the
reign of James I he writes:

[44] *History*, vol. ii, p. 286.
[45] *Treatise*, pp. 598-9.
[46] *History*, vol. v, p. 269.

High pride of family then prevailed; and it was by a dignity and stateliness of behaviour, that the gentry and nobility distinguished themselves from the common people. Great riches acquired by commerce were more rare, and had not as yet been able to confound all ranks of men, and render money the chief foundation of distinction.[47]

Can one detect a note of regret in this passage? Writing to his kinsman Alexander Home, who was researching into the Hume genealogy, Hume passed on all the information he had, and added:

I am not of the opinion of some, that these matters are altogether to be slighted. Though we should pretend to be wiser than our ancestors, yet it is arrogant to pretend that we are wiser than the other nations of Europe, who, all of them, except perhaps the English, make great account of their family descent. I doubt that our morals have not much improved since we began to think riches the sole thing worth regarding.[48]

If pressed on this question—whether it is better for social ranking to be based on birth or on wealth—I believe Hume would have opted for one of his characteristic compromises. A hierarchy based on birth has the disadvantage that it discourages commerce, since ambitious men will aim for titles rather than commercial profit;[49] a hierarchy based on wealth generates less deference among the lower orders, and is therefore a less secure support of political authority.[50] A mixed system, somewhere perhaps between the French and the British, offers the best combination of virtues.

Social ranking arises naturally everywhere, because it corresponds to intrinsic human traits; moreover once established it has, according to Hume, valuable social functions (from which it follows that attempts to destroy rank, though ultimately doomed to fail, may in the short term be socially damaging). We have glanced briefly at one such function: the moderating effect of rank on individuals' economic aspirations. We shall look now at the political effects of social hierarchy. Hume's view here is quite subtle, and needs to be stated carefully. On the one hand, social hierarchy acts in general as a support to political authority; on the other, it may act as a check, especially on the authority of a monarch. Political stability depends on achieving the right balance between these two effects.

To consider the supporting function first, men of high status— the nobility and the gentry—will tend naturally to behave in ways

---

[47] *History*, vol. iv, p. 504.

[48] *Letters*, vol. i, p. 276. I read 'doubt' here in its old sense of 'suspect'.

[49] See above, ch. 5, pp. 109-10.   [50] See below, pp. 137-8.

favourable to established authority. They will do so partly because they have the greatest interest in seeing the existing system of justice preserved, and partly because they are likely to be most thoroughly imbued with conservative attitudes by upbringing.[51] These men will then carry the lower orders with them, transforming respect for rank into respect for the political order which rank supports; 'a regard to birth, rank, and station, has a mighty influence over men, and enforces the decrees of the magistrate.'[52] That is why Hume says, in the passage cited above, that he does not fear popular insurrections unless 'raised and supported by persons of higher quality'. In the latter case, the natural regard for rank is engaged against the established authority. One of Hume's worries about contemporary politics was that 'men of rank' had no incentive to hold political office, because there was little financial reward for doing so, and few opportunities for distributing patronage, while at the same time the politician exposed himself to the insults of the Opposition. So noblemen declined office and made their feelings public. 'These sentiments loosen the attachment of their inferiors', Hume remarked.[53]

On the one hand, therefore, a social hierarchy produces men who serve naturally as a cement to the political system; on the other hand the same men, having independent sources of support, can act as a check on the central authority. They will tend to throw their weight behind an established ruler when his authority is threatened, but against him when he tries to engross more power than he is entitled to have. This, I believe, explains apparent inconsistencies in Hume's view of the English gentry during the Civil War period. He says, on one side, 'from innumerable instances, it appears how deep rooted, in the minds of the English gentry of that age, was the principle of loyalty to their sovereign'.[54] On the other side:

A reasonable compliance with the court was slavish dependence; a regard to the king, servile flattery; a confidence in his promises, shameless prostitution. This general cast of thought ... never predominated more than during the reign of Charles. The present house of commons, being entirely composed of country gentlemen, who came into parliament with all their native prejudices about them, and whom the crown had no means of influencing, could not fail to contain a majority of these stubborn patriots.[55]

[51] See *History*, vol. v, p. 227.
[52] 'Of the Origin of Government', *Essays*, p. 37.
[53] See *Letters*, vol. ii, pp. 161, 180-1.
[54] *History*, vol. v, p. 419.
[55] *History*, vol. v, p. 114.

But this striking contrast of attitudes is softened when we notice that the second passage refers to the period when the king's position was not itself in question, though he was locked in dispute with the Commons over the extent of his prerogative. In these circumstances the gentry were carrying out (perhaps with excessive ardour) their oppositional function. The first passage relates to the commonwealth period when the new king was attempting to capture power, and the gentry had gone over to their supporting role, as they had from the beginning of the war. The general principle of loyalty to the crown, therefore, did not exclude practical opposition to the king at times when his authority seemed to be secure.

The checking function was made possible by the fact that the nobility were economically independent of the crown, and held social sway over their inferiors. Their independence derived from their possession of landed property, which was protected by law, and which the king was not entitled to confiscate. In return they were morally (though not legally) obliged to aid their dependents, meaning all those relatives, tenants, and employees who were subordinated to them. Hume disapproved of publicly-administered systems of poor relief,[56] and clearly looked to the landowners to fill this role. 'A rich man', he wrote, 'lies under a moral obligation to communicate to those in necessity a share of his superfluities.'[57]

This delicately-balanced relationship between king, nobility, and people was threatened, in Hume's eyes, by the rapid growth of the public debt, which by throwing an increasing burden of taxation on to land would eventually destroy the independence of the nobility and gentry. The hypothetical result gives us the clearest idea of how Hume would have responded to a fully commercial society in which landowners had been displaced from their position of eminence by financiers. The relevant passage, although excessively rhetorical, is worth quoting at length, because it summarizes a number of themes in Hume's social thought, as well as indicating that his economic concerns were ultimately subordinate to social and political considerations.

In this unnatural state of society, the only persons who possess any revenue beyond the immediate effects of their industry, are the stockholders, who draw almost all the rent of the land and houses, besides the produce of all the customs

---

[56] See *History*, vol. iii, p. 317.
[57] *Treatise*, p. 482.

and excises. These are men who have no connections with the state, who can enjoy their revenue in any part of the globe in which they choose to reside, who will naturally bury themselves in the capital, or in great cities, and who will sink into the lethargy of a stupid and pampered luxury, without spirit, ambition, or enjoyment. Adieu to all ideas of nobility, gentry, and family. The stocks can be transferred in an instant: and, being in such a fluctuating state, will seldom be transmitted during three generations from father to son. Or were they to remain ever so long in one family, they convey no hereditary authority or credit to the possessor; and by this means the several ranks of men, which form a kind of independent magistracy in a state, instituted by the hand of nature, are entirely lost; and every man in authority derives his influence from the commission alone of the sovereign. No expedient remains for preventing or suppressing insurrections but mercenary armies: no expedient at all remains for resisting tyranny: elections are swayed by bribery and corruption alone: and the middle power between king and people being totally removed, a grievous despotism must infallibly prevail. The landholders, despised for their poverty, and hated for their oppressions, will be utterly unable to make any opposition to it.[58]

I have suggested already that Hume's social attitudes ought to be understood in relation to the outlook of the eighteenth-century aristocracy. A brief excursus into social history is therefore necessary at this point. A delineation of English society in the mid-eighteenth century will provide the background against which opinions of Hume's that seem puzzling fall into place.

One historian has described this society as 'an open aristocracy based on property and patronage',[59] and such a characterization neatly picks out the main features that deserve our attention. It was, first of all, a ranked society in which men were conscious of their social status, and aware of the distance that separated them from other ranks. Social position was based on the ownership of property, with landed property being pre-eminent. Historians usually distinguish four broad social categories: the nobility proper, titled and owning large estates; the gentry, owning smaller estates and living chiefly from the rent these provided; the middle rank, comprising working farmers (tenants and freeholders),

----

[58] 'Of Public Credit', *Essays*, pp. 362-3. Hume's views here no doubt reflect the influence of Montesquieu, who had argued in *The Spirit of the Laws* that the nobility constitute the essential 'intermediate power' which prevents monarchy from degenerating into despotism. For Hume's warm response to Montesquieu's book, see *Letters*, vol.i, pp. 133-8. Montesquieu's opinions may conveniently be examined in M. Richter, *The Political Theory of Montesquieu* (Cambridge, 1977), esp. pp. 184-7, 211-14.

[59] H. Perkin, *The Origins of Modern English Society, 1780-1880* (London, 1969), p. 17. For the account that follows I have also drawn upon: D. Marshall, *Eighteenth Century England* (London, 1962); G. Mingay, *English Landed Society in the Eighteenth Century* (London, 1963); W. A. Speck, *Stability and Strife: England 1714-1760* (London, 1977), ch. 2; H. J. Habbakuk, 'England' in A. Goodwin (ed.), *The European Nobility in the Eighteenth Century* (London, 1967).

merchants, manufacturers, and professional men; and the labouring poor, artisans and farm workers. The boundaries between these groups were far from sharp, however, and although it was not easy for a person to move rapidly up the social hierarchy, there were numerous links between the landed groups and the middle order, through marriage and also the sending of younger sons into trades or professions. Hume's own career illustrates the fluidity of the boundaries. Born into the lesser gentry, he was sent first to train as a lawyer, then apprenticed for a short while to a Bristol merchant. Through state employment he finally achieved an income which gave him a comfortable gentlemanly status, though he did not of course reconvert this into an estate, as he probably would if he had raised a family. Having crossed and recrossed the border between the gentry and the middle rank, and having many friends of professional status, he was less aware of this division than of the distance separating him from 'the great' and 'the poor' on either side.

Although land remained the chief badge of position in eighteenth-century England, the liaisons formed between land on the one side and trade and industry on the other prevented any antipathy from developing between the two groups. Besides marriages contracted between landowners and the daughters of wealthy merchants and manufacturers (sometimes the salvation of a landed estate), the landowners themselves were increasingly drawn into industrial activity. They mined for coal and other minerals, built roads and canals, and sometimes started their own manufacturing concerns.[60] A passion for 'improvement', both in agriculture and in industry, was widespread in this group, and correspondingly they lacked that disparaging attitude towards commerce which became characteristic of the British upper classes in later generations.

Finally something must be said about the role played by patronage in linking together the various strata of this society, using the term not merely in its narrow political sense but more broadly to refer to the distribution of appointments and other privileges throughout the social fabric. As one historian puts it:

[60] See Mingay, *English Landed Society*, ch. 8; and R. S. Neale, '"The Bourgeoisie, Historically, Has Played a Most Revolutionary Part"' in E. Kamenka and R. S. Neale (eds.), *Feudalism, Capitalism and Beyond* (London, 1975). For evidence that Scottish land-owners followed the same path as their English counterparts, see T. C. Smout, 'Scottish Landowners and Economic Growth 1650-1850', *Scottish Journal of Political Economy*, xi (1964), 218-34.

If government patronage controlled the more lucrative, private patronage controlled the more numerous appointments: most church-livings, salaried county, borough and parish offices, merchants' and lawyers' clerks, estate agents, chaplains, secretaries, tutors and governesses, and the whole pyramid of domestic service, sometimes extending to the very labourers on the estate or home farm.[61]

Who would expect to receive the benefits of patronage? First, one's family, immediate and widely extended; second, tenants and villagers; third, political associates and supporters; fourth, those of one's acquaintance who were recognized to be specially deserving. Owning property, therefore, carried with it a host of expectations and obligations, none of them legally enforcible but all of them socially binding. Hume himself, although not in a position to dispense a great many favours, used his influence as a matter of course on behalf of his family and friends—for instance in purchasing an army commission for his nephew,[62] trying to obtain a parish living for his nephew's tutor,[63] and seeking a position in the navy for a deserving but unfortunate acquaintance.[64] 'Friendship' was the term characteristically used to denote the relationship between men that gave rise to these claims and obligations,[65] and it is worth reminding ourselves of the elasticity of its root, 'friend'. Besides 'one joined to another in mutual benevolence and intimacy', its most common modern meaning, it can refer to 'a sympathiser, patron or supporter' or to 'one who is on the same side in warfare, politics, etc.'.[66] The eighteenth-century idea of friendship plainly fused these different meanings, so that when Hume speaks of men seeking benefits for themselves and their friends he is referring in a shorthand way to the whole network of patronage, not merely to close personal friendships.

This social context helps us to make sense of aspects of Hume's thought that may on the surface appear paradoxical. Hume's ideology was the ideology of an open and progressive aristocracy, which was willing to accept newcomers into its midst, and which was generally well-disposed towards improvement in agriculture and industry. It was neither an exclusive estate, nor a rising class trying to displace an established class, but a group whose privileged position lacked any formal legal basis. It was, to use

[61] Perkin, *Origins of Modern English Society*, pp. 44-5.
[62] See *Letters*, vol. ii, pp. 292-3.
[63] See *Letters*, vol. ii, p. 213.
[64] See *Letters*, vol. ii, pp. 219-21.
[65] See Perkin, *Origins of Modern English Society*, p. 49.
[66] *Shorter Oxford English Dictionary* (Oxford, 1967), p. 752.

terms that I shall later argue are anachronistic, simultaneously liberal and conservative: receptive to intellectual and practical innovations, committed to personal freedom and the impartial rule of law, yet at the same time firmly attached to a ranked social order and to a political constitution that reflected and upheld that order. In this light we can understand, for example, how Hume could be committed both to the preservation of a social hierarchy and to an economic order that was largely free of political controls. From a nineteenth-century viewpoint these two attitudes appear to belong to incompatible ideologies, but to eighteenth-century eyes free commercial activity did not seem to threaten the system of ranks; rather it contributed harmoniously to the growth of a progressive, 'civilized' society. Again, Hume's views about the respective scope of justice and benevolence fall naturally into place here. Justice—the protection of established property rights— was the basis on which the whole social order was erected, since position depended on property ownership. This meagre legal framework was, however, supplemented by the patronage net- work, whose obligations Hume classified as matters of private benevolence. Thus the balance he struck between a restricted notion of justice and a broader notion of benevolence faithfully reflected the working of eighteenth-century society, where much was left to personal morality that in other epochs has been legally enforced. One could multiply examples indefinitely, but I hope enough has been said to show that Hume's social opinions, peculiar in some respects to our eyes, would in the aristocratic milieu of the mid-eighteenth century have appeared quite un- remarkable.

7

Forms of Government

We have already taken notice of Hume's ambition to found a science of politics. It is one of the three applied sciences mentioned at the beginning of the *Treatise*, and in *Enquiry* I it is held up (along with such disciplines as chemistry) as an example of a science which treats of general facts in contrast to particularizing disciplines such as history.[1] Elsewhere Hume comments on the fact that political behaviour reveals a greater degree of uniformity than such other areas of human experience as artistic taste and scientific development.[2] These two points taken together—that politics may be studied scientifically, and that it tends to follow regular patterns, making prediction possible—should prepare us for the bold claim encapsulated in the title of his essay: 'That Politics may be reduced to a Science', and for the assertion it contains that the consequences of laws and governments depend so little on individual temperament that one can draw conclusions in this area with as much certainty as in mathematics.[3]

But when it comes to the actual analysis of political life, Hume's performance is much more modest than these aspirations would lead us to expect. The essay just referred to, rather than laying down foundations for a general science of politics, contents itself with establishing five maxims about the consequences of particular forms of government (for instance that a hereditary monarchy is less socially divisive than an elective monarchy).[4] Moreover the opening sections of this essay need to be read alongside Hume's remark, in 'Of Civil Liberty', that 'the world is still too young to fix many general truths in politics, which will remain true to the latest posterity', and his similar observation, in 'Of Some Remarkable Customs', that 'all general maxims in politics ought to be established with great caution; and that

---

[1] *Enquiry* I, pp. 164-5.
[2] 'Of Eloquence', *Essays*, p. 98.
[3] See the passage cited above, ch. 5, p. 101.
[4] This fact has led one commentator to suggest that, rather than trying to validate the use of abstract reasoning in politics, Hume is attempting in this essay to demonstrate its absurdity. See J. Conniff, 'Hume's Political Methodology: A Reconsideration of "That Politics May Be Reduced to a Science"', *Review of Politics*, xxxviii (1976), 88-108.

irregular and extraordinary appearances are frequently discovered in the moral, as well as in the physical world'.[5]

We can understand Hume's hesitancy about the possibilities of a political science in the light of two aspects of his thought that we have already examined. The first concerns the degree to which human nature is itself uniform; the second, the connections between government, the economy, the social structure, and culture. Each poses problems for a generalizing science of politics, as we shall now see.

Hume claims that forms of government have consequences that do not depend on 'the humours and tempers of men'. But since governments are themselves composed of men, this can only be true in a limited sense. Hume must mean that, when considering how men will behave politically, we can take for granted a class of motives that are uniform and that will always outweigh other motives that are socially variable. We saw earlier that he believed human beings shared a substratum of basic characteristics upon which were laid traits peculiar to particular social milieux. The implication now being drawn is that only the substratum counts in politics. Motives like ambition and avarice are universally present, and they dominate political life. That is why political writers take it as axiomatic that every man should be considered a knave, as governed entirely by self-interest. Such assumptions make it possible to produce generalizations about the effects of different sets of political institutions.

It is not, however, always clear where the dividing line between basic substratum and social overlay should be drawn; Hume has this in mind when he expresses doubts about advancing general maxims in politics:

We have not as yet had experience of three thousand years; so that not only the art of reasoning is still imperfect in this science, as in all others, but we even want sufficient materials upon which we can reason. It is not fully known what degree of refinement, either in virtue or vice, human nature is susceptible of, nor what may be expected of mankind from any great revolution in their education, customs, or principles.[6]

Machiavelli is then held up as an example of a 'great genius' who generalized erroneously from limited political experience.

The first problem, therefore, is that political science requires assumptions about human nature, but particular assumptions are

---

[5] 'Of Civil Liberty', *Essays,* p. 89; 'Of Some Remarkable Customs', *Essays,* p. 372.
[6] 'Of Civil Liberty', *Essays,* p. 89.

hard to justify because we cannot distinguish conclusively between traits that really are universal and those that only appear to be. The second problem arises from the complex set of interrelationships between government and other facets of society. When examining Hume's account of social change, we saw that he forewent any simple monocausal account of the growth of civilization in favour of a multicausal analysis which traced the interactions between political change, economic development, changes in the social structure, and cultural refinement. This implies that one cannot consider the effects of forms of government without taking into account the economic, social, and cultural environment in which they are operating. One set of institutions may be most effective in promoting economic expansion *given* a commercial economy, say, but it may be impossible to plant those institutions in a primitive economy with the intention of developing it. So rather than producing a political science whose propositions take the form 'G (form of government) has consequences C', Hume should aim to generate propositions of the form 'Under conditions S, G has consequences C', where C may or may not be such as to constitute a change in S. Thus (*a priori*) a particular combination of S and G may be self-reinforcing or self-destructive; Hume's science of politics potentially has a dynamic aspect.

It may still be possible to find cases where the effects of political institutions can be analysed in a quite general way, irrespective of circumstances, and these are the cases that Hume has in mind when he uses the analogy of mathematics in 'That Politics may be reduced to a Science'. But such cases will be comparatively rare, and the political scientist will more often be in the business of producing limited generalizations, or of comparing two sets of institutions operating in the same environment. Hume often, for instance, compares the performance of monarchies and republics in modern, civilized societites, while being clear that his conclusions do not apply to earlier social conditions. He also limits the scope of his political science in two more specific ways. First, he points out that it is easier to predict the consequences of constitutional governments than of absolute governments, since in the latter case a great deal must depend on the character of the person who holds the reins of power.[7] Second, for a similar reason, conclusions can be reached more easily about domestic

---

[7] 'That Politics may be reduced to a Science', *Essays,* pp. 13-14.

policy than about foreign policy, which depends on the decisions of a small number of people.[8]

Hume's ambition is therefore not to produce a general ranking of forms of government according to some moral criterion, but to make a number of more limited comparisons. He will have achieved his aim if he can say that, in given circumstances and in one particular respect, form A is better than form B. We should bear in mind here his underlying belief that all forms of government which meet his minimum standard of performance are to be judged equally legitimate, and his view that radical changes of regime are rarely desirable. The practical point of a science of politics will be to indicate the best direction of (gradual) change where change is unavoidable or can be carried out without disturbing existing habits of obedience. For that purpose limited generalizations are sufficient, and indeed are less dangerous than bold statements to the effect that such-and-such a government is the best possible.

This political science aims to discover the consequences, and to a lesser extent the preconditions, of various forms of government. It should therefore begin with a general classification of types of government. Hume, however, never offers a clear and systematic classification, but tends instead to distinguish governments according to whatever criterion is most salient for a particular argument. His terminology is inconsistent and confusing. What follows is an attempt to present his main findings in a more orderly way.

Like many of his contemporaries Hume was struck by the comparisons that could be drawn between modern Britain and modern France,[9] and this formed the basis of one of his major lines of division: between 'absolute monarchies', where authority resided ultimately in the hands of a single man (though it might be delegated to subordinate officials), and 'free governments', where authority was divided among several bodies, at least one of which was based on popular representation. As Forbes has pointed out, this contrast formed the basis for many popular panegyrics on 'English liberty' as against 'French tyranny'.[10] But

---

[8] 'Of the Rise and Progress of the Arts and Sciences', *Essays*, pp. 113-14; 'Of Commerce', *Essays*, p. 260.

[9] Plamenatz has observed that in this period 'the English and the French, who were then the richest and the most powerful peoples in the West, were very much given to bold generalizations often based on nothing better than a comparison between their two countries'. (*Man and Society*, (London, 1963), vol. i, p. 328.)

[10] Forbes, *Hume's Philosophical Politics*, ch. 5.

Hume came to see that a second, cross-cutting division was more important than the first: that between government conducted according to a general and uniform set of laws, and government conducted according to the particular edicts of the current power-holder or -holders—between 'regular' and 'arbitrary' government.[11] As noted earlier, the history of civilization could from one point of view be seen to consist in the transition from arbitrary to regular government.

If we superimpose the two divisions, we have four possible forms of government. First, there are governments that are both absolute and arbitrary. Hume refers to these as 'barbarous monarchies' or 'despotisms', and examples were provided by the government of the Roman emperors[12] and of the sultans of Turkey, Egypt, and other eastern nations.[13] In the simplest form, a chieftain simply issued orders to his followers, but in a larger state it became necessary for the monarch to appoint subordinate officials to whom he granted the same arbitrary power as he himself exercised. 'It is not, therefore, to be supposed, that a barbarous monarch, unrestrained and uninstructed, will ever become a legislator, or think of restraining his *Bashaws* in every province, or even his *Cadis* in every village.'[14] Although despotism was characteristic of the East, and of earlier periods in the West, it was not confined to them. Under Cromwell's government in England the same lineaments began to emerge. According to Hume, when wide legal powers were conferred on the Protector's twelve major-generals in 1655,

All reasonable men now concluded, that the very mask of liberty was thrown aside, and that the nation was forever subjected to military and despotic government, exercised not in the legal manner of European nations, but according to the maxims of Eastern tyranny. Not only the supreme magistrate owed his authority to illegal force and usurpation; he had parcelled out the people into so many subdivisions of slavery, and had delegated to his inferior ministers the same unlimited authority which he himself had so violently assumed.[15]

---

[11] In this he was undoubtedly influenced by Montesquieu, who in a manner parallel to Hume's classified governments as 'republics', 'monarchies', or 'despotisms', and argued that the moral gulf between monarchy and despotism was wider than that between monarchy and republic. See especially Books II and III of *The Spirit of the Laws* (Richter, *The Political Theory of Montesquieu*, pp. 178-96).

[12] 'Of the Liberty of the Press', *Essays*, pp. 9-10; 'Of the First Principles of Government', *Essays*, p. 29.

[13] 'Of the First Principles of Government', *Essays*, p. 29; 'Of the Rise and Progress of the Arts and Sciences', *Essays*, pp. 116-17; *History*, vol. v, p. 454.

[14] 'Of the Rise and Progress of the Arts and Sciences', *Essays*, p. 117.

[15] *History*, vol. v, p. 454.

The effects of barbarous monarchy are plain enough to Hume.[16] Because exertions of authority are always unpredictable under that system, the people are oppressed and insecure. They have little incentive to work, trade, or acquire property; and for the same reason the arts and sciences will be neglected. In short, this form of government represents only a small improvement over the state of nature and retains many of its cultural features.

According to Hume ancient writers were accustomed to regard all monarchical governments as arbitrary in the sense described.[17] Modern experience has shown, however, that monarchy may also take a civilized form, where the king, although possessing absolute authority, governs according to general laws. 'It may now be affirmed of civilized monarchies, what was formerly said in praise of republics alone, *that they are a government of Laws, not of Men.*'[18] Indeed, this has become the norm among modern European nations. The factors which differentiate civilized from barbarous monarchies are, first, that all subordinate officials are placed under the restraint provided by the rule of law, and, second, that the monarch himself, although formally unlimited in his powers, does in fact play a restricted role, being content to uphold the great bulk of the laws which he finds in existence when he assumes office. This form of government therefore depends less upon the personal character of the sovereign than a barbarous monarchy, enabling 'the government, by the force of its laws and institutions alone, without any extraordinary capacity in the sovereign, to maintain itself in order and tranquillity'.[19] For this reason such governments provide their people with peace and security, enable industry and the arts to flourish, and in general 'answer most of the ends of political society'.[20]

To delve a little further into the distinguishing features of a civilized monarchy, we need to examine first what Hume means by 'a government of laws, not of men'. He has in mind those features traditionally conjured up by the phrase 'the rule of law': justice dispensed equally to all-comers, no imprisonment without

---

[16] 'Of the Rise and Progress of the Arts and Sciences', *Essays*, pp. 116-20, 125.

[17] *History*, vol. i, p. 394. Hume had plainly overlooked Aristotle's discussion of kingship and tyranny.

[18] 'Of Civil Liberty', *Essays*, p. 95. The reference here may be to Harrington, who had asked (and answered affirmatively) 'whether a commonwealth be rightly defined to be a government of laws and not of men, and monarchy to be a government of some man, or few men, and not of laws?' (J. G. A. Pocock (ed.), *The Political Works of James Harrington* (Cambridge, 1977), p. 396.)

[19] *History*, vol. iii, p. 20.

[20] 'Of the Rise and Progress of the Arts and Sciences', *Essays*, p. 127.

trial, no confiscation of property without the owner's consent, judges independent of the will of the sovereign, and so forth. Discussing the government of Elizabeth I (whose general character according to Hume was that of an absolute monarchy) he notes various institutions whose existence was prejudicial to the rule of law, especially the Star Chamber 'which possessed an unlimited discretionary authority of fining, imprisoning, and inflicting corporal punishment', and whose members enjoyed office at the sovereign's pleasure. 'There needed but this one court in any government to put an end to all regular, legal, and exact plans of liberty,' Hume remarks.[21] Thus the rule of law exists to the extent that such institutions with arbitrary power are checked or eliminated (though Hume, as we shall see, doubted whether the elimination could ever be total).

But what can check the authority of the sovereign himself in a civilized monarchy? In general, Hume says, nothing but 'custom, example, and the sense of his own interest'. An enlightened prince will see that he can enjoy more security and opulence by allowing his country to be governed by general laws than by acting arbitrarily in his own immediate interests; he will also, like every other citizen, absorb the customs and conventions of his age, including conventions governing the conduct of the monarch.[22] There will also be contingent checks on his power, which vary from case to case. In Tudor England, for example, the main checks were the sovereign's dependence on parliament for revenue and the lack of a standing army. A rather different example is provided by the Chinese government where, Hume says, the emperor has no effective military force at his disposal and so can only preserve domestic peace by placing his subordinates under the restraint of general laws. To the extent that civilized monarchy depends on these contingent factors, its survival cannot be guaranteed, but in Hume's view that is true of all forms of government.

Civilized monarchy is therefore compatible with liberty when that is taken to mean the absence of arbitrary coercion.[23] This

[21] *History*, vol. iv, p. 346.

[22] The difficulties experienced by the early Stuarts, and especially Charles I, were held by Hume to stem from the fact that they had been educated into a different understanding of royal power from their subjects. Of Charles he writes: 'In any other age or nation, this monarch had been secure of a prosperous and a happy reign. But the high idea of his own authority which he had imbibed, made him incapable of giving way to the spirit of liberty which began to prevail among his subjects.' (*History*, vol. v, p. 64.) See also his comments on James in 'Of the Protestant Succession', *Essays*, p. 490.

[23] A view of freedom recently defended by F. A. Hayek. See his *The Constitution of Liberty* (London, 1960), esp. ch. 1.

is one of Hume's main uses of the term, which he often en-
capsulates in phrases such as 'regular and equitable plan of
liberty', 'regular, legal and exact plans of liberty', 'regular plan
of law and liberty'. The linking of regularity, law, and liberty in
these expressions shows that liberty on this interpretation is not
limited by constraint as such, but by arbitrary constraint, applied
without due process of law. But Hume also, without warning,
uses 'liberty' in two other ways: to mean simply the absence of
constraint (particularly in matters such as freedom of speech and
religious belief), and to describe one particular form of government, which he labels 'free'. It is plain that civilized monarchies
cannot, by definition, embody freedom in the third sense, and
they need not (indeed Hume believes that they are unlikely to, for
empirical reasons) embody much of it in the second. The scope for
confusion should be apparent: the establishment of a strong
monarchical government may promote liberty in Hume's first
sense while diminishing it in the two latter senses. For instance
Hume describes the Anglo-Saxons as 'one of the freest nations
of which there remains any account in the records of history' (on
account of the weakness of royal authority, taking liberty in sense
three), but then on the same page describes the destruction of that
'freedom' and the growth of absolutism as preparing the way for
'a regular and equitable plan of liberty' (liberty in sense one).[24]
When he speaks of the preconditions for liberty in Britain, in
particular, it is not always clear whether he has in mind the
transition from barbarous to civilized government, or the later
emergence of a free constitution. As Forbes has pointed out,[25]
current Whig ideology regarded these two forms of liberty as
inseparable; but for Hume they were not, and to state his position
clearly he needed a more precise terminology than was readily
available in his political environment.

Further discussion of the consequences of civilized monarchy is
best conducted by comparison with free government; so let us
now examine Hume's view of the latter. For once he gives us a
clear and explicit definition:

The government, which, in common appellation, receives the appellation of
free, is that which admits of a partition of power among several members, whose
united authority is no less, or is commonly greater, than that of any monarch;
but who, in the usual course of administration, must act by general and equal
laws, that are previously known to all the members, and to all their subjects.[26]

[24] *History*, vol. ii, p. 513.
[25] Forbes, *Hume's Philosophical Politics*, ch. 5.
[26] 'Of the Origin of Government', *Essays*, p. 39.

Free governments are, therefore, by definition governments of law; they fall on the 'regular' side of the line dividing 'arbitrary' from 'regular' government. They also incorporate a division of powers between two or more separate bodies, characteristically between a more popular legislative body and a more exclusive executive body. The king, if there is one, has less effective authority than the other institutions taken together.

Free governments fall into two categories, limited monarchies and pure republics. The rationale for Hume's classification is that, in most respects, limited monarchies behave more like republics than like absolute monarchies. He describes Britain, the prime example of a monarchical free government, as predominantly republican 'though with a great mixture of monarchy'.[27] This is an important assumption, because it allows Hume to juxtapose comparisons drawn between ancient republics and monarchies with comparisons between modern Britain and the European monarchies.

All free governments face the problem of conciliating their various component bodies. In limited monarchy the main difficulty is to limit the power of the king without reducing him to complete impotence—a problem which Hume discusses at length when dealing with the British political system and which we shall take up in the next chapter. In republics the difficulty is to prevent the aristocratic part of the government from being swamped by the popular element. The ancient republics were plagued by this problem: 'In those days there was no medium between a severe, jealous aristocracy, ruling over discontented subjects, and a turbulent, factious, tyrannical democracy.'[28] In republican Rome, the reconciliation was achieved by the patrician body avoiding a head-on clash with the plebeian body, but instead seeking to influence it covertly—the nobles using their prestige, wealth, and political skills to sway the plebs.[29] In theory, Hume argues, it should be possible for a system of checks to be established more formally in a republic than in a monarchy, but since in practice this is difficult to achieve successfully, republican constitutions 'are the source of all disorder, and of the blackest crimes, where either skill or honesty has been wanting in their original frame and institution'.[30]

---

[27] 'Of the Liberty of the Press', *Essays*, p. 10. This essay does however highlight one important way in which limited monarchies and republics do *not* behave alike.

[28] 'Of the Populousness of Ancient Nations', *Essays*, p. 413.

[29] 'Of Some Remarkable Customs', *Essays*, pp. 375-8.

[30] 'That Politics may be reduced to a Science', *Essays*, p. 14.

Hume has no sympathy for democratic republics, that is governments where the popular majority are in effective control either directly or through representatives. This is of course what we should expect given his views about the proper political role of the aristocracy. Of ancient Athens he writes:

The Athenian Democracy was such a tumultuous government as we can scarcely form a notion of in the present age of the world. The whole collective body of the people voted in every law, without any limitation of property, without any distinction of rank, without control from any magistracy or senate; and consequently without regard to order, justice, or prudence.[31]

Hume's complaints against democratic assemblies are that they are disorderly; that they are unable to pursue a steady line of policy; that they disregard the common precepts of morality; that they are susceptible to enthusiasms, religious or otherwise; and that they are liable to be bought by the rich, to be swayed by orators, and eventually to capitulate before a strong leader. These themes reappear in his discussions of the role of parliament during the English Civil War. For instance, 'popular assemblies, as, by their very number, they are in a great measure exempt from the restraint of shame, so when they also overleap the bounds of law, naturally break out into acts of the greatest tyranny and injustice.'[32] Or again:

Many persons of family and distinction had, from the beginning of the war, adhered to the parliament: but all these were, by the new party, deprived of authority; and every office was entrusted to the most ignoble part of the nation. A base populace, exalted above their superiors; hypocrites, exercising iniquity under the visor of religion: these circumstances promised not much liberty or lenity to the people; and these were now found united in the same usurped and illegal administration.[33]

Of the particularly distasteful 'Barebone's parliament' he wrote: 'In this notable assembly were some persons of the rank of gentlemen; but the far greater part were low mechanics; Fifth Monarchy men, Anabaptists, Antinomians, Independents; the very dregs of the fanatics.'[34] And he had no doubt of the outcome of such disorderly institutions; 'illegal violence, with whatever pretences it may be covered, and whatever object it may pursue, must inevitably end at last in the arbitrary and despotic government of a single person.'[35] Cromwell's dictatorship was the natural result of the democratic excesses of that period.

---

[31] 'Of the Populousness of Ancient Nations', *Essays*, p. 374.
[32] *History*, vol. v, pp. 295-6.   [33] *History*, vol. v, p. 358.
[34] *History*, vol. v, p. 441.   [35] *History*, vol. v, p. 435.

To guard republics against the deformation threatened by democracy, Hume proposed four safeguards. First, the legislature should be a representative body rather than an assembly of the people; this was one of the 'universal axioms' listed in the essay 'That Politics may be reduced to a Science'. Second, the representatives, whilst listening to the opinions of their constituents, should preserve their independence of mind and not become mere delegates; Hume made this clear in his remarks about instructions to members of parliament.[36] Third, the electorate should be restricted by a property qualification for the suffrage. Fourth, the popular body should be balanced by a strong and more selectively-based executive body (though as we have seen, Hume sees the preservation of this balance as one of the difficulties inherent in a republican government).

All of these features are contained in Hume's sketch of the ideal republic which he describes as a 'perfect commonwealth', though we have yet to see whether he ranks republics unreservedly above monarchies in his order of preference. The main peculiarity of this sketch is that Hume favours a devolved form of government whereby electors choose county representatives to meet in local assemblies, who then themselves choose senators to compose the national assembly. The county assemblies together possess the legislative power and the senate the executive power (the latter are to choose a protector and ministers from among their number). The advantage of this scheme, Hume claims, is that it allows the people to debate laws without the usual drawbacks of large popular assemblies (the county assemblies have 100 members each). 'If the people debate, all is confusion: if they do not debate, they can only resolve; and then the senate carves for them. Divide the people into many separate bodies, and then they may debate with safety, and every inconvenience seems to be prevented.'[37] Notice however that 'the people' in this context have already been filtered through two processes of selection. First, there is a property qualification for the suffrage—Hume raised the requirement from 'all the freeholders in the county parishes, and those who pay scot and lot in the town parishes' in the edition of 1752, to 'all the freeholders of ten pounds a year in the county, and all the householders worth 200 pounds in the town parishes' in editions from 1753-68, and finally to 'all the freeholders of twenty pounds a year in the county, and all the householders worth 500 pounds

---

[36] See 'Of the First Principles of Government', *Essays*, pp. 32-3.
[37] 'Idea of a Perfect Commonwealth', *Essays*, pp. 508-9.

in the town parishes'.[38] Second, the ordinary voters have merely to choose their representatives, no more. 'The lower sort of people and small proprietors are good enough judges of one not very distant from them in rank or habitation: and therefore, in their parochial meetings, will probably choose the best, or nearly the best representative: but they are wholly unfit for county meetings, and for electing into the higher offices of the republic.'[39] Hume views his republic as striking a balance between aristocracy and 'well-tempered democracy', and the tempering is clearly very thorough. The 'democratic' element really consists in the admission of the middle rank of people to a small share of power in a government that remains predominantly aristocratic in character.

We have now examined the three major forms of government that Hume distinguishes: barbarous monarchy, civilized monarchy, and free government (with its two subdivisions, limited monarchy and republic). It is worth asking whether anything fills the fourth box in Hume's matrix: can an arbitrary government be republican or quasi-republican? The answer is that it can, but according to Hume such a form of government is unstable and tends to convert itself spontaneously into one of the other forms. A republic, he says, may be barbarous when it first appears, but the people will quickly see the advantage of placing legal checks on their magistrates; hence 'it necessarily, by an infallible operation, gives rise to Law ... A republic without laws can never have any duration.'[40] One might also want to include here feudal government as conceived by Hume—though it defies easy classification within the framework we are employing. He himself describes feudalism as 'that prodigious fabric, which for several centuries preserved such a mixture of liberty and oppression, order and anarchy, stability and revolution, as was never experienced in any other age or any other part of the world'.[41] It was nominally regulated by a body of law, but the law was applied in such a haphazard way that the system fell closer to the 'arbitrary' end of his spectrum. He calls feudalism 'barbarous' and remarks that 'if the feudal government was so little favorable to the true liberty even of the military vassal, it was still more destructive of the independence and security of the other members

---

[38] For the variant readings, see *The Philosophical Works of David Hume*, ed. T. H. Green and T. H. Grose (London, 1874-5), vol. iii, p. 482.

[39] 'Idea of a Perfect Commonwealth', *Essays*, p. 508.

[40] 'Of the Rise and Progress of the Arts and Sciences', *Essays*, pp. 118-19.

[41] *History*, vol. i, p. 441.

of the state, or what in a proper sense we call the people'.[42] At the same time it did not correspond to the stereotype of barbarous monarchy, for the king's power was constantly being checked by the independent power of the nobility; 'the lives, the personal liberty, and the properties of all his subjects were less secured by law against the exertion of his arbitrary authority than by the independent power and private connections of each individual.'[43] This check was not, however, regularized as it was under a civilized limited monarchy, but depended upon the prevailing balance of power between king and barons—each side having military and financial resources to use against the other. The result was not favourable to peace and security:

On the whole, though the royal authority was confined within bounds, and often within very narrow ones, yet the check was irregular, and frequently the source of great disorders; nor was it derived from the liberty of the people, but from the military power of many petty tyrants, who were equally dangerous to the prince and oppressive to the subject.[44]

Feudalism, therefore, although in some respects unique, might reasonably be located in Hume's framework as a barbarous version of limited monarchy. Hume does not himself classify it in this way, preferring to stress the peculiarities of the system (as the above citations show), but my suggestion is consistent with the remainder of his thought.

We are thus left with three 'regular' or 'civilized' forms of government—absolute monarchy and the two versions of free government—and one stable and two unstable forms of barbarism. Hume's main evaluative contention is that the gulf between the civilized and the barbarous forms is vastly wider than any differences in performance between the civilized governments themselves. The choice between absolute monarchy and free government, in other words, is a matter of fine discrimination between forms of government each of which discharges the main function of government—regular enforcement of the rules of justice—perfectly adequately. This has the practical implication that one should never attempt to change the form of a civilized government if there is any appreciable risk that a relapse into barbarism might ensue; here his moral beliefs reinforce an attitude of quiescence which he has argued for already on epistemological grounds.[45] So

---

[42] *History*, vol. i, p. 448.
[43] *History*, vol. i, pp. 470-1.
[44] *History*, vol. i, pp. 471-2.
[45] See above, ch. 4, pp. 93-4.

in turning to Hume's comparisons between the civilized forms, we should bear in mind that they were intended mainly to satisfy the curious observer rather than to guide the practical activities of politicians.

Hume endorses the opinion current in his time that free governments offer more encouragement to commerce than absolute governments; though he adds that the reason for this is not what it is commonly supposed to be. To engage in commerce men need above all to know that their private property is secure, but this assurance is now almost as complete under a civilized European monarchy as under a republic. Absolute governments do, however, discourage commerce by fostering a social system where rank depends on 'birth, titles, and place', which cannot be acquired by commercial success. Traders will give up commerce 'in order to purchase some of those employments, to which privileges and honours are annexed'.[46] Given Hume's enthusiasm for a society with a strong commercial sector, this comparison clearly counts in favour of free government.

The second comparison is more evenly balanced. Hume challenges the view that the arts and sciences can only flourish under a free government, though he concedes that they must first have arisen under such a regime. Civilized monarchy can only come into existence through borrowing its laws and institutions from a republic, and at the same time it may take over the culture and learning which the republic has fostered. Hume says, for that reason, that the monarchical form of government 'owes all its perfection to the republican', meaning that in broad historical terms civilized monarchies are parasitic on republics.[47] It does not follow, of course, that republics will continue to outstrip monarchies culturally. In fact, Hume maintains, monarchies tend to encourage the arts and republics the sciences, since to advance politically in a monarchy one needs 'wit, complaisance, or civility' to ingratiate oneself with the court, whereas in a republic one has to impress the people, for which purpose 'industry, capacity, or knowledge' is needed.[48] The connection between these qualities and the arts and the sciences respectively remains obscure to me, and it may be felt that Hume is here simply attempting to insert the common observation, that science flourished in Britain and the arts in France, into a plausible-sounding theory. His general

[46] 'Of Civil Liberty', *Essays*, pp. 93-4.
[47] 'Of the Rise and Progress of the Arts and Sciences', *Essays*, pp. 124-7.
[48] Ibid., p. 127.

attitude is in any case clear: from a cultural point of view absolute and free governments are on a par.

In the third place, Hume compared the fiscal policies which each form of government might be expected to pursue. France, 'the most perfect model of pure monarchy', had a ramshackle tax system which discouraged the industry of the poor, but according to Hume this was not inherent in the monarchical system, and a wise minister might rectify it. Free governments, on the other hand, were liable to contract an ever-increasing public debt. This had happened in Holland as well as in Britain, and seemed to Hume an inbuilt 'source of degeneracy' in these states;[49] we have already examined his reaction to this policy.[50] Fiscal policy was therefore a consideration tending to tip the balance back in favour of absolute government.

Finally, free governments had the advantage of liberty itself— liberty in the sense of rights enjoyed by the subject against the government. Hume makes particular mention of three aspects of liberty which appeared to be associated with free government: religious liberty, liberty of the press, and habeas corpus. It is interesting to notice, however, that in the latter two cases the connection is made specifically with limited monarchy. Indeed as far as freedom of the press is concerned, Hume argues that an absolute monarchy (France) and a pure republic (Holland) coincide in allowing only a limited amount of freedom, whereas in England this freedom has to be unrestricted to allow the republican part of the constitution to maintain an adequate watch over the monarchical part.[51] Similarly the law of habeas corpus 'seems necessary for the protection of liberty in a mixed monarchy; and as it has not place in any other form of government, this consideration alone may induce us to prefer our present constitution to all others'.[52] Thus the argument about freedom seems not only to count in favour of free government in general, but more specifically in favour of limited monarchy as opposed to republican government.

But how strong is the argument in Hume's eyes? We must observe that in each of the three areas referred to, Hume tempers his praise of liberty with a cautionary note. His next sentence concerning habeas corpus reads: 'It must, however, be confessed, that there is some difficulty to reconcile with such extreme liberty

---

[49] 'Of Civil Liberty', *Essays*, pp. 96-7.
[50] See above, ch. 6, pp. 131-2.
[51] 'Of the Liberty of the Press', *Essays*, pp. 8-11.
[52] *History*, vol. vi, p. 204.

the full security and the regular police of a state, especially the police of great cities.' On the subject of press freedom he enters a similar reservation: 'It must however be allowed, that the unbounded liberty of the press, though it be difficult, perhaps impossible, to propose a suitable remedy for it, is one of the evils attending those mixed forms of government.'[53] Even religious toleration was not an unmixed blessing: 'But in proportion as the practice of submitting religion to private judgment was acceptable to the people, it appeared in some respects dangerous to the rights of sovereigns, and seemed to destroy that implicit obedience on which the authority of the civil magistrate is chiefly founded.'[54] In each case Hume is reminding us that liberty, though good in itself, may be subversive of another, greater good, namely political order, and when that point is reached liberty must be sacrificed. This point of view is well summed up in a passage near the end of his *History* where Hume makes clear how he differs from the established Whig interpretation of English history:

> Forgetting that a regard to liberty, though a laudable passion, ought commonly to be subordinate to a reverence for established government, the prevailing faction has celebrated only the partisans of the former, who pursued as their object the perfection of civil society, and has extolled them at the expense of their antagonists, who maintained those maxims that are essential to its very existence.[55]

The question Hume asks of free government, and especially of limited monarchy, is whether it can allow men to enjoy the fruits of liberty without endangering the stability of the state. This question colours his treatment of British politics, as we shall discover in the following chapter.

But now let us draw the threads together and try to decide whether Hume has an overriding preference for any one form of government. We have seen that free governments are preferred for encouraging commerce, but absolute monarchies may be able to pursue a more frugal fiscal policy. Free governments, especially limited monarchies, allow more personal freedom, but it seems moot whether this is a great advantage in Hume's eyes. These are the reasons offered for and against particular types of government. What of his explicit statements? His attempt to describe 'the most

---

[53] 'Of the Liberty of the Press', *Essays*, p. 12. This was a late addition to the essay and displaced a much more favourable assessment of press freedom in earlier versions. The change clearly reflects Hume's response to current events in Britain, as we shall see in the next chapter. Forbes describes this, with justice, as 'the most striking example of a retreat in the later Hume from a liberal to a less liberal position'. (*Hume's Philosophical Politics*, p. 184.)

[54] *History*, vol. iii, p. 202.   [55] *History*, vol. vi, pp. 365-6.

perfect of all' commonwealths issues in a republican model, and that might seem decisive evidence. But Hume's sympathetic adaption of Harrington's *Oceana* in that essay stands in rather stark contrast to the verdict in his *History*. 'Harrington's Oceana was well adapted to that age, when the plans of imaginary republics were the daily subjects of debate and conversation; and even in our time, it is justly admired as a work of genius and invention. The idea, however, of a perfect and immortal commonwealth, will always be found as chimerical as that of a perfect and immortal man.'[56] It is impossible not to wonder how seriously Hume's 'perfect commonwealth' was meant to be taken. A similar ambiguity colours a letter written to his nephew in 1775, where after agreeing with Millar that 'the Republican Form of [Government] is by far the best', he goes on to argue that it is 'only fitted for a small state' (explicitly contradicting what he had said in 'Idea of a Perfect Commonwealth') and that any attempt to move in that direction in England will produce 'only Anarchy, which is the immediate Forerunner of Despotism'.[57] This last remark reflects a verdict that Hume had returned much earlier in his life on British government. 'There is no doubt but a popular government may be imagined more perfect than an absolute monarchy, or even than our present constitution. But what reason have we to expect that any such government will ever be established in Great Britain, upon the dissolution of our monarchy?' A republic in Britain would be first of all chaotic and then by way of reaction tyrannical. So 'though liberty be preferable to slavery, in almost every case; yet I should rather wish to see an absolute monarch than a republic in this Island'.[58]

These are Hume's rather confusing remarks about the merits of republics. On the other side of the balance must be laid a few observations, such as his claim concerning Chinese government: 'Perhaps a pure monarchy of this kind, were it fitted for defence against foreign enemies, would be the best of all governments, as having both the tranquillity attending kingly power, and the moderation and liberty of popular assemblies.'[59] There is his remark in a letter to the Abbé le Blanc that his *History* 'discovers the Consequences of puritanical and republican Pretensions. You wou'd have remark'd in my Writings, that my principles are,

[56] *History,* vol. v, pp. 531-2.
[57] *Letters,* vol. ii, p. 306.
[58] 'Whether the British Government Inclines More to Absolute Monarchy or to a Republic', *Essays,* pp. 52-3.
[59] 'Of the Rise and Progress of the Arts and Sciences', *Essays,* p. 123.

all along, tolerably monarchical, and that I abhor, that low Practice, so prevalent in England, of speaking with Malignity of France.'[60] There is also his puzzling observation that, after the Revolution, 'we in this island have ever since enjoyed, if not the best system of government, at least the most entire system of liberty, that ever was known amongst mankind'.[61] This last suggests a willingness on Hume's part to detach the question of the best form of government from the question of the extent of liberty enjoyed, perhaps reflecting his view that liberty was a blessing that carried with it dangers to political stability.

Over all it appears that Hume had a slight preference for free government, but this preference was expressed in such a cautious way that it could have very little practical impact. We should remind ourselves here that Hume's generalizations about government were designed to be severely limited in scope. Given ideal circumstances—a suitable population and the chance to devise a form of government from scratch—a republic would be the best solution. But in actual cases these preconditions would not be met. Instead there would be a population of a given size, at a particular stage of economic development, with inherited dispositions and loyalties, and so forth. Hume's main lesson here was a conservative one: 'In the particular exertions of power, the question ought never to be forgotten, What is best? But in the general distribution of power among the several members of a constitution, there can seldom be admitted any other question than, What is established?'[62]

Leaving aside for now the question of commerce, Hume's hesitant preference for free government can be understood in terms of two continua. The first ran between arbitrary and regular government. Because absolute monarchy depended in the last resort on the personality of the sovereign, it was impossible for that form of government ever to embody the rule of law perfectly; 'monarchy, when absolute, contains even something repugnant to law. Great wisdom and reflection can alone reconcile them'. But at the same time Hume recognized that the executive branch of government had to retain some prerogative to deal with unpredictable emergencies.

No government at the time [1640] appeared in the world, nor is perhaps to be found in the records of any history, which subsisted without the mixture of some

---

[60] *Letters*, vol. i, p. 194.
[61] *History*, vol. vi, p. 363.
[62] *History*, vol. iv, p. 344.

arbitrary authority committed to some magistrate; and it might reasonably, beforehand, appear doubtful, whether human society could ever reach that state of perfection, as to support itself with no other control than the general and rigid maxims of law and equity.[63]

The question to be asked of free government, therefore, was whether it had reduced prerogative to the point where the basic security of the state was in danger. Could a government such as that of contemporary Britain deal with mob uprisings, for example? Had these government, in other words, moved further along the arbitrary/regular continuum than was compatible with imperfect human nature?

The second continuum ran between authority and liberty, in the second sense distinguished above. Free governments, particularly limited monarchies, gave their subjects a great deal of latitude in thought, speech, and behaviour. This again was a great blessing in itself, but it had to be balanced against the need to retain respect for established authority.[64] We recall that Hume was worried about the public promulgation of doctrines of resistance to government. Could a government allow its philosophers and men of letters to speculate freely while still managing to instil habits of obedience in the mass of the population?

These anxieties about free government coloured Hume's attitude towards the British political system. Unlike most of his contemporaries, who regarded the British form of government as obviously the best, and as far superior to French 'tyranny', Hume regarded it as a lucky and somewhat precarious historical accident. It was a system to be treasured while it existed, but it should not be expected to last indefinitely. Requesting his publisher to re-insert the words 'and happy' into his description of the British constitution as 'that singular and happy Government which we enjoy at present', he remarked that 'the English government is certainly happy, though probably not calculated for Duration, by reason of its excessive Liberty'.[65] This was certainly a jaundiced remark, occasioned by a particular set of events, but it reflected a persistent theme in Hume's thought. Because he thought absolute monarchy in the French style very little inferior on

---

[63] *History*, vol. v, pp. 170-1. Hume goes on to say that in retrospect parliament's action in restricting royal prerogative has been vindicated; but this has brought both advantages and disadvantages; the principle established is 'noble, though dangerous'. These cautious judgements reflect the delicate balance he is trying to strike between prerogative and the rule of law.

[64] See 'Of the Origin of Government', *Essays*, pp. 38-9.

[65] *Letters*, vol. ii, p. 261.

balance to free government, he could view the passing of limited monarchy with comparative equanimity. Absolute monarchy, he said, 'is the easiest death, the true *Euthanasia* of the British constitution'.[66]

If there was little to choose between civilized monarchy and free government, there was even less to choose between a limited monarchy and a republic. Hume never made this comparison explicitly, but we can extrapolate from what he says elsewhere, using the two continua as guide-lines. It will be seen that republics are potentially more 'regular' than limited monarchies, while the latter are likely to permit a greater degree of liberty. In limited monarchies, the relationship between crown and parliament cannot be strictly defined, and a good deal must depend on the personal character of the monarch. On the other hand, we are told that such monarchies are distinguished by their adherence to the rule of habeas corpus, and by the extensive freedom of speech that they permit. Hume uses this point in ironic fashion when writing to his nephew about the virtues of republics: '[One] great Advantage of a Commonwealth over our mixt Monarchy is, that it [woud consid]erably abridge our Liberty, which is growing to such an Extreme, as to be incom[patible wi]th all Government.'[67] When considering the matter more seriously, he claims, as noted above, that attempting to install a republic in Britain would have particularly disastrous consequences.[68]

Once again, the speculative view that republics and limited monarchies were much on a par was not meant to convey the practical implication that it mattered little if the monarchy disappeared in Britain. On the contrary, Hume's point was that since (civilized) forms of government differed so little in their merits, there was all the more reason to uphold the form of government that happened to be established in a particular country. Whatever the theoretical merits of republics, 'it is needless to reason any further concerning a form of government which is never likely to have place in Great Britain, and which seems not to be the aim of any party amongst us. Let us cherish and improve our ancient government as much as possible, without encouraging a passion for such dangerous novelties'.[69] Despite his scepticism,

[66] 'Whether the British Government Inclines More to Absolute Monarchy or to a Republic', *Essays*, p. 53.

[67] *Letters*, vol. ii, p. 306.

[68] Hume's distance from the republican tradition as a whole has been documented by Moore in 'Hume's Political Science and the Classical Republican Tradition'.

[69] 'Of the First Principles of Government', *Essays*, p. 33.

Hume could claim to be a better friend to the British constitution than those self-proclaimed 'patriots' who undertook to defend it on grounds of abstract principle. But to see how this claim might be borne out, we need to look in greater detail at Hume's interpretation of the development and present structure of the British political system.

8

Politics in Britain

To make sense of Hume's attitudes towards British politics, we must first try to disentangle the complex web of ideology that surrounded political activity in the middle part of the eighteenth century. The complexity of the web can largely be attributed to the fact that a political division based on current interests (between Court and Country) became superimposed on an older division of principle (between Whig and Tory) which had first appeared in a different political setting. Hume was keenly aware of the anachronistic nature of the second cleavage, as we shall see in due course, but that did not mean he could entirely avoid the terms in which political debate was conducted by his contemporaries. He wanted to make an impact on that debate, which meant addressing the ideological stances of Whig and Tory, even if only to persuade each of them that their views were obsolete. If the juxtaposition of Court/Country and Whig/Tory spelt confusion, Hume was forced to thread his way through the maze as best he could.

The terms 'Whig' and 'Tory' came into common use during the controversy over James, Duke of York's exclusion from the succession in 1679-80. By the time of the Revolution, the main lines of division were established. The Tories were the party of Church and King; they were generally committed to the doctrines of absolute authority in the monarch, of divine ordination and indefeasible hereditary succession, of passive obedience in the subject; they supported the Church of England and opposed extensions of toleration.[1] The Whigs, on the other hand, were the party of limited government; they maintained that sovereignty rested jointly in the hands of King, Lords, and Commons, and that the king's authority was checked by an original contract with the people—most often understood as a historical contract enshrined in the ancient constitution of the realm. They embraced the doctrine of resistance to arbitrary government and favoured religious toleration.[2]

---

[1] For a fuller account, see H. T. Dickinson, *Liberty and Property: Political Ideology in Eighteenth Century Britain* (London, 1977), ch. 1, sect. I.

[2] See Dickinson, *Liberty and Property,* ch. 2, sect. I.

Those, in very broad outline, were the pre-Revolutionary stances of the two parties. It has often been thought that the Revolution dealt a decisive blow to Tory ideology, since most Tories, notwithstanding their official doctrines, supported the removal of James II. But recent scholarship has shown that Tory propagandists began at once to refashion their creed to meet the new circumstances; a popular manoeuvre was to argue that a regime established *de facto* had Divine blessing and therefore commanded allegiance, even though *de jure* authority still belonged to the deposed monarch.[3] The Whigs, conversely, although loud in their praise of the Revolution, took care that it should not set a precedent for further resistance to government, and tried to prevent the contractual doctrine from being developed in a republican or democratic direction. As one authority has put it:

> ... the Whig establishment held that the Original Contract was a strictly histori-
> .cal, regularly renewable phenomenon, that the Revolution was virtually an act
> of self-defence, provoked by James II, who had saved everyone a great deal of
> trouble by withdrawing in circumstances which made his action tantamount
> to an abdication. It was now the permanent basis of the constitution, yet it offered
> no precedent for the future, unless another king should arise as tyrannical and
> irresponsible as James. There was no particular stress on popular rights, except
> as expressed through parliament.[4]

Despite differences in fundamental ideology, therefore, both Tories and Whigs managed to acquiesce in the settlement of 1688; their remaining practical differences revolved around the succession (until the Hanoverians were established in 1714) and the protection of the established Church. None the less, at the level of parliamentary politics, the division remained crucial during the first two decades of the eighteenth century. Aspiring politicians attached themselves firmly to one or other camp, and elections were fiercely contested.[5] Old arguments were kept alive in the heat of debate, as Whigs accused Tories of Jacobitism and Tories accused Whigs of subverting the Church.

What finally made nonsense of the old ideological division was the Whig ascendancy after 1720. Commanding victories at the polls meant that the Whigs could monopolize positions of power, and the disheartened Tories stopped contesting elections. A governing oligarchy could not remain saddled with an ideology

---

[3] See Kenyon, *Revolution Principles*, ch. 3; Dickinson, *Liberty and Property*, ch. 1, sect. III.

[4] Kenyon, *Revolution Principles*, p. 45.

[5] J. H. Plumb, *The Growth of Political Stability in England, 1675-1725* (London, 1967) ch. 5; Speck, *Stability and Strife*, ch. 6.

that emphasized the limits to executive power and the right of revolution. Instead we witness the growth of a Court or establishment ideology in contraposition to the Country ideology adopted by back-benchers and other politicians excluded from power. Contemporary opinion recognized the cleavage between Court and Country, but it should be emphasized that this was not a party division for electoral purposes; elections, when they were contested, were still fought under the labels of Whig and Tory. Almost all the Court faction were Whigs, and most of the Country faction were Tories, but this fact (though important from the ideological point of view) was simply a by-product of the political supremacy of the Whigs.

The ideological debate between Court and Country revolved around competing interpretations of the British constitution. Both sides agreed that the constitution depended on a balance between king and parliament, but they differed over where it was to be struck and how it was to be maintained. The Court party saw the king's authority as threatened by the growing power of the Commons, and argued that it must be fortified in various ways: the king must be left free to choose his ministers, granted sufficient funds to keep him financially independent of parliament, and allowed to retain a standing army. In particular, the monarch must be allowed to extend his patronage to members of parliament, since only in this way could the various branches of government be brought into harmony with each other.[6] The Country party, by contrast, argued for the independence of parliament, meaning in practice the exclusion of 'placemen' from parliamentary seats. They sought to check the king's prerogative, and wished to replace the standing army with a citizen militia.[7]

Alongside this political division, which fairly plainly reflected the divergent interests of the two groups, ran a secondary division in social outlook, which can plausibly be seen as mirroring the social composition of Court and Country parties. Very broadly, the Court faction was drawn from the great landowners and financiers, while the Country opposition was made up of gentry and clergymen.[8] Ideologically, the Court party embraced wholeheartedly the financial revolution of the post-1688 period, involving the creation of the Bank of England, the funding of the

---

[6] Dickinson, *Liberty and Property*, ch. 4; I. Kramnick, *Bolingbroke and his Circle* (Cambridge, Mass., 1968), ch. 5.

[7] Dickinson, *Liberty and Property*, ch. 5; Kramnick, *Bolingbroke*, ch. 6; Speck, *Stability and Strife*, ch. 10.

[8] Speck, *Stability and Strife*, ch. 6.

national debt through the issue of government stocks, and so forth.[9] The Country party remained hostile, its hostility taking the ideological form of animosity towards financiers, stockjobbers, and other moneyed men, and the practical form of attempts to reduce the national debt and (equally unsuccessful) attempts to exclude all but bona fide landowners from the House of Commons.[10] To support this position, their spokesmen argued that ownership of land uniquely qualified a man to hold political office, while the Court, more in tune with actual developments, saw political stability as flowing from the harmonious inter-marriage of landed and commercial interests which was embodied in its own membership.

A curious result of this transformation of the Whig oligarchy into a Court faction, and the Tory backbenchers into a Country opposition, was the inversion of their traditional readings of English political history. It is worth stressing that throughout the period we are considering, the interpretation given to historical events remained crucial to political argument, for reasons that are plain enough. So long as one party claimed that royal power derived from an original contract between king and people, while the other insisted that it descended directly from heaven (though the king might choose to consult the people about its exercise), it was essential to decide whether there had in fact been an 'ancient constitution' limiting the powers of the monarch. Certain topics in English history were staple fare: the Anglo-Saxon constitution, the Norman invasion, Magna Carta, government under the Tudors, the causes of the Civil War, and lastly, of course, the nature of the Revolution. Whigs such as James Tyrrell gave one version of these events, Tories such as Robert Brady another.[11] But for Court Whigs, a reading of English history which stressed the time-honoured limits on kingly authority was an embarrass-ment. Their strategem in consequence was to date the achieve-ment of 'liberty' and limited government to the Revolution, while accepting what would traditionally have been seen as a Tory view of earlier events. 'To bring the government of England back to its first principles is to bring the people back to absolute slavery', wrote one of Walpole's journalists.[12] Conversely, the Country

---

[9] Kramnick, *Bolingbroke*, ch. 2.

[10] Kramnick, *Bolingbroke*, ch. 3; Dickinson, *Liberty and Property*, ch. 5.

[11] Kenyon, *Revolution Principles*, ch. 2; Dickinson, *Liberty and Property*, ch. 1, sect. I, ch. 2, sect. I; J. G. A. Pocock, *The Ancient Constitution and the Feudal Law* (Cambridge, 1957), esp. ch. 8.

[12] Cited in Kramnick, *Bolingbroke*, p. 131.

party began to revive ancient constitutionalism. Bolingbroke, their leading spokesman, rediscovered the free government of the Anglo-Saxons, contrasted Elizabeth's limited monarchy with James I's absolutist pretensions, and so forth.[13] In essence, therefore, Court Whigs and Country Tories had exchanged versions of the historical record, with the modification that the Court spokesmen saw a radical departure in constitutional practice occurring in 1688, ushering in the regime of freedom which they themselves were supervising.[14]

With this introduction we can understand why Hume's *History* should have been of such great political significance to him. His aim in writing it, we may assume, was first of all, to strike a blow at traditional Whig and Tory ideologies, by revealing the shakiness of the historical foundations on which they rested;[15] and secondly, to intervene in the debate between Court and Country, by examining the mechanisms which kept the British constitution in balance.[16] The first and larger task was essentially negative: certain historical myths had to be swept away. The second task was more positive, for Hume believed that the emergence of the modern constitution could be traced back through the latter part of the historical record, and so lessons might be extracted from it which could be applied to contemporary politics. Let us begin, then, by glancing briefly at Hume's account of earlier periods of English history, before looking more closely at his understanding of the modern constitution.

It will be seen at once that Hume has no truck with the idea of an ancient constitution, and that in general his version of early history comes closer to traditional 'Tory' than to traditional 'Whig' accounts. He argued that, rather than there being a single constitution which various monarchs had tried to subvert, there had been *several* constitutions before the current settlement.[17] The Anglo-Saxon constitution, though its shape was hard to determine, had been predominantly aristocratic in character; the king was weak, and justice was dispensed rather unevenly by individual

---

[13] Kramnick, *Bolingbroke*, pp. 177-81; Forbes, *Hume's Philosophical Politics* pp. 240-6.

[14] J. G. A. Pocock, 'Machiavelli, Harrington, and English Political Ideologies in the Eighteenth Century' in his *Politics, Language and Time* (London, 1972).

[15] For a statement of this intention, see 'Of the Coalition of Parties', *Essays*, pp. 478-9.

[16] Cf. C. N. Stockton, 'Hume—Historian of the English Constitution', *Eighteenth Century Studies*, iv (1970-1), 277-93; Forbes, *Hume's Philosophical Politics*, ch. 8. For a general assessment, see E. C. Mossner, 'An Apology for David Hume, Historian', *Publications of the Modern Language Association of America*, lvi (1941), 657-90.

[17] *History*, vol. iv, p. 345; 'Of the Coalition of Parties', *Essays*, pp. 482-3.

members of the nobility.[18] The Norman invasion saw the establishment of strong monarchical government, with the barons being to a great extent subordinated to the crown, and the commons being excluded from any share of legislative power.[19] The system was, moreover, largely despotic in nature; the Normans, Hume wrote, were 'incapable of any true or regular liberty; which requires such improvement in knowledge and morals, as can only be the result of reflection and experience, and must grow to perfection during several ages of settled and established government'.[20] Magna Carta marked the change from barbarous monarchy to what I suggested above might be called the barbarous version of limited monarchy. The barons challenged the power of the king, though without reaching any formal constitutional arrangement for sharing authority. Hume was willing to concede that the Charter might be regarded as 'a kind of original contract' to which nobility and people might appeal when resisting extensions of royal power,[21] but his main aim was to show how ill-defined and chaotic the feudal regime was:

The king conducted himself by one set of principles, the barons by another, the commons by a third, the clergy by a fourth. All these systems of government were opposite and incompatible: each of them prevailed in its turn, as incidents were favorable to it: a great prince rendered the monarchical power predominant; the weakness of a king gave reins to the aristocracy; a superstitious age saw the clergy triumphant; the people, for whom chiefly government was instituted, and who chiefly deserve consideration, were the weakest of the whole.[22]

Attempts to find a free and democratic 'ancient constitution' were therefore doomed to fail. It should be recognized instead that the phrase denoted merely whatever arrangements had existed prior to the moment of utterance and that 'the English constitution, like all others, has been in a state of continual fluctuation'.[23] Moreover the various systems of government up to the end of the medieval period were all predominantly barbarous rather than civilized, and so provided no ideals against which present arrangements might be judged.

Hume claimed that his portrait of Tudor government marked a breakthrough in historical research. It was usual for partisans of liberty—first the Whigs and later the Country ideologues—to

---

[18] *History*, vol. i, pp. 152-66.
[19] *History*, vol. i, pp. 449-57.
[20] *History*, vol. i, p. 244.
[21] *History*, vol. ii, p. 4.
[22] *History*, vol. ii, pp. 277-8.
[23] *History*, vol. iv, p. 345.

depict the Tudors, and especially Elizabeth, as model consti-
tutionalists who paid a proper regard to the revived powers of
the House of Commons. Hume overturned this picture, maintaining that 'scarcely any sovereign before Elizabeth, and none
after her, carried higher, both in speculation and practice, the
authority of the crown'.[24] The Commons were supine, confining
their attention to domestic affairs and tolerating the limitations
imposed by the queen on their freedom of speech.[25] The queen
had at her disposal a battery of instruments which, if she had
chosen to deploy them frequently, would have nullified the rule
of law.[26] Yet for all that 'Elizabeth continued to be the most
popular sovereign that ever swayed the sceptre of England;
because the maxims of her reign were conformable to the principles of the times, and to the opinion generally entertained with
regard to the constitution'.[27] This was the crux of Hume's argument. Elizabeth was able to enjoy her extensive powers because
her subjects did not expect or demand any liberties that were
inconsistent with royal authority. At one stroke Hume had
demolished both the idea of the Elizabethan era as a golden age
of popular liberty and the alternative view that Elizabeth's absolutist pretensions involved trampling upon the established
liberties of her subjects.

This analysis of the Tudor period formed the background
against which Hume diagnosed the difficulties confronting the
first two Stuarts. His central theme was that James I and Charles
I claimed no major powers which were not already held by their
predecessors.[28] Why, then, did the Stuarts fail to secure what the
Tudors had secured with ease, and eventually succumb to the
power of parliament? Hume's answer had three parts to it.
Firstly, the Commons began to claim more extensive liberties
than they had enjoyed under the Tudors. This resulted partly
from the ambiguity of the constitution as it existed at the time—so

---

[24] *History*, vol. iv, p. 119.   [25] *History*, vol. iv, pp. 172-5.
[26] *History*, vol. iv, pp. 345-60.   [27] *History*, vol. iv, p. 140.
[28] Hume at first accepted the popular view that the Stuarts had encroached on rights
enjoyed under the Tudors; but his research into the earlier period led him to revise his
interpretation. Compare the account of the Stuarts in 'Of the Parties of Great Britain'
with the accounts given in the *History* and in 'Of the Coalition of Parties'. When he began
his *History*, he thought that 'the most curious, interesting, and instructive Part of our
History' began with James I (*Letters*, vol. i, p. 168), but later he wished that he had
started with Henry VII 'to have shown how absolute the authority was, which the English
kings then possessed, and that the Stuarts did little or nothing more than continue matters
in the former tract, which the people were determined no longer to admit'. (*Letters*, vol. i,
p. 264.)

that the parliamentary party could claim some historical warrant for their demands—and partly from a general shift in political attitudes, connected with a changing distribution of property and the rise of the 'middling rank' (the latter favouring stricter limitations on royal authority[29]). Secondly, James and Charles both proved too weak to maintain the monarchy at the height to which Elizabeth had raised it. Their minor encroachments on popular liberty were ill-judged, and aroused the suspicions of the populace; they were unwilling to take forceful measures to quell opposition; and above all they had neither the military force nor the financial resources to remain independent of parliament— the Commons learnt to use the supply question to extend their authority. Thirdly, neither of these factors would have been sufficient to cause a revolution if religion had not become enmeshed with politics. The dispute between king and parliament could have been resolved if it had been conducted purely in secular terms; but once religious enthusiasm was yoked to the cause of political liberty, civil war became unavoidable.[30]

Hume drew two separate lessons from these events. One was that the system of limited monarchy which developed subsequently in England must be regarded as a historical accident. That was true, in the first place, because the three factors which together led to the downfall of absolute monarchy—an insurgent House of Commons, a weak monarchy, and the spread of religious enthusiasm—might not have occurred simultaneously. On the Continent, the trend ran everywhere in the direction of absolutism;[31] England was a stark exception to a general rule. In the second place, the emergence of limited government could not reasonably have been foreseen by those who opposed the Stuarts. That it was *intended* by the more enlightened of them Hume conceded, but no one could reasonably have believed in advance that the course of opposition which the parliamentarians chose to pursue would issue eventually in such a benign system of government. Hume was therefore even-handed in dispensing praise equally to the partisans of liberty, whose bold actions had such fortunate results, and to the supporters of the established regime whose views 'ought, beforehand, to have appeared more solid, more safe, and more legal'.[32] For both these reasons, his

[29] See above, ch. 6, p. 126.
[30] *History*, vol. iv, pp. 565-8; vol. v, p. 145.
[31] *History*, vol. iv, pp. 393, 453-4.
[32] 'Of the Coalition of Parties', *Essays*, p. 485. see also *History*, vol. iv, pp. 344-5.

account of the emergence of limited government in England stands in sharp contrast to the Whiggish interpretation which views it as the deliberate outcome of the actions of far-sighted men taking a stand against royal absolutism. We should learn to recognize 'the great mixture of accident, which commonly concurs with a small ingredient of wisdom and foresight, in erecting the complicated fabric of the most perfect government'.[33]

Hume's second lesson had to do with the conditions needed to make limited monarchy work successfully. As the power of the Commons increased, and that of the Stuarts declined, there came a point at which a constitutional balance might have been struck. Before the outbreak of the Civil War, Charles had ceased to claim rights, such as the right to raise revenue without parliamentary consent, and the right to assemble and dismiss parliament at will, which were incompatible with free government.[34] Why, then, was no accommodation reached? The reason, as we have already seen, was partly that the wound had 'been poisoned by the infusion of theological hatred',[35] partly that the Commons were no longer prepared to trust Charles as an individual. But beyond these particular facts lay a more general problem for limited monarchy: how could the king retain any effective power without possessing either a fairly extensive prerogative or a standing army? What alternative source of power was available to him? Hume's answer, essential to his general understanding of the British constitution, was that the king must be able to wield influence within parliament, and particularly in the lower House; and that the mechanism which enabled him to do so was patronage.[36] For the mechanism to work, the king must be granted a reasonably generous revenue, and members of the Commons must be prepared to accept office in the king's employment. Under Charles, however, 'every attempt which had been made to gain the popular leaders, and by offices to attach them to the crown, had failed of success, either for want of skill in conducting it, or by reason of the slender preferments which it was then in the king's power to confer'.[37]

This analysis of Hume's clearly had relevance to contemporary politics. But before considering how the lessons of history were to be applied in the present, we should round off the historical narrative. When the crown was restored in 1660, Hume believed,

---

[33] *History*, vol. ii, p. 514.
[34] *History*, vol. v, pp. 148-50.
[35] *History*, vol. v, p. 145.
[36] *History*, vol. v, pp. 539-40.
[37] *History*, vol. v, p. 189.

it was clearly on the understanding that the king would henceforth be subject to parliamentary limitation, even though some aspects of royal authority (for example the king's dispensing power) were not properly defined until the Revolution. On that account his treatment of the later Stuarts was less sympathetic than his treatment of their predecessors, in whose defence it could be said that they had to govern at a time when the constitution was changing and uncertain.[38] (Hume remarked: 'I am sensible, that the History of [the] two first Stuarts will be most agreeable to the Tories: That of the two last, to the Whigs.'[39] James II made two fatal errors, namely attempting to encroach too far on the liberties which the people had come to enjoy, and attacking the established religion. He lacked, in Hume's opinion, just one essential quality: 'a due regard and affection to the religion and constitution of his country'.[40] William's motives in coming to England were laudable, and the Revolution itself was a most fortunate event, not only because it freed the country from an 'exceptionable administration' but because 'by deciding many important questions in favor of liberty, and still more by that great precedent of deposing one king, and establishing a new family, it gave such an ascendant to popular principles, as has put the nature of the English constitution beyond all controversy'.[41] But although the Revolution had this advantage, it had the corresponding disadvantage that the hereditary principle was weakened, and 'how could stability be preserved in any monarchical government ... unless men had so passionate a regard for the true heir of their royal family'?[42] Hume therefore gave a dispassionate account of the arguments offered in 1688 by the Tories (who favoured passing the crown to James's son, appointing a regent meanwhile) and by the Whigs (who maintained that in exceptional circumstances the right of choosing a monarch reverted to the community as a whole).[43] In his general assessment of the case for and against the Protestant succession,[44] he maintained that the arguments, as they might have appeared to someone shortly after the Revolution, were finely balanced. A settlement in the Stuart line would have offered the advantage of preserving hereditary succession, and the disadvantage of pro-

---

[38] *Letters*, vol. i, pp. 217-18.
[39] *Letters*, vol. i, p. 180.
[40] *History*, vol. vi, p. 353.
[41] *History*, vol. vi, p. 363.
[42] 'Of the Protestant Succession', *Essays*, p. 487.
[43] *History*, vol. vi, pp. 359-60.
[44] 'Of the Protestant Succession', *Essays*, pp. 487-98.

ducing a king whose religious sympathies lay with the Roman Catholic Church. The Hanoverian settlement had the advantage of fixing limits to royal authority conclusively, and the disadvantage of installing a king with foreign possessions.

In dealing with the events of 1688, therefore, Hume steered a judicious course between Whig and Tory perspectives. He approved the removal of James, but refused to concede either a general right on the part of the political community to choose its sovereign or an indefeasible right of hereditary succession. What of the general balance of his *History*? It will be seen that on most key points Hume leans towards traditional Tory rather than traditional Whig interpretations. He remarks himself that the political ascendancy of the Whigs 'has proved destructive to the truth of history, and has established many gross falsehoods', citing Rapin Thoyras, Locke, Sidney, and Hoadley as examples of historians of whom this might be said.[45] I believe that this remark expresses Hume's position more accurately than his well-known observation that 'my views of *things* are more conformable to Whig principles; my representations of *persons* to Tory prejudices',[46] which misled Mossner into claiming that Hume's 'Toryism' essentially consisted in his affection for the Stuart family.[47] In fact, on the major topics that we have surveyed—Anglo-Saxon government, the Conquest, Magna Carta, Tudor government and so forth—Hume consistently took the traditional Tory line.

We must bear in mind, however, that at the time at which Hume was writing, traditional modes of interpretation had become confused by the new division between Court and Country. So although Hume's *History* was antagonistic to older Whig views, it was broadly in line with the interpretation favoured by Court Whigs, such as those attached to Walpole. Indeed one of Hume's main purposes was to show that the old division had become irrelevant and should be replaced by a straightforward contest between Court and Country parties—a contest which need not and should not be rooted in conflicting accounts of English history. To understand his strategy, we must pay some

[45] *History*, vol. vi, p. 365.

[46] *Letters*, vol. i, p. 237.

[47] E. C. Mossner, 'Was Hume a Tory Historian? Facts and Reconsiderations', *Journal of the History of Ideas*, ii (1941), 225-36. Mossner analyses changes made by Hume in successive editions of his *History*, counting them as 'Tory' if they indicate sympathy for the Stuarts or antipathy towards the parliamentarians, and 'Whig' in the opposite case. He offers a more judicious, though still incomplete, assessment in 'An Apology for David Hume, Historian'.

attention to his views about party conflict, and about the nature of the division between Whig and Tory in particular.

In his essay 'Of Parties in General' Hume classified parties as personal ('founded on personal friendship') or as real ('founded on some real difference of sentiment or interest'). Real parties might be further divided into parties based on interest (those whose members shared common interests which they hoped to advance politically), parties based on principle (those whose members shared the same political or religious convictions), and parties based on affection (those whose members were attached to a particular person or family challenging for power). Once government in Britain began to assume the form of a limited monarchy, he asserted, a division arose spontaneously between two factions which might naturally be labelled the Court and Country parties.[48] Each was partly a party of interest and partly a party of principle. Because a mixed constitution involved a shifting balance of power between king and parliament, some would stand to gain from extensions of royal power and others to gain from extensions of parliamentary power. Equally, because of differences in personal temperament, some would be inclined to stress obedience to authority in their political ideology, and others to stress the value of freedom, even though all might agree that a balance had to be struck between these values and that a mixed government embodied such a balance. By superimposing these two tendencies we can find the source of the Court/Country division. Although the division is partly one of principle, it is important to notice that it involves no absolute contradiction, but rather concerns the relative emphasis to be laid on each of two values recognized by both parties. For that reason Court and Country parties should normally be able to compromise their differences in practice.

The division between Court and Country might, however, harden into a rigid opposition for one of two reasons. First, an irreconcilable difference of principle might supervene upon existing differences in outlook. This had happened during the period of the Civil War, when religious disagreement—between the established clergy and the nonconformists—had changed Court and Country parties into Cavaliers and Roundheads respectively.[49] Second, if there were any dispute about the suc-

---

[48] *History*, vol. iv, p. 565; 'Of the Parties of Great Britain', *Essays*, pp. 66-7.
[49] 'Of the Parties of Great Britain', *Essays*, pp. 67-8.

cession to the throne, the two parties might become to a degree parties of affection, attached to different persons or families. Again, there would be little chance for compromise once a division of this sort had come into being. Both factors were involved in the formation of Whig and Tory parties. Arising originally from the Court and Country factions under James II,[50] the Whigs acquired a set of speculative principles and later an affection for the house of Hanover, the Tories an opposed set of principles and an affection for the Stuarts. The two sets of principles could be summed up, respectively, in the doctrines of the original contract and of passive obedience. To persuade Whigs and Tories to abandon their historic affiliations and to reform themselves simply into Court and Country parties, Hume had first to expose the absurdity and irrelevance of these doctrines. His campaign had both a philosophical and an historical dimension, as he recognized himself.[51] That was inevitable given that the doctrines in question involved both philosophical claims (concerning the basis of political obligation) and historical claims (concerning the 'ancient constitution', or lack thereof, and so forth). To settle the philosophical issue, Hume offered his own account of allegiance to government, which legitimized resistance in 1688 without opening the door to rebellion as wide as the social contract theory threatened to do, and so was calculated to appeal to moderate men of both parties.[52] The historical dispute was to be resolved by Hume's supposedly non-partisan *History*, which laid to rest the Whig myth of the ancient constitution, while at the same time emphasizing the blessings which flowed from the system of government that was finally consolidated by the Revolution.

If both philosophical and historical baggage could be stripped away, Whigs and Tories would be revealed for what they essentially were: a Tory was 'a lover of monarchy, though without abandoning liberty, and a partisan of the family of Stuart', while a Whig was 'a lover of liberty, though without renouncing monarchy, and a friend to the settlement in the Protestant line'.[53] To convert these factions into true Court and Country parties, it was necessary finally to remove the contrast in affection for the two royal houses. Such affections were in their nature not susceptible

---

[50] *History*, vol. vi, p. 219.
[51] 'Of the Coalition of Parties', *Essays*, p. 479.
[52] See above, ch. 4 *passim*.
[53] 'Of the Parties of Great Britain', *Essays*, p. 70.

to direct rational argument, but Hume thought he might wean the Tories away from their loyalty to the Stuarts by an appeal to their conservatism. Whatever might have been the case shortly after the Revolution—and we have seen that Hume thought the Stuart and Hanoverian cases quite evenly balanced at that time— the Hanoverians had now been in power for more than half a century; they had acquired a title to govern which was so strong that to dispute it would be to risk plunging the nation back into the horrors of a civil war.[54]

If Hume's campaign were to be fully successful, only Court and Country parties would remain. These were inevitable in a free government, and their flourishing was indeed a sign of constitutional health. When Hume advocated 'The Coalition of Parties' he meant only that party differences of the kind discussed above should disappear.

> The only dangerous parties are such as entertain opposite views with regard to the essentials of government, the succession of the crown, or the more consider-able privileges belonging to the several members of the constitution; where there is no room for any compromise or accommodation, and where the controversy may appear so momentous as to justify even an opposition by arms to the pretensions of antagonists.[55]

Yet his attitude towards parties even of the safe variety remained ambivalent. They helped to preserve the free constitution (since they were watchful that neither crown nor parliament should encroach on the other's rights), but at the same time they engendered factional strife and encouraged shameless self-seeking under the guise of party principle. Hume wrote to Montesquieu that, in preferring complex to simple forms of government, the latter had overlooked their disadvantage, namely that they were liable to be deranged by 'le contraste et l'opposition des parties'.[56] When discussing practical political affairs, Hume always urged Court and Country to moderate their arguments. For instance, they should not attack and defend ministers as though these individuals were wholly responsible for the destruction or salvation of the constitution.

> Would men be moderate and consistent, their claims might be admitted; at least might be examined. The *country party* might still assert, that our constitution, though excellent, will admit of maladministration to a certain degree; and there-

---

[54] 'Of the Coalition of Parties', *Essays*, p. 486; 'Of the Protestant Succession', *Essays*, pp. 497-8.
[55] 'Of the Coalition of Parties', *Essays*, p. 478.
[56] *Letters*, vol. i, p. 138.

fore, if the minister be bad, it is proper to oppose him with a *suitable* degree of zeal. And, on the other hand, the *court party* may be allowed, upon the supposition that the minister were good, to defend, and with *some* zeal too, his administration. I would only persuade men not to contend, as if they were fighting *pro aris et focis,* and change a good constitution into a bad one, by the violence of their factions.[57]

In the last resort Hume was prepared to accept parties; his ideal commonwealth contains an official opposition whose job it is to scrutinize and criticize the government's policies;[58] but he does so reluctantly, and with a strong sense of the evils that necessarily accompany them.[59]

If we turn now to examine where Hume stood in the contemporary ideological debate between Court and Country, we find that he cannot consistently be placed in either camp: some of his views seem to reflect Court attitudes, others Country attitudes. He was, of course, self-consciously a man without party, and so was not obliged to force his opinions into one or other of the conventional moulds. On the general question of whether the monarchy or parliament was gaining in strength to the detriment of the balanced constitution, Hume expressed himself very cautiously. The monarch's wealth was indeed such as to give him considerable political influence; the fact that the total amount of property in the hands of commoners was greater did not change things because, *pace* Harrington, 'much less property in a single hand will be able to counterbalance a greater property in several'.[60] On the other hand the king was constrained by the fact that he had to exercise his power within the limits of the law; and his position was weakened by a general loss of respect for established authority, so that he had to rely increasingly on 'private interest and influence' to gain his ends. Hume's summing up is judicious in the extreme:

Unless there happen some extraordinary convulsion, the power of the crown, by means of its large revenue, is rather upon the increase; though at the same time, I own that its progress seems very slow, and almost insensible. The tide has run long, and with some rapidity, to the side of popular government, and is just beginning to turn towards monarchy.[61]

[57] 'That Politics may be reduced to a Science', *Essays*, pp. 26-7.
[58] 'Idea of a Perfect Commonwealth', *Essays*, p. 505.
[59] Compare the general survey of attitudes towards party in C. Robbins, ' "Discordant Parties": A Study of the Acceptance of Party by Englishmen', *Political Science Quarterly*, lxxiii (1958), 505-29.
[60] 'Whether the British Government Inclines More to Absolute Monarchy or to a Republic', *Essays*, p. 49.
[61] Ibid., p. 52.

It is difficult to believe that ideologues of either party could have derived much support from such a deliverance.[62]

On the more specific issue of royal patronage, Hume's views were close to those of the Court writers around Walpole. We have already observed how important a role he gave to patronage in maintaining the balance between king and Commons; all the Stuart kings faced difficulties because they lacked the resources to offer positions and employments to members of parliament, or because those members were unwilling to accept the offers made. On the other hand:

> In our present constitution, many accidents which have rendered governments every where, as well as in Great Britain, much more burdensome than formerly, have thrown into the hands of the crown the disposal of a large revenue, and have enabled the king, by the private interest and ambition of the members, to restrain the public interest and ambition of the body. While the opposition (for we must still have an opposition, open or disguised,) endeavors to draw every branch of administration under the cognizance of parliament, the courtiers reserve a part to the disposal of the crown; and the royal prerogative, though deprived of its ancient powers, still maintains a due weight in the balance of the constitution.[63]

Since patronage was the only resource available to the king to prevent the Commons from engrossing his powers entirely, the argument should not be about whether patronage as such was desirable, but about its proper extent.[64] Unfortunately this issue could not be settled in general terms, for much depended on the character and standing of a particular king or minister—a popular monarch would have less need of patronage, and so forth.[65] Hume's aim was once again to induce Court and Country spokesmen to moderate the terms of their argument, but he was in this case particularly insistent that the Country party should cease ranting about 'corruption' and 'dependence' when what they were referring to was really the secret cement of the constitution.

On standing armies, however, Hume lined up on the Country side. Under James I 'the public was entirely free from the danger and expense of a standing army', while the militia was well-

---

[62] Notwithstanding the fact that the essay in question was reprinted in the *Craftsman*, an organ of Country opinion. For discussion, see Forbes, *Hume's Philosophical Politics*, p. 211.

[63] *History*, vol. v, p. 540.

[64] Hume distinguished between 'pensions and bribes' which were always to be condemned, and the disposal of 'places, honours and preferments' which was acceptable for the reason given. See *History*, vol. vi, pp. 203-4; 'Of the Independency of Parliament', *Essays*, p. 46, fn. 1.

[65] 'Of the Independency of Parliament', *Essays*, pp. 44-7.

organized and adequate for the defence of the realm.[66] The events of his successor's reign illustrated 'the danger of mercenary armies',[67] and a measure declaring them illegal under Charles II was 'necessary for the full security of liberty and a limited constitution'.[68] Hume was therefore displeased at the sizeable standing army maintained during his lifetime, claiming that 'it is evident that this is a mortal distemper in the British government, of which it must at last inevitably perish'.[69] His ideal commonwealth has a militia modelled on that of Switzerland, without which 'it is vain to think that any free government will ever have security or stability'.[70]

His opinions about the proper extent of royal prerogative are harder to pin down. We have already examined his general attitude towards prerogative in a free government: although authority should as far as possible be exercised in accordance with the rule of law, some discretionary power must remain to deal with emergencies of various sorts. By the constitutional changes which had been introduced in Britain since the accession of the Stuarts, 'the liberty and independence of individuals has been rendered much more full, entire and secure; that of the public more uncertain and precarious'.[71] To consider some particular cases, Hume welcomed the restrictions placed on the king's prerogative in summoning and dismissing parliaments[72] and he also applauded the abolition of his dispensing power (i.e. his power to exempt particular individuals from the operation of a law), which was 'a branch of prerogative incompatible with all legal liberty and limitations'.[73] He was more guarded about the right of arbitrary imprisonment. A law prohibiting such imprisonment was in general a valuable adjunct of a mixed monarchy, but it had the disadvantage that in times of unrest the executive's hands were tied. If parliamentary agreement was necessary to confer special powers on the government, what if parliament itself should be the source of the disorder?[74] So although Habeas Corpus increased the freedom of the subject, it was

---

[66] *History*, vol. iv, p. 512.
[67] *History*, vol. v, p. 382.
[68] *History*, vol. vi, p. 204.
[69] 'Idea of a Perfect Commonwealth', *Essays*, p. 513.
[70] Ibid., pp. 506, 511.
[71] *History*, vol. iv, p. 500.
[72] *History*, vol. v, pp. 149-50.
[73] *History*, vol. vi, p. 310.
[74] *History*, vol. v, p. 39.

difficult to reconcile with 'the full security and the regular police of a state, especially the police of great cities'.[75] (The significance of the final clause will be apparent shortly.) Hume also endorsed the use of royal prerogative in certain special cases. Charles II assumed discretionary powers to control the rebuilding of London after the Great Fire, and this, though strictly illegal, brought 'great advantages' to the city.[76] A contemporary example was the pressing of seamen, where the crown exercised a power uncontrolled by law, which was actually preferable to having a similar power conferred by parliamentary authority.[77] These must be the sort of cases Hume has in mind when he suggests in general 'that ... many inconveniencies must necessarily result from the abolishing of all discretionary power in every magistrate; and that the laws, were they ever so carefully framed and digested, could not possibly provide against every contingency', although he adds that the extent of the discretionary power needed will depend on the 'accuracy and refinement' of the laws in question.[78]

On the question of prerogative, therefore, Hume steered a judicious mid-course between enthusiastic support and outright condemnation. Prerogative must always exist, but in a limited monarchy its exercise should be confined to cases of urgent public necessity—such as national disasters—and cases where public security is endangered. This reminds us of his general theme, that liberty, 'the perfection of civil society', must ultimately be subordinated to authority, its necessary condition of existence. In terms of contemporary debate, it shows Hume searching for a middle ground between the defenders and the opponents of royal authority. Indeed, to review his position in relation to Court and Country ideologies on the four issues so far discussed, we find that on the general balance of the constitution and on royal prerogative he took a 'moderate' position between the two camps; on patronage he leant towards the Court position; and on standing armies he sided with the Country ideologues. A more carefully balanced standpoint it would be hard to imagine! As to the affiliation of his social thought, it will be seen that its broad outlines coincide with those of Court ideology, in so far as Hume generally welcomes luxury and commerce, has no inclination to exclude moneyed men from political power, and so forth. Into the

[75] *History*, vol. vi, p. 204.
[76] *History*, vol. vi, pp. 50-1.
[77] 'Of Some Remarkable Customs', *Essays*, pp. 378-80.
[78] *History*, vol. iv, p. 418.

other scale, however, must be thrown his attitude towards the national debt. Hume's obsessive concern with increases in the debt makes him read at times like a Country propagandist, and in this context, of course, he reveals that his general sympathy for the commercial revolution does not extend to a hypothetical social state where the stockholders have taken charge.[79]

Having observed Hume's delicate balancing act—designed, we have seen, to further soften conflict between the two parties— what should be said in general about his view of the British political system? He seems to have been impressed above all by the *peculiarity* and the *fragility* of the system. Its peculiarity could only be brought out historically, be seeing that it had arisen, largely by accident, from a combination of factors not likely to be found together again. Its fragility was mainly attributable to the fact that it rested on an irregular and informal balance between parliament and executive. It is worth cataloguing the various possible ways in which, according to Hume, the system might collapse, even making allowance for a certain amount of rhetorical exaggeration on his part. It might be torn apart by conflict between the parties which it necessarily engendered,[80] it might drift into absolute monarchy because of increases in the financial power of the crown;[81] it might, on the other hand, turn into a republic if members of parliament were to begin receiving in- structions from their constituents;[82] it might (indeed it 'must inevitably') be destroyed by the continued presence of a standing army;[83] it might, finally, be crippled by a mounting public debt.[84] In short, its chances of longevity were slim, and they could only be improved by politicians coming to a better under- standing of the mechanisms which kept the system in balance. Hume's attitude to the death of the constitution was not simple, but I think it can best be summed up as follows: considered in the abstract, limited monarchy on the British model is slightly but not vastly superior to absolute monarchy, and much on a par with republican government in its modern form. But the trans- ition to either of these forms, involving changes in deeply-rooted habits of allegiance, would be extremely painful, and for that

[79] See above, ch. 6, pp. 137-8.
[80] 'Of Parties in General', *Essays*, p. 55.
[81] 'Whether the British Government Inclines More to Absolute Monarchy or to a Republic', *Essays*, pp. 52-3.
[82] 'Of the First Principles of Government', *Essays*, pp. 32-3.
[83] 'Idea of a Perfect Commonwealth', *Essays*, p. 513.
[84] 'Of Civil Liberty', *Essays*, pp. 96-7.

reason alone the constitution is eminently worth defending. So despite his pessimism, he would do his best to see that the system survived.

In this light we can understand Hume's angry reaction to the radical movement of the 1760s and 1770s, a reaction which cannot merely be attributed to the crustiness of an elderly man. His ire was aroused particularly by the series of events sparked off by the trial of John Wilkes for libel, following a newspaper article critical of George III's government, and the subsequent attempts by the House of Commons to prevent Wilkes taking his seat in parliament. These episodes were accompanied by popular demonstrations and riots, often of a violent nature, in support of Wilkes, and later by a series of petitions to the King from electors up and down the country, listing a large number of grievances including the treatment handed out to Wilkes.[85]

The Wilkes affair brought three issues in particular into the political arena: the extent of press freedom, the role (if any) of extra-parliamentary political activity, and the relationship between members of parliament and their electors. In each instance Hume responded unhesitatingly and passionately in favour of the political establishment. He radically revised the essay 'Of the Liberty of the Press' for the edition of 1770, removing a long conclusion favourable to press freedom and inserting instead the abrupt observation that the 'unbounded liberty of the press' was an evil attending mixed government. The thought behind this observation was revealed in a letter to Turgot written after the riots of 1768:

Here is a People thrown into Disorders (not dangerous ones, I hope) merely from the Abuse of Liberty, chiefly the Liberty of the Press; without any Grievance, I do not only say, real, but even imaginary; and without any of them being able to tell one Circumstance of Government which they wish to have corrected.[86]

As to the extra-parliamentary opposition, Hume could only see them as the 'mob' which through its 'madness' threatened to undermine the established institutions of government. 'Our Government has become an absolute Chimera', he wrote;[87] and later, 'there must necessarily be a Struggle between the Mob and the Constitution'.[88] Popular leaders employed 'Lyes, Calumnies, Imposture, and every infamous Art' to influence their followers.[89] Hume advocated a vigorous policy of repression, including the impeachment of the Mayor and Sheriffs of London and the

---

[85] For a general account, see G. F. E. Rude, *Wilkes and Liberty* (Oxford, 1962), *passim*.

[86] *Letters*, vol. ii, p. 180.   [87] *Letters*, vol. ii, p. 210.

[88] *Letters*, vol. ii, p. 218.   [89] *Letters*, vol. ii, p. 216.

suspension of habeas corpus.[90] More flamboyantly (though perhaps less seriously) he hoped that 'some hundreds of Patriots will make their Exit at Tyburn, and improve English Eloquence by the dying Speeches'.[91] As for the campaign of petitions, Hume made his opinion clear in a letter to his publisher William Strahan:

Tho' I have renounced the World, I cannot forbear being rouzd with Indignation at the Audaciousness, Impudence, and Wickedness of your City Address. To punish it as it deserves woud certainly produce a Fray; but what signifies a Fray, in comparison of losing all Authority to Government.[92]

Although these remarks contain their share of rhetorical exaggeration, it is clear that Hume saw a real threat to the balance of the British constitution in the events surrounding the Wilkes affair. That balance was essentially held between two sections— the Crown and Parliament—of a small group of politically active men. The events in question pushed a much larger fraction of the population on to the political stage. In the process, Hume feared, the authority of government would be challenged, and the preponderance of liberty in the constitution, already excessive, would become intolerable. 'So much Liberty is incompatible with human Society: And it will be happy, if we can escape from it, without falling into a military Government, such as Algiers or Tunis.'[93] Reflecting on the whole affair in retrospect, Hume listed the powers of government that had been forfeited:

The right of displacing the Judges was given up; General Warrants are lost; the right of Expulsion the same; all the co-ercive Powers of the House of Commons abandon'd; all Laws against Libels annihilated; the Authority of Government impair'd by the Impunity granted to the Insolence of Beckford, Crosby, and the Common Council; the revenue of the civil List diminished. For God's sake, is there never to be a stop put to this inundation of the Rabble?[94]

The Wilkes affair represented a new departure in politics for Hume. His beliefs about government were formed on the underlying assumption that politics was an activity properly confined to a fairly select social group; in that sense his political thought was informed by an aristocratic ideology as much as was his social thought. This assumption was revealed in his consistent hostility

---

[90] *Letters*, vol. ii, p. 218.
[91] *Letters*, vol. ii, p. 210.
[92] *Letters*, vol. ii, pp. 217-8.
[93] *Letters*, vol. ii, p. 210.
[94] *Letters*, vol. ii, pp. 244-5.

to democratic forms of government,[95] but it was not brought to bear on contemporary politics until a popular movement forced Hume to express himself bluntly. Had he lived at a time when the major debates were not about the proper balance between executive and legislative within the governing elite, but about the relationship between government and the people as a whole, the aristocratic cast of his thought would have appeared in a much more striking light. His reactions to the Wilkes affair are thus a valuable indication of how he might have responded to the more explicit radicalism of the period of the French Revolution. If Hume's political attitudes seem urbane when compared to the more strident conservatism of Burke, for instance, that has more to do with the contingencies of his time than with differences in underlying ideology. This theme will be taken up again in the concluding chapter when I consider Hume's relationship to the conservative tradition as a whole.

[95] See above, ch. 7, pp. 151-3.

CONCLUSION

Conclusion

I said in my introduction that the fascination of Hume's political thought lies in seeing how a revolutionary philosophy is married to an establishment ideology to yield what is probably the best example we have of a secular and sceptical conservative political theory. The two contributory elements—the philosophy and the ideology—have now been disentangled, but it remains to look explicitly at how each contributes to Hume's over-all standpoint. At the same time we must see in what sense Hume can be described as a conservative, and assess his place in relation to the conservative tradition as a whole. I have already hinted that labels like 'liberal' and 'conservative' may be inappropriate when applied to an eighteenth-century thinker, and that suggestion will be borne out by looking at how the French Revolution—a novel phenomenon in European history—changed the terms of political debate and gave rise to political traditions such as liberalism and conservatism in the form that we now recognize. Hume might therefore be described as a conservative before his time—except, paradoxically, that his version of conservatism could not have served as an adequate response to the dramatic events of 1789.

It may now be helpful to summarize the philosophical and ideological elements in Hume's political thought. I have explored the connections between Hume's epistemology, his moral theory, and his social and political thought through an examination of his account of judgement. In contradistinction both to traditional rationalism and to traditional empiricism, Hume argued that important classes of judgement—including judgements about causation and about the external world—could be grounded neither in reason nor in sense-experience, but derived rather from the natural workings of the imagination. These judgements could therefore be 'justified' only in the weak sense of showing that human beings could not help but make them, and equally the possibilities for correcting and improving judgement were confined within the bounds set by the imagination. I have labelled this basic epistemological position 'mitigated scepticism'. In turning to his moral theory, we discovered both novelty and continuity of argument. Again in contrast to traditional rationalism and empiricism, Hume insisted that moral judgement necessarily involved an element of feeling. He invoked the mechanism of sympathy to explain how human beings could respond to the beneficial and injurious character-traits of their fellows. But besides taking up this anti-cognitivist stance—famously summarized in his doctrines that reason is the slave of the passions and that no proposition containing an 'ought' could be deduced from a set of propositions each of which contains only an 'is'— Hume emphasized the part played by the imagination in directing both passions and moral sentiments. Indeed moral judgement was only possible on condition that the person making the judgement conceived its target in the appropriately general way. Given that men tended to share the same basic moral responses—that was true except of those whose feelings had been completely distorted by superstition or enthusiasm—differences in judgement depended upon the better or worse functioning of the imagination. As in the case of empirical judgement, a distinction could be drawn between the 'wise' and the 'vulgar', even though neither could judge on the basis of reason or observation alone.

The political implications of these doctrines emerge when Hume applies them to judgements about justice and allegiance to government. These are of course species of moral judgement, but their targets have the distinctive property of being 'artificial virtues'. Hume argues that there is no natural motive for respecting property rights or obeying those in authority, and so nothing at which a moral feeling could originally have been directed. Instead the virtues of justice and allegiance arise artificially, as a result of conventions established by men to allow themselves to pursue their interests more adequately. But although the existence of rules of justice can in this way be traced to the pressures of self-interest, the particular rules that are chosen depend on the workings of the imagination, which allows men to agree on a natural assignment of property rights. Equally, when explaining why an authority is necessary to enforce respect for property rights, Hume points to the weakness of the imagination which makes us prefer a smaller present gain to a greater future gain. Once the decision to establish government has been made, however—for reasons of self-interest—the imagination provides us with rules for assigning authority to particular persons, which partly parallel the rules of justice. Both in the case of justice and in the case of allegiance to government, therefore, the imagination enables large numbers of men to co-ordinate their behaviour without explicit agreement by prompting them to adopt the same conventions concerning property and authority.

The chain of argument I have sketched is philosophical, in the sense that it refers to the status and character of various kinds of human belief; yet it establishes the terms on which Hume's thinking about politics is conducted. How is this so? First, it sets limits to the kind of argument that can be produced in politics. It excludes the possibility of advancing normative claims that are either rationally self-evident or capable of empirical demonstration. In this respect Hume's position necessarily differs both from a traditional natural law standpoint and from utilitarianism. According to the theory of natural law, certain politically relevant principles could be known to be true. If we consider Locke as a representative of this position, he thought it demonstrable that men had a natural right of property to those things that they had transformed by their labour, and also had a natural obligation to obey any government to which they had consented and which acted within the boundaries set by natural law. Since these propositions were provable, anyone who disagreed with them could be shown with certainty to be in error. Political argument could start from certain fixed assumptions, or, putting the same point in material terms, every legitimate political system had to meet certain definite requirements. To use Locke as an example again, any government which taxed property without obtaining the consent of the property-owners was *ipso facto* illegitimate. Now, of course, this still left a good deal open to conventional resolution—Locke did not claim, for instance, that one specific form of government was required by natural law. But Hume swept away the fixed assumptions altogether. Nothing in politics could be demonstrated in the sense of being derived deductively from self-evident premisses. If political arrangements were not wholly arbitrary, the reason was that men as a matter of fact imagined and felt in similar ways. Even here qualification was needed, since there were men whose feelings and understanding were distorted beyond the reach of argument. If confronted with such a person— a 'gloomy, hair-brained enthusiast' for example—Hume would simply have accepted that no arguments could be offered to persuade him to change his opinions. As for those beliefs shared by all men in normal circumstances, they abounded with contradictions and absurdities which could not be removed by offering a rational alternative. Hume had removed the argumentative bedrock provided by natural law.[1]

[1] The conclusions Hume reached—for instance, the rules of property that he endorsed— were not necessarily at odds with those reached by the natural lawyers. Hume acknow-

The utilitarian approach to politics is of course rather different. Once the single principle of utility has been accepted as the supreme normative standard, all political questions become empirical. Does this or that rule of property promote the general happiness more effectively? Is this or that form of government more beneficial to its subjects? Assuming with the utilitarians that 'happiness' is an empirically identifiable state, these questions can in principle be answered by producing factual evidence. How does Hume's position differ from this? He does not, to begin with, accept the principle of utility as a supreme normative standard. In his account of moral judgement, the contribution of personal qualities to the general welfare is given some weight, but it is not regarded as the sole criterion of merit.[2] Nor did Hume think that compelling reasons could be offered for making it the criterion. It was not, for instance, irrational that we should praise actions more highly when their beneficial results fell on those connected to us by ties of kinship or acquaintance. This was a feature of natural judgement which reason alone could not alter. Second, Hume could not have accepted the calculative approach to action which seems a necessary component of any utilitarian theory worthy of the name.[3] Whether this takes the form of saying that men should always act so as to produce the greatest happiness possible, or of saying that rules should be adopted whose general observance would create the most happiness, utilitarians assume a model of man as a creature capable of altering his behaviour according to a calculation of relative advantage. Hume rejected this assumption for reasons that were partly epistemological and partly ideological. On the one hand, he suggested that certain

---

ledged this when, in a gesture of reconciliation, he said that his rules of justice might be described as laws of nature. The fact remains that his mode of deriving these rules, and the underlying epistemology that it implies, is far removed from theirs.

[2] This point was recognized by Bentham. Although maintaining that 'I felt as if scales had fallen from my eyes' when reading the third book of the *Treatise*, where 'the foundations of all *virtue* are laid in *utility*', he later berated Hume for inconsistency, in following the principle of utility on some occasions and 'the IPSE DIXIT principle, under the name of the moral sense' on others (the latter was Bentham's term of ridicule for non-utilitarian standards). I owe this observation to D. G. Long, 'Bentham on Property' in A. Parel and T. Flanagan (eds.), *Theories of Property: Aristotle to the Present* (Waterloo, Ontario, 1979).

[3] I am excluding here degenerate versions of utilitarianism which maintain that the socially best policy is for everyone to follow the rules and practices which he is now accustomed to follow, on the grounds that, although some other set might in theory be more productive of happiness, the cost of change would in every case outweigh the benefit received. Utilitarians admittedly always face the problem of deciding what to propose for a population who are not themselves utilitarian in moral outlook; but this version amounts to complete capitulation.

modes of behaviour—for instance certain ways of allocating property—were prompted by associations that formed naturally in the mind, rather than by any sort of means-end calculation. So, for example, a decision to allow the first possessor of a piece of property to retain it would appear just, without it being shown that this decision promoted some further end; moreover Hume saw nothing reprehensible in such a judgement. On the other hand, he stressed the value of habitual behaviour to creatures who were liable to be deflected from the rules of justice and allegiance by private or group interest. This provided a positive reason for not attempting to alter conventional rules on the grounds that some other set might, if accepted, be more productive of utility.

Hume's mitigated scepticism therefore led him to approach political questions in a different spirit from natural law thinkers, for whom political argument could begin from certain rationally demonstrable principles, and from utilitarians, for whom political arguments could in principle be resolved empirically. Instead political theory had to accept human judgement at face value, as non-rational and corrigible only to a small degree. A position of this kind must in a diffuse sense be conservative, not because it is yet committed to any particular set of institutions or social arrangements, but because it must remain closely tied to conventionally-accepted judgements. We do not so far have an argument for a graded society or for a monarchical government, but we do have an argument for accepting those arrangements if they can be shown to correspond to men's natural sentiments. Notice that Hume, besides ruling out most familiar arguments for radical change, is also ruling out arguments designed to show that the existing order is preferable to any other on rational grounds. So conservatism of this sort, besides being anathematic to radicals, is also likely to be looked on with suspicion by those who prefer a stronger defence of the status quo. Johnson called Hume 'a Tory by chance' and, although in Johnson's case this had particular reference to Hume's religious views, the general sentiment— that Hume is on the right side, but not for quite the right reasons— is likely to be shared by conservatives of a more orthodox kind.

Having traced the main connections between Hume's philosophy and his political ideas, let me now run over his main ideological commitments in equally summary fashion. We began with his conception of human nature, about which he held a view midway between the pessimism of, say, Hobbes, and the optimism of, say, Rousseau or Godwin. Men were on the whole neither egoists nor altruists, but tended to be partially benevolent—benevolent towards those in their immediate social vicinity. They were sociable creatures, lovers of company and conversation, but at the same time jealous of their reputation and social standing. For this reason, rather than from any innate desire for consumption, they tried to increase their private stock of wealth and commodities, and had to be restrained within the bounds of justice by various forces, including custom, love of reputation, and political artifice (but significantly excluding religion). These forces were strong but not irresistible, and a return to the state of nature remained a permanent possibility, a reminder of the bleaker side of Hume's account of the human condition.

As a social theorist, Hume reveals a sharp awareness of social change, but at the same time a firm predilection for civilized, commercial societies. This is grounded less on the greater material wealth of these societies than on the refinement of human character that they encourage, and on their potential military strength— so Hume inverts the arguments of those republicans who defended simple agricultural societies on the grounds that they fostered virtue and military prowess. Hume was also a modernizer in his economic views: he believed that wages, prices, manufacturing, and trade should all be left to the working of the market, that taxes should be imposed with caution and moderation, and that public borrowing should be discouraged. But although in these respects his views appear to foreshadow the *laissez-faire* ideology of nineteenth-century liberals, they must be taken in conjunction with his commitment to a social hierarchy with landowners standing at its head. Hume regarded social ranking as natural, and had no complaint about the inequality of opportunity that resulted from men being born into different stations. On the contrary a degree of social deference helped to stabilize the political system, where the aristocracy had the dual function of supporting and checking the central authority. So his approval of commerce and economic freedom was conditional on its being compatible with the preservation of social order.

Hume's political preferences were expressed with characteristic caution, but he was at least firmly committed to the existence of 'regular' government—that is, government conducted according to a general and uniform set of laws. Regular governments might be monarchical or 'free', and, unlike many of his contemporaries, he saw no overwhelming reasons for preferring the latter class, of which Britain was the most conspicuous member. Governments of this kind depended on the aristocracy retaining their leading role, and must avoid democratic degeneration. In general they offered both the benefits and the dangers of freedom, and their success depended on being able to preserve freedom while still retaining authority over their subjects. Since the choice between absolute monarchies and free governments was fairly narrow, continuity of regime became the overriding concern—so Hume defended the mixed constitution in Britain less because it was intrinsically preferable to the alternatives than because it was the established constitution which commanded the allegiance of the people.

To defend the constitution Hume tried to destroy certain myths which surrounded it—the myth of the ancient constitution, the myth of the contract enforced in 1688, and so forth. The free constitution was a modern achievement, fostered by a House of Commons that encroached upon the extensive authority enjoyed by the Tudor monarchy, and finally established by the settlement made with William and Mary. The hidden secret of the constitution was the patronage network which gave the crown sufficient influence over parliament to prevent deadlock between the two bodies. The balance was a delicate one, and men were naturally inclined to throw their weight on one side or the other—hence the emergence of Court and Country parties. Hume's polemical aim was to prevent this unavoidable party contest from deranging the machinery of government. He stood aside from the contest itself, and his views on contemporary issues did not fit the stereotyped pattern characteristic of either party.

I have described Hume's set of beliefs as an establishment ideology, and that description is intended to draw attention to two of its complementary features. First, from a social point of view, Hume's thought reflected the outlook of the eighteenth-century aristocracy both in its assumptions about human behaviour and in its general vision of society. It is important to realize that the members of this order were not benighted reactionaries, but men who were on the whole favourably disposed towards economic progress, cultural refinement, and learning. To understand the progressive aspects of Hume's thought, it is not necessary to conjure up a rising bourgeoisie whose ideas he might have adopted, but enough merely to grasp the open and progressive nature of the aristocracy itself. Of course this outlook was premised on the assumption that economic progress did not threaten the privileged position of the landowners; when such a threat appeared, as seemed to happen with the rise of the stock-jobbers, prominent in the demonology of the early eighteenth century, Hume closed ranks with the rest of the establishment.

Second, from a political point of view, Hume defended the apparatus of government established in 1688 and the men who controlled it, though not of course either of the warring factions into which they tended to divide. He pictured himself as the true friend of the constitution, and since this was largely the preserve of the great landowning families, the social and political aspects of his ideology complemented each other. He thought that the constitution could be made more secure by stripping away the historical myths that encrusted it and by a realistic appraisal of its workings. In both respects he may have underestimated the extent to which a mythical veiling was necessary: his defence was too low-key for a partisan audience. But his commitment to the political establishment was clear enough.

If we ask whether this establishment ideology should be characterized as predominantly liberal or conservative in nature, we face the difficulty that we are trying to apply nineteenth-century labels (the terms themselves did not come into use until the early part of that century) to an eighteenth-century context. This is not simply a matter of historical niceties. For the contrast between liberal and conservative ideology to make sense, there has to be a perceived incompatibility between liberal demands for personal freedom, the rule of law, careers open to talents, etc., and conservative commitments to institutional continuity, authority, social hierarchy, and so forth. In eighteenth-century Britain no such incompatibility was obvious; the prevailing system largely embodied both sets of features. It was the Revolution in France that forced people to reveal their ultimate commitments. Either one was for the Revolution—in which case liberty and equality came before social order and institutional continuity— or one was against, in which case what could now be identified as conservative values came uppermost. We can say simply that to be liberal was to believe in the values of the French Revolution (or at least those manifested in its earlier stages) even in cases where the pursuit of those values might threaten social stability; whereas to be conservative was to believe in the preservation (or restoration, as the case might be) of the *ancien régime*, embodying social hierarchy, the traditional authority of the king and the church, and so forth. Conservatives now attempted consciously to arrest change, believing that even gradual change might erode an order that could no longer be taken for granted; the complacency of the eighteenth century was shattered.[4] Liberals, on the other hand, became radicals, believing that their demands could not be met without overthrowing (albeit peacefully) the old social system.

When we speak of conservatism and liberalism, therefore, we think of ideologies developed in opposition to one another in response to the French Revolution. If we try to interpret Hume's political thought using these as points of reference, we find that it contains elements that appear to be liberal and others that appear to be conservative. The point can be illustrated crudely through a series of contrasts. For instance:

(a) He believed that men would follow rules of justice without coercion (a 'liberal' view); *but* he also believed that they did so largely as a result of custom and other conventional factors (a 'conservative' view).

(b) He believed in economic freedom and the growth of commerce (a 'liberal' view); *but* he also believed in the preservation of social hierarchy (a 'conservative' view).

(c) He believed in political freedom and the rule of law (a 'liberal' view); *but* he also believed in encouraging deference to established authority (a 'conservative' view).

(d) He believed that the freedoms enjoyed uniquely in Britain were desirable (a 'liberal' view); *but* he also believed that the British system was for that reason inherently unstable (a 'conservative' view).

Summing this up, Hume believed that those things which liberals characteristically value are indeed valuable, *provided* that those things which conservatives characteristically value can be securely enjoyed at the same time. Putting the point in that way may suggest that Hume must ultimately side with the conservatives: liberty is the jam, security the bread. Or to cite again his attack on the Whig historians:

Forgetting that a regard to liberty, though a laudable passion, ought commonly to be subordinate to a reverence for established government, the prevailing faction has celebrated only the partisans of the former, who pursued as their object the perfection of civil society, and has extolled them at the expense of their antagonists, who maintained those maxims that are essential to its very existence.[5]

---

[4] For some perceptive remarks about the specific character of conservatism, see K. Mannheim, 'Conservative Thought' in *Essays on Sociology and Social Psychology* (London, 1953), pp. 74-164.

[5] *History*, vol. vi, pp. 365-6.

But to say that liberty must ultimately yield to security is not to say much unless one believes that such values are genuinely likely to conflict. In the mid-eighteenth century it seemed possible to avoid making the choice. The conservative elements in Hume's thought appear much more in what he takes as given than in what he finds it necessary to defend explicitly. He does not need to argue for social hierarchy or continuity in government, since their existence could be taken for granted (we must often discover his attitudes by examining his reactions to past events when these values *were* threatened). Thus it is too simple (though tempting) to say that he was a fair-weather liberal whose real commitments were conservative. What one may properly say is that Hume had ideological commitments which, had they been passed through the prism of an event such as the French Revolution, would have turned him into a genuine conservative.

We may delve a little further here with the aid of a three-sided comparison between Hume, Adam Smith, and Edmund Burke. The simple view of these men is that Smith was a liberal, Burke a conservative, and Hume some mixture of the two. I shall suggest that this appearance is largely accidental, and that all three agreed closely in matters of basic ideology. Notice first that they shared to a great extent the same formative political experience— Hume lived from 1711 to 1776, Smith from 1723 to 1790, Burke from 1729 to 1797—with the single important difference that Burke lived to feel the full force of the French Revolution, which of course provoked his most celebrated book (Smith's more muted response will be noted below). The three men moved in overlapping circles, and were personally acquainted with each other. Moreover each at some time expressed admiration for the others' work. The substantial similarities in outlook which deserve our attention can be considered under three headings: a belief in economic freedom, a belief in social hierarchy, and a commitment to the political establishment of eighteenth-century Britain. The combination of these three elements produced that distinctive ideology whose relation to later patterns of thought I have been trying to clarify.

To take the belief in economic freedom first: all three men accepted the notion of a self-regulating market through which the interests of producer and consumer were naturally harmonized, and the consequent general presumption against state interference with production, trade, wage and price levels, and so forth. There is no need to document Adam Smith's opinions on these matters, nor is there space to enter all those qualifications which have to be made to the view of Smith as a pure apostle of *laissez-faire*.[6] My concern at the moment is with the broad picture rather than the details. Hume's economic ideas have already been described: the extent to which Smith was influenced by Hume's essays in composing *The Wealth of Nations* is hard to determine,[7] but the large area of agreement between the two men is plain enough. Burke's economic views may need slightly fuller documentation, since he wrote very little specifically on economics. It may come as a surprise to anyone who is inclined to interpret Burke in the light of nineteenth-century conservatism that Smith is reported to have said of him: 'Burke is the only man I ever knew who thinks on economic subjects exactly as I do, without any previous communications having passed between us.'[8] Burke claimed in his turn that 'he was also consulted, and the greatest deference was paid to his opinions by Dr Adam Smith, in the progress of the celebrated work on the Wealth of Nations'. This is from the preamble to *Thoughts and Details on Scarcity*, where Burke, in response to contemporary events, puts the case against government interference with agricultural wages, prices, and merchandizing. The idea of the self-regulating market is simply presented:

The balance between consumption and production makes price. The market settles, and alone can settle, that price. Market is the meeting and conference of the *consumer* and the *producer*, when they mutually discover each other's wants. Nobody, I believe, has observed with any reflection what market is, without being astonished at the truth, the correctness, the celerity, the general equity, with which the balance of wants is settled. They who wish the destruction of that balance, and would fain by arbitrary regulation decree, that defective production should not be compensated by encreased price, directly lay their *axe* to the root of production itself.[9]

The consequence drawn is that 'it is better to leave all dealing, in which there is no force or fraud, collusion or combination, entirely to the persons mutually concerned in the matter contracted for',[10] and the concerns of the state should be confined to 'the exterior establishment of its religion; its magistracy; its revenue; its

---

[6] For the qualifications, see L. Robbins, *The Theory of Economic Policy in English Classical Political Economy* (London, 1952); J. Viner, 'Adam Smith and Laissez Faire' in *The Long View and the Short* (Glencoe, Ill., 1958); A. S. Skinner, 'The Functions of Government' in *A System of Social Science: Papers Relating to Adam Smith* (Oxford, 1979).

[7] See W. L. Taylor, *Francis Hutcheson and David Hume as Predecessors of Adam Smith* (North Carolina, 1965), where specific areas of disagreement between the two men are noted.

[8] J. Rae, *Life of Adam Smith*, ed. J. Viner (New York, 1965), pp. 387-8.

[9] E. Burke, *Thoughts and Details on Scarcity* (London, 1800), pp. 25-6.

[10] Ibid., p. 7.

military force by sea and land; the corporations that owe their existence to its fiat; in a word, to every thing that is *truly and properly* public, to the public peace, to the public safety, to the public order, to the public prosperity'.[11]

If the depth of Burke's commitment to economic freedom may be unfamiliar, his attachment to the virtues of social hierarchy is surely not. His praise of distinctions of rank, both as a source of social stability and as a prop to political authority, is fulsome. Although he believed that hereditary landownership was particularly important in these respects, he had no wish to exclude other sources of distinction. In a famous passage where he describes how a 'natural aristocracy' is formed, he speaks of professional life and trade as suitable breeding-grounds, along with other conditions open only to those who have inherited their high status.[12] Here he follows Hume, in substance if not in tone, for Hume also believed in the virtues of a ranked society, and thought that the best order was one which mixed ranking by birth with ranking by achievement.[13] In Smith's case, the simple view might suggest that an economic liberal would regard social hierarchy as an impediment to the free working of a market economy. On the contrary, Smith saw the desire for social pre-eminence as perhaps the strongest motive impelling men to economic activity. Like Hume's, his discussion of the distinction of ranks is conducted mainly in the tone of a dispassionate observer. Social gradation has a 'natural' origin in our tendency to admire the advantages enjoyed by the rich and powerful.[14] Rank may be based on personal merit, age, wealth, or birth.[15] Of these 'birth and fortune are evidently the two circumstances which principally set one man above another. They are the two great sources of personal distinction, and are therefore the principal causes which naturally establish authority and subordination among men.'[16] In the abstract it may seem to us that personal merit does not receive its proper recognition, but, Smith says,

[11] Ibid., pp. 45-6. For further discussion of Burke's economic ideas, see D. Barrington, 'Edmund Burke as an Economist', *Economica*, xxi (1954), 252-8; W. C. Dunn, 'Adam Smith and Edmund Burke: Complementary Contemporaries', *Southern Economic Journal*, vii (1941), 330-46.

[12] E. Burke, *An Appeal from the New to the Old Whigs* (New York, 1962), pp. 104-5.

[13] See above, ch. 6, pp. 132-8.

[14] A. Smith, *The Theory of Moral Sentiments*, ed. D. D. Raphael and A. L. Macfie (Oxford, 1976), pp. 52-3.

[15] A. Smith, *The Wealth of Nations*, ed. R. H. Campbell, A. S. Skinner, and W. B. Todd (Oxford, 1976), pp. 710-13.

[16] Smith, *The Wealth of Nations*, p. 714.

Nature has wisely judged that the distinction of ranks, the peace and order of society, would rest more securely upon the plain and palpable difference of birth and fortune, than upon the invisible and often uncertain difference of wisdom and virtue. The undistinguishing eyes of the great mob of mankind can well enough perceive the former: it is with difficulty that the nice discernment of the wise and the virtuous can sometimes distinguish the latter. In the order of all those recommendations, the benevolent wisdom of nature is equally evident.[17]

Thus Smith, too, embraces the ranked social structure of his age, not trying to show that the ranking is 'fair' according to some criterion of distributive justice, but arguing that the system has a function that is not perceived by those who contribute to its maintenance. Ranking is simultaneously natural and beneficial. Like Hume, Smith could take the hierarchy largely for granted. It was left to Burke to respond to a deliberate attempt to sweep it away.

Finally all three men converged in support of the political system established at the Revolution of 1688 and maintained in its essentials throughout the eighteenth century. Over specific questions—the respective merits of standing armies and militias, for instance—they differed.[18] But over the broad outlines—that is to say, a government subject to the rule of law, resting on a balance between crown and parliament, and with the great land-owning families effectively preponderant—they agreed. Burke was of necessity a party man, and as such was more inclined to use conventional Whig rhetoric in his pronouncements. Hume and Smith, although commonly alleged to be Tory and Whig respectively in their sympathies, really stood apart from the party battles and offered a detached defence of the establishment. The nature of Hume's defence has already been examined in detail. Smith wrote much less than Hume explicitly about politics, but when his scattered remarks are brought together a remarkably similar pattern of argument emerges.[19] Like Hume, Smith was mainly impressed by the contrast between civilized and barbarous

---

[17] Smith, *The Theory of Moral Sentiments*, p. 226. It is worth noting that this passage was added in the sixth edition of the book, serving to counterbalance a longer section (Part I, section III, ch. 3) in which Smith argued that our tendency to admire the rich and powerful rather than the truly meritorious was a source of moral corruption. In his old age he was prepared to concede part of the radical case, while still insisting that this corruption of sentiments met a social need.

[18] For comparisons between Hume and Smith in particular, see D. Winch, *Adam Smith's Politics: An Essay in historiographic revision* (Cambridge, 1978); D. Forbes, 'Sceptical Whiggism, Commerce, and Liberty' in A. S. Skinner and T. Wilson (eds.), *Essays on Adam Smith* (Oxford, 1975).

[19] Winch, *Adam Smith's Politics*, has rendered students of Smith's work a particularly valuable service here.

governments, and much more narrowly in favour of 'free' governments among the civilized category. He also echoed Hume's account of the part played by patronage in conciliating crown and parliament in the mixed monarchy of Britain. His statements about the need for a 'natural aristocracy' to lend support to government (and in particular to command the armed forces) are remarkably reminiscent of Burke's, even if, as Forbes has suggested, Smith lays less stress on the hereditary component of such an aristocracy.[20]

Hume, Smith, and Burke shared an establishment ideology which, in retrospect, may look either liberal or conservative, depending on which aspects are turned towards us. The 'liberal' face is represented by their belief in economic freedom, and some of their political commitments—those to personal freedom and the rule of law, for instance. The 'conservative' face is represented by their belief in social hierarchy, and by other political commitments, such as their view of the proper role in government of crown and nobility.[21] By considering Smith and Burke alongside Hume we can see how one face of the ideology may obscure the other. In Smith's case the point is a simple one. His reputation as a liberal (in the nineteenth-century sense) rests on the fact that his best-known book was a book largely about economics, where the 'liberal' face of his thought was necessarily prominent. Once Smith's social and political views are assembled and brought into the balance, the ideological distance that separates him from Hume virtually disappears.

In Burke's case the point is rather more complex. He is the mirror image of Smith in so far as he wrote a great deal about society and government and very little about economics—and so quite naturally has been regarded as a conservative. But we

---

[20] Forbes, 'Sceptical Whiggism, Commerce, and Liberty', p. 196.

[21] Interestingly enough both faces can be seen in the attitude of the three men towards the American Revolution. All were sympathetic to the grievances felt by the colonists (Smith perhaps the most, and Burke the least, but the differences were not great). All argued that the most beneficial economic relationship between Britain and America was one of free trade; but at the same time all looked at the problem with one eye on domestic politics. A military force sufficient to crush the rebellion would, they thought, require an increase in taxation and an accompanying extension of crown patronage large enough to unbalance the constitution. Alternatively, a military defeat would undermine the authority of government at home. Thus a 'liberal' endorsement of freedom at the international level went hand-in-hand with a 'conservative' concern for the stability of the domestic political establishment. For Hume's views, see *Letters*, vol. ii, esp. pp. 287-8, 300-1, 304-5, 308. For convenient accounts of Smith's and Burke's, see Winch, *Adam Smith's Politics*, ch. 7 and F. O'Gorman, *Edmund Burke: His Political Philosophy* (London, 1973), ch. 3 respectively.

need to add something further to this observation. Burke's most celebrated and distinctive essays were conceived in response to the French Revolution and its English supporters. In the process of responding, he transmuted the old establishment ideology into a form that is recognizably conservative in the post-revolutionary sense; the elements are virtually the same, but the over-all effect is subtly different. Allowance must of course be made for the fact that Burke wrote more as a politician than as a philosopher. Setting that point aside for the moment, how did Burke's experience set him apart from a pre-revolutionary thinker such as Hume?[22]

In order to respond to the revolutionaries and their English disciples, Burke had to defend assumptions which Hume took for granted. These new thinkers—recognizably liberal in the modern sense—stood for equality of rights, representative government, and so forth. They did not, in other words, accept the mixed constitution in the form which it had assumed during the eighteenth century; nor did they endorse the social privileges and the political power of the landed aristocracy. To argue against them effectively, Burke had to show that these arrangements were positively valuable. It was moreover not enough to claim that the value of the existing institutions lay precisely in the fact that they were long established and so commanded the loyalties of the people. As Burke observed, his opponents were more concerned with what was abstractly right than with what might be expedient in the short term—or perhaps, rather, they assumed that what was abstractly right would *ipso facto* win popular allegiance. Burke needed to justify the old order on terms set by the revolutionaries—bearing out Novalis's remark that he had written a revolutionary book against the Revolution. He therefore adduced arguments that are rarely or never to be found in Hume. He claimed, for instance, that prejudices, customs, laws, political institutions, and so forth were the repositories of the collective wisdom of the ages, and as such were not to be judged at the bar of individual reason—a claim that went far beyond Hume's observation that long experience was necessary to discover the best laws for a society. He argued that political leadership required special skills not to be found in the general run of men outside the aristocracy; so an arrangement regarded by Hume as convenient was seen by Burke as rationally defensible. Above all, he

[22] For further light on the gulf that separated Hume from later conservatives see S. Wolin, 'Hume and Conservatism' in D. W. Livingston and J. T. King (eds.), *Hume: A Re-evaluation* (New York, 1976).

portrayed the social and political hierarchy that he wanted to defend as corresponding to a natural order of things. That view is expressed in a famous passage which begins 'Society is indeed a contract', and continues, in part:

Each contract of each particular state is but a clause in the great primaeval contract of eternal society, linking the lower with the higher natures, connecting the visible and invisible world, according to a fixed compact sanctioned by the inviolable oath which holds all physical and all moral natures, each in their appointed place.[23]

It may be felt that claims of this kind are merely rhetorical flourishes on Burke's part, and that his difference with Hume is really the difference between an engaged politician and a philosopher. Although this is part of the truth, I should prefer to develop the point in another way. The arguments that Burke needed to use—given that he was to answer the revolutionaries in their own terms—were arguments of the kind that Hume had excluded on philosophical grounds. It was impossible for Burke to conduct the whole of his campaign from a position of epistemological scepticism. Sceptical arguments could be effectively deployed to undercut the claims made by radicals—before the event, as it were—but they could not be used to show that the arrangements proposed by the revolutionaries were positively undesirable, or to argue for a restoration of the *ancien régime*. Those who have thought to find a natural law theory in Burke have not been wholly mistaken, because a theory of this kind would have provided the appropriate epistemological basis for some of the claims that he wanted to make. Burke, however, was not enough of a philosopher (at least when he wrote the *Reflections*) to lay a coherent groundwork for his argument in natural law. He had been schooled in the same empiricist tradition as Hume and Smith, and in his later writings ideas from the two traditions are thrown together as the polemical needs of the moment require.

It is interesting to compare Adam Smith's much softer response to the Revolution in France. We may tentatively derive it from the section added in 1790 to *The Theory of Moral Sentiments*— tentatively because the new section was first drafted early in 1789, and it is only supposition (though perhaps reasonable supposition) that later additions were made in response to French developments.[24] In the passage in question, Smith speaks of discontented

[23] E. Burke, *Reflections on the Revolution in France* (London, 1967), pp. 93-4.
[24] See the editors' note in Smith, *The Theory of Moral Sentiments*, p. 321.

men who propose 'to new-model the constitution, and to alter, in some of its most essential parts, that system of government under which the subjects of a great empire have enjoyed, perhaps, peace, security, and even glory, during the course of several centuries together'.[25] He contrasts the man of public spirit who 'will accommodate, as well as he can, his public arrangements to the confirmed habits and prejudices of the people; and will remedy as well as he can, the inconveniencies which may flow from the want of those regulations which the people are averse to submit to', with the man of system who

is so oftern enamoured with the supposed beauty of his own ideal plan of government, that he cannot suffer the smallest deviation from any part of it. He goes on to establish it completely and in all its parts, without any regard either to the great interests, or to the strong prejudices which may oppose it. He seems to imagine that he can arrange the different members of a great society with as much ease as the hand arranges the different pieces upon a chess-board.[26]

If the 'men of system' are taken to represent the French revolutionaries and their sympathizers, Smith is offering a critique of revolutionary aspirations that is perfectly in keeping with Hume's (and his own) philosophical stance. He is pointing out that the revolutionaries claim a kind of knowledge which they cannot possibly possess, while at the same time they discount those useful 'habits and prejudices' which stabilize the workings of a large society. But notice that Smith does not claim that these habits and prejudices contain any mysterious collective wisdom; nor does he offer a defence of any particular set of social arrangements when he charges the revolutionaries with acting as though men could be pushed about as easily as chess pieces. Smith's is the authentic voice of sceptical conservatism, and although Burke was happy to borrow sceptical arguments when it suited his purpose, he wanted simultaneously to present a non-sceptical defence of the old order of Europe.

To return finally to Hume, I have tried to establish the following theses concerning his political thought. (1) Hume's politics may usefully be seen as deriving partly from his unconventional position in philosophy, and partly from his much more conventional ideological assumptions. (2) The philosophical position by itself leads to a sceptical kind of conservatism which is concerned to exclude certain types of argument for radical change rather than to defend any set of political arrangements in particular.

[25] Smith, *The Theory of Moral Sentiments*, p. 232.
[26] Ibid., pp. 233-4.

(3) The ideology is a characteristically eighteenth-century combination of beliefs that would later be channelled into liberalism and conservatism respectively. (4) The proto-conservative beliefs were those that Hume and others took most for granted, and so it was possible (as in the case of Smith) for the ideology to show a liberal face. (5) The conservatism came to the fore when existing social and political arrangements were challenged from below, as happened to Hume in a small way with the Wilkes affair, and to Burke in a much larger way with the French Revolution. (6) Nevertheless the sheer magnitude of the challenge posed by the Revolution forced Burke to defend the old ideology in a manner incompatible with Hume's philosophy, and in so doing to found the tradition of full-blooded conservatism.

If genuine conservatism involves the conscious defence of the old regime against hostile forces threatening to destroy it, Hume cannot be counted a conservative. His epistemology incapacitates him from offering a defence of the appropriate kind; and his ideology is shot through with eighteenth-century optimism about the harmony of freedom and authority, economic progress and social stability, and so forth. The gulf that divides Hume from his conservative successors may be seen in their contrasting attitudes towards religion. Hume refused to look upon religion as a force contributing to social stability, and religious assumptions played no part in his philosophy. In both respects his conservative successors disagreed with him profoundly. It would perhaps be an exaggeration to say that nineteenth-century conservatism needed a religious underpinning; but the philosophical foundations that were employed—whether a revived version of natural law, an organic cosmology, or a providential account of history—were all strengthened considerably by religious assumptions. It is odd to discover that some of the originators of German romanticism spoke with admiration of Hume;[27] but his appeal plainly lay in his destructive attack on Enlightenment rationalism, and he could have made no constructive contribution to the revival of fideism.

That is not quite the end of the story, however, for the conservative tradition broadly conceived has always made room for sceptics of a Humean kind, alongside those I have called 'full-blooded' conservatives. Indeed if we were to examine conservatism as a political rather than an intellectual tradition, and

---

[27] See I. Berlin, 'Hume and the Sources of German Anti-Rationalism' in G. P. Morice (ed.), *David Hume: Bicentenary Papers* (Edinburgh, 1977).

particularly if we were to concentrate attention on British politics, it might well appear that the sceptical stream of thought has been the dominant one.[28] The characteristics of sceptical conservatism are, first, that it draws its ideology from its surroundings and makes no attempt to justify it—so that although it always has an ideology, the content changes imperceptibly over time; second, that it is deeply suspicious of all rationalist schemes for change; third, that it is prepared to reform when reform seems urgent, and when it can be carried through without unduly disturbing existing institutions and habits of thought—it follows Hume's recommendation that the wise magistrate should 'adjust his innovations as much as possible to the ancient fabric, and preserve entire the chief pillars and supports of the constitution'.[29] Conservatives of this kind will not share all of Hume's ideology, for they will recognize that it was appropriate to other times and circumstances. They will almost certainly not share his philosophy in a technical sense. But they might be persuaded that Hume's mitigated scepticism provides the most adequate underpinning for an approach to politics which they have adopted quite spontaneously.

---

[28] Cf. A. Quinton, *The Politics of Imperfection* (London, 1978), where the sceptical aspects of the conservative tradition are emphasized.

[29] See above, ch. 4, p. 97.

Bibliography

ARDAL, P.S., *Passion and Value in Hume's Treatise* (Edinburgh, Edinburgh University Press, 1966).

'Convention and Value' in G. P. Morice (ed.), *David Hume: Bicentenary Papers* (Edinburgh, Edinburgh University Press, 1977).

ARKIN, M., 'The Economic Writings of David Hume—a Reassessment', *South African Journal of Economics*, xxiv (1956), 204-20.

ATKINSON, R. F., 'Hume on the Standard of Morals' in K. R. Merrill and R. W. Shahan (eds.), *David Hume: Many-Sided Genius* (Norman, University of Oklahoma Press, 1976).

BARRINGTON, D., 'Edmund Burke as an Economist', *Economica*, xxi (1954), 252-8.

BAXTER, I. F. G., 'David Hume and Justice', *Revue Internationale de Philosophie*, xlvii (1959), 112-31.

BEITZINGER, A. J., 'Hume's Aristocratic Preference', *Review of Politics*, xxviii (1966), 154-71.

BERLIN, I., 'Hume and the Sources of German Anti-Rationalism' in G. P. Morice (ed.), *David Hume: Bicentenary Papers* (Edinburgh, Edinburgh University Press, 1977).

BREAZEALE, D., 'Hume's Impasse', *Journal of the History of Philosophy*, xiii (1975), 311-33.

BRICKE, J., 'Hume's Associationist Psychology', *Journal of the History of the Behavioural Sciences*, x (1974), 397-409.

'Emotion and Thought in Hume's *Treatise*' in T. Penelhum and R. A. Shiner (eds.), *New Essays in the History of Philosophy* (Guelph, Ontario, Canadian Association for Publishing in Philosophy, 1975).

BROWNSEY, P. F., 'Hume and the Social Contract', *Philosophical Quarterly*, xxviii (1978), 132-48.

BRYSON, G., *Man and Society: The Scottish Enquiry of the Eighteenth Century* (Princeton, Princeton University Press, 1945).

BURKE, E., *Thoughts and Details on Scarcity* (London, F. and C. Rivington, 1800).

An Appeal from the New to the Old Whigs (New York, Bobbs-Merril, 1962).

Reflections on the Revolution in France (London, J. M. Dent and Sons, 1967).

CHITNIS, A. C., *The Scottish Enlightenment: a Social History* (London, Croom Helm, 1976).

CLIVE, J., 'The Social Background of the Scottish Renaissance' in N. T. Phillipson and R. Mitchison (eds.), *Scotland in the Age of Improvement* (Edinburgh, Edinburgh University Press, 1970).

CONNIFF, J., 'Hume's Political Methodology: A Reconsideration of "That Politics May be Reduced to a Science"', *Review of Politics*, xxxviii (1976), 88-108.

CONNON, R. W., 'The Textual and Philosophical Significance of Hume's MS Alterations to *Treatise* III' in G. P. Morice (ed.), *David Hume: Bicentenary Papers* (Edinburgh, Edinburgh University Press, 1977).

DAY, J. P., 'Hume on Justice and Allegiance', *Philosophy*, xl (1965), 35-56.

DICKINSON, H. T., 'The Eighteenth-Century Debate on the "Glorious Revolution"', *History*, lxi (1976), 28-45.

Liberty and Property: Political Ideology in Eighteenth Century Britain (London, Methuen, 1977).

DUNN, W. C., 'Adam Smith and Edmund Burke: Complementary Contemporaries', *Southern Economic Journal*, vii (1941), 330-46.

ELSTER, J., *Ulysses and the Sirens: Studies in Rationality and Irrationality* (Cambridge, Cambridge University Press, 1979).

FORBES, D., 'Politics and History in David Hume', *Historical Journal*, vi (1963), 280-95.

Hume's Philosophical Politics (Cambridge, Cambridge University Press, 1975).

'Sceptical Whiggism, Commerce, and Liberty' in A. S. Skinner and T. Wilson (eds.), *Essays on Adam Smith* (Oxford, Clarendon Press, 1975).

'Hume's Science of Politics' in G. P. Morice (ed.), *David Hume: Bicentenary Papers* (Edinburgh, Edinburgh University Press, 1977).

'Linking the Philosophical and Political', *Political Studies*, xxv (1977), 272-3.

FURLONG, E. J., 'Imagination in Hume's *Treatise* and *Enquiry Concerning the Human Understanding*', *Philosophy*, xxxvi (1961), 62-70.

GREEN, T. H. and GROSE, T. H. (eds.), *The Philosophical Works of David Hume* (London, Longmans, 1874-5).

GREIG, J. Y. T. (ed.), *The Letters of David Hume* (Oxford, Clarendon Press, 1932).

GRENE, M., 'Hume: Sceptic or Tory?', *Journal of the History of Ideas*, iv (1943), 333-48.

HABBAKUK, H. J., 'England' in A. Goodwin (ed.), *The European Nobility in the Eighteenth Century* (London, A. and C. Black, 1967).

HAYEK, F. A., *The Constitution of Liberty* (London, Routledge and Kegan Paul, 1960).

— 'The Legal and Political Philosophy of David Hume' in V. C. Chappell (ed.), *Hume: A Collection of Critical Essays* (London, Macmillan, 1968).

HIRSCHMAN, A. O., *The Passions and the Interests* (Princeton, N. J., Princeton University Press, 1977).

HORNE, T. A., *The Social Thought of Bernard Mandeville* (London, Macmillan, 1978).

HUME, D., *The History of England from the Invasion of Julius Caesar to the Abdication of James the Second* (London, Frederick Warne & Co., 1884).

— *Dialogues Concerning Natural Religion*, ed. H. D. Aiken (New York, Hafner Publishing Co., 1948).

— *Writings on Economics*, ed. E. Rotwein (Edinburgh, Nelson, 1955).

— *Essays Moral, Political and Literary* (Oxford, Oxford University Press, 1963).

— *A Letter from a Gentleman to his Friend in Edinburgh*, ed. E. C. Mossner and J. V. Price (Edinburgh, Edinburgh University Press, 1967).

— *Enquiries Concerning Human Understanding and Concerning the Principles of Morals*, ed. L. A. Selby-Bigge, 3rd edn. revised P. H. Nidditch (Oxford, Clarendon Press, 1975).

— *A Treatise of Human Nature*, ed. L. A. Selby-Bigge, 2nd edn. revised P. H. Nidditch (Oxford, Clarendon Press, 1978).

HUTCHESON, F., *A System of Moral Philosophy* (Glasgow, R. and A. Foulis, 1755).

KEMP SMITH, N., *The Philosophy of David Hume* (London, Macmillan, 1941).

KENYON, J. P., *Revolution Principles: The Politics of Party 1689-1720* (Cambridge, Cambridge University Press, 1977).

KING, J. T., 'The Place of the Language of Morals in Hume's Second *Enquiry*' in D. W. Livingston and J. T. King (eds.), *Hume: A Re-evaluation* (New York, Fordham University Press, 1976).

KLIBANSKY, R. and MOSSNER, E.C. (eds.), *New Letters of David Hume* (Oxford, Clarendon Press, 1954).

KRAMNICK, I., *Bolingbroke and his Circle* (Cambridge, Mass., Harvard University Press, 1968).

KUYPERS, M. S., *Studies in the Eighteenth Century Background of Hume's Empiricism* (New York, Russell, 1966).

KYDD, R., *Reason and Conduct in Hume's Treatise* (New York, Russell, 1964).

LARKIN, P. W., *Property in the Eighteenth Century* (Cork, Cork University Press, 1930).

LETWIN, S., *The Pursuit of Certainty* (Cambridge, Cambridge University Press, 1965).

LOCKE, J., *Two Treatises of Government*, ed. P. Laslett (New York, Mentor, 1965).

LONG, D. G., 'Bentham on Property' in A. Parel and T. Flanagan (eds.), *Theories of Property: Aristotle to the Present* (Waterloo, Ontario, Wilfrid Laurier University Press, 1979).

MACKIE, J. L., *Hume's Moral Theory* (London, Routledge and Kegan Paul, 1980).

MACPHERSON, C. B., *The Political Theory of Possessive Individualism* (Oxford, Clarendon Press, 1962).

Democratic Theory: Essays in Retrieval (Oxford, Clarendon Press, 1973).

'The Economic Penetration of Political Theory', *Journal of the History of Ideas*, xxxix (1978), 101-18.

MANNHEIM, K., 'Conservative Thought' in K. Mannheim, *Essays on Sociology and Social Psychology* (London, Routledge & Kegan Paul, 1953).

MARSHALL, D., *Eighteenth Century England* (London, Longman, 1962).

MARSHALL, G., 'David Hume and Political Scepticism', *Philosophical Quarterly*, iv (1954), 247-57.

MEEK, R. L.., *Social Science and the Ignoble Savage* (Cambridge, Cambridge University Press, 1976).

MILL, J. S., 'Bentham' in J. S. Mill, *Essays on Politics and Culture*, ed. G. Himmelfarb (New York, Doubleday Anchor, 1963).

MILLER, D., *Social Justice* (Oxford, Clarendon Press, 1976).

'Hume and Possessive Individualism', *History of Political Thought*, i (1980), 261-78.

MINGAY, G., *English Landed Society in the Eighteenth Century* (London, Routledge and Kegan Paul, 1963).

MOORE, J., 'Hume's Theory of Justice and Property', *Political Studies*, xxiv (1976), 103-19.

'Hume's Political Science and the Classical Republican Tradition', *Canadian Journal of Political Science*, x (1977), 809-39.

MOSSNER, E. C., 'Was Hume a Tory Historian? Facts and Reconsiderations', *Journal of the History of Ideas*, ii (1941), 225-36.

'An Apology for David Hume, Historian', *Publications of the Modern Language Association of America*, lvi (1941), 657-90.

The Life of David Hume (Edinburgh, Nelson, 1954, revised edn. Oxford, Clarendon Press, 1980).

'Philosophy and Biography: The Case of David Hume' in V. C. Chappell (ed.), *Hume: A Collection of Critical Essays* (London, Macmillan, 1968).

MURPHY, J. G., 'Hume and Kant on the Social Contract', *Philosophical Studies*, xxxiii (1978), 65-79.

NEALE, R. S., '"The Bourgeoisie, Historically, Has Played a Most Revolutionary Part"' in E. Kamenka and R. S. Neale (eds.), *Feudalism, Capitalism and Beyond* (London, Edward Arnold, 1975).

NOXON, J., *Hume's Philosophical Development* (Oxford, Clarendon Press, 1973).

O'GORMAN, F., *Edmund Burke: His Political Philosophy* (London, Allen and Unwin, 1973).

PASSMORE, J. A., *Hume's Intentions* (Cambridge, Cambridge University Press, 1952).

'Hume and the Ethics of Belief' in G. P. Morice (ed.), *David Hume: Bicentenary Papers* (Edinburgh, Edinburgh University Press, 1977).

PERKIN, H., *The Origins of Modern English Society, 1780-1880* (London, Routledge and Kegan Paul, 1969).

PLAMENATZ, J., *Man and Society* (London, Longmans, 1963).

PLUMB, J. H., *The Growth of Political Stability in England, 1675-1725* (London, Macmillan, 1967).

POCOCK, J. G. A., *The Ancient Constitution and the Feudal Law* (Cambridge, Cambridge University Press, 1957).

'Burke and the Ancient Constitution', *Historical Journal*, iii (1960), 125-43.

'Machiavelli, Harrington, and English Political Ideologies in the Eighteenth Century' in J. G. A. Pocock, *Politics, Language and Time* (London, Methuen, 1972).

The Machiavellian Moment (Princeton, Princeton University Press, 1975).

'Early Modern Capitalism—the Augustan Perception' in E. Kamenka and R. S. Neale (eds.), *Feudalism, Capitalism and Beyond* (London, Edward Arnold, 1975).

(ed.), *The Political Works of James Harrington* (Cambridge, Cambridge University Press, 1977).

'The Mobility of Property and the Rise of Eighteenth Century Sociology' in A. Parel and T. Flanagan (eds.), *Theories of Property: Aristotle to the Present* (Waterloo, Ontario, Wilfrid Laurier University Press, 1979).

POPKIN, R. H., 'David Hume: His Pyrrhonism and his Critique of Pyrrhonism' in V. C. Chappell (ed.), *Hume: A Collection of Critical Essays* (London, Macmillan, 1968).

PRICE, H. H., 'The Permanent Significance of Hume's Philosophy', *Philosophy*, xv (1940), 7-37.

PRICE, K. B., 'Does Hume's Theory of Knowledge Determine his Ethical Theory?', *Journal of Philosophy*, xlvii (1950), 425-34.

QUINTON, A., *The Politics of Imperfection* (London, Faber and Faber, 1978).

RAE, J., *Life of Adam Smith*, ed. J. Viner (New York, Augustus M. Kelley, 1965).

RAPHAEL, D. D., *The Moral Sense* (London, Oxford University Press, 1947).

(ed.), *British Moralists 1650-1800* (Oxford, Clarendon Press, 1969).

'The Impartial Spectator', *Proceedings of the British Academy*, lviii (1972), 3-22, reprinted in A. S. Skinner and T. Wilson (eds.), *Essays on Adam Smith* (Oxford, Clarendon Press, 1975).

'Hume and Adam Smith on Justice and Utility', *Proceedings of the Aristotelian Society*, lxiii (1972-3), 87-103.

'Hume's Critique of Ethical Rationalism' in W. B. Todd (ed.), *Hume and the Enlightenment* (Edinburgh, Edinburgh University Press, 1974).

'"The true old Humean Philosophy" and its Influence on Adam Smith' in G. P. Morice (ed.), *David Hume: Bicentenary Papers* (Edinburgh, Edinburgh University Press, 1977).

RICHTER, M., *The Political Theory of Montesquieu* (Cambridge, Cambridge University Press, 1977).

ROBBINS, C., '"Discordant Parties": A Study of the Acceptance of Party by Englishmen', *Political Science Quarterly*, lxxiii (1958), 505-29.

ROBBINS, L., *The Theory of Economic Policy in English Classical Political Economy* (London, Macmillan, 1952).

ROBISON, W. L., 'David Hume: Naturalist and Meta-Sceptic' in D. W. Livingston and J. T. King (eds.), *Hume: a Re-evaluation* (New York, Fordham University Press, 1976).

ROLL, E., *A History of Economic Thought* (London, Faber, 1961).

ROTWEIN, E., 'David Hume, Philosopher-Economist' in K. R. Merrill and R. W. Shahan (eds.), *David Hume: Many-sided Genius* (Norman, University of Oklahoma Press, 1976).

RUDE, G. F. E., *Wilkes and Liberty* (Oxford, Clarendon Press, 1962).

RUSSELL, B., 'A Reply to my Critics' in P. Schilpp (ed.), *The Philosophy of Bertrand Russell* (Evanston and Chicago, Northwestern University, 1944).

'Philosophy and Politics' in B. Russell, *Unpopular Essays* (London, Allen and Unwin, 1950).

SHORTER OXFORD ENGLISH DICTIONARY (Oxford, Clarendon Press, 1967).

SKINNER, A. S., 'The Functions of Government' in A. S. Skinner, *A System of Social Science: Papers Relating to Adam Smith* (Oxford, Clarendon Press, 1979).

SMITH, A., *The Theory of Moral Sentiments*, ed. D. D. Raphael and A. L. Macfie (Oxford, Clarendon Press, 1976).

The Wealth of Nations, ed. R. H. Campbell, A. S. Skinner, and W. B. Todd (Oxford, Clarendon Press, 1976).

Lectures on Jurisprudence, ed. R. L. Meek, D. D. Raphael, and P. G. Stein (Oxford, Clarendon Press, 1978).

SMOUT, T. C., 'Scottish Landowners and Economic Growth 1650-1850', *Scottish Journal of Political Economy*, xi (1964), 218-34.

A History of the Scottish People 1560-1830 (London, Fontana, 1972).

SPECK, W. A., *Stability and Strife: England 1714-1760* (London, Edward Arnold, 1977).

STEIN, P., 'Law and Society in Eighteenth-Century Scottish Thought' in N. T. Phillipson and R. Mitchison (eds.), *Scotland in the Age of Improvement* (Edinburgh, Edinburgh University Press, 1970).

STEPHEN, L., *English Thought in the Eighteenth Century* (London, Smith, Elder & Co., 1876).

STEWART, J. B., *The Moral and Political Philosophy of David Hume* (New York, Columbia University Press, 1963).

STOCKTON, C. N., 'Hume—Historian of the English Constitution', *Eighteenth Century Studies*, iv (1970-1), 277-93.

'Economics and the Mechanism of Historical Progress in

Hume's *History*' in D. W. Livingston and J. T. King (eds.),
Hume: a Re-evaluation (New York, Fordham University Press,
1976).

STROUD, B., *Hume* (London, Routledge and Kegan Paul, 1977).

TAYLOR, M., *Anarchy and Co-operation* (London, Wiley, 1976).

TAYLOR, W. L. *Francis Hutcheson and David Hume as Predecessors
of Adam Smith* (North Carolina, Duke University Press, 1965).

THOMPSON, M. P., 'Hume's Critique of Locke and the
"Original Contract"', *Il Pensiero Politico*, x (1977), 189-201.

VINER, J., 'Adam Smith and Laissez Faire' in J. Viner, *The
Long View and the Short* (Glencoe, Ill., The Free Press, 1958).

WEBER, M., *The Protestant Ethic and the Spirit of Capitalism*
(London, Allen and Unwin, 1930).

WILBANKS, J., *Hume's Theory of Imagination* (The Hague,
Nijhoff, 1968).

WINCH, D., *Adam Smith's Politics: An Essay in historiographic revision*
(Cambridge, Cambridge University Press, 1978).

WOLIN, S., 'Hume and Conservatism' in D. W. Livingston and
J. T. King (eds.), *Hume: A Re-evaluation* (New York, Fordham
University Press, 1976).

Index

DATE DUE

GAYLORD			PRINTED IN U.S.A.